**MALMARNA &
FURTHER AFIELD**
See pages 100–133

**EXCURSIONS FROM
STOCKHOLM**
See pages 134–145

LILLA VÄRTAN

DJURGÅRDEN

SALTSJÖN

DJURGÅRDEN
See pages 84–99

0 metres	500
0 yards	500

EYEWITNESS TRAVEL GUIDES

STOCKHOLM

EYEWITNESS TRAVEL GUIDES

STOCKHOLM

Main Contributor: KAJ SANDELL

DK PUBLISHING

LONDON • NEW YORK • MUNICH
MELBOURNE • DELHI

Produced by Streiffert Förlag AB, Stockholm
CHIEF EDITOR Bo Streiffert
PROJECT EDITOR Guy Engström
EDITORS Monica Nilsson, Guy Engström
DESIGNER Bo Streiffert
PICTURE RESEARCH Guy Engström

Dorling Kindersley Ltd
MANAGING EDITOR Anna Streiffert
ART DIRECTOR Gillian Allan

MAIN CONTRIBUTOR Kaj Sandell

CONTRIBUTORS
Lisa Carlsson, Jan & Christine Samuelson
Christina Sollenberg Britton, Stockholm Information Service

MAPS Stig Söderlind

PHOTOGRAPHERS Jeppe Wikström, Erik Svensson

ILLUSTRATIONS
Urban Frank, assisted by Jan Rojmar

Reproduced by PDC Tangen, Norway
Printed and bound by South China Printing Co. Ltd., China

First American Edition, 2000

01 02 03 04 05 10 9 8 7 6 5 4 3 2

Published in the United States by DK Publishing, Inc.,
375 Hudson Street, New York, New York 10014
Reprinted with revisions 2001
Copyright 2000, 2001 © Dorling Kindersley Ltd, London

Published in Great Britain by Dorling Kindersley Limited.

A CATALOGING IN PUBLICATION RECORD IS AVAILABLE
FROM THE LIBRARY OF CONGRESS.

ISSN 1542-1554
ISBN 0-7894-9418-3

FLOORS ARE REFERRED TO THROUGHOUT IN ACCORDANCE WITH EUROPEAN USAGE;
IE THE "FIRST FLOOR" IS THE FLOOR ABOVE GROUND LEVEL.

See our complete product line at
www.dk.com

**The information in this
Dorling Kindersley Travel Guide is checked regularly.**
Every effort has been made to ensure that this book is as up-to-date as
possible at the time of going to press. Some details, however, such as
telephone numbers, opening hours, prices, gallery hanging
arrangements and travel information are liable to change. The
publishers cannot accept responsibility for any consequences arising
from the use of this book, nor for any material on third party websites,
and cannot guarantee that any website address in this book will be
a suitable source of travel information. We value the views and
suggestions of our readers very highly. Please write to: Publisher,
DK Eyewitness Travel Guides, Dorling Kindersley, 80 Strand,
London WC2R 0RL, Great Britain.

◁ **Dawn at Skeppsbron, on the eastern side of Gamla Stan**

CONTENTS

Wooden sculpture on the
17th–century warship *Vasa*

INTRODUCING
STOCKHOLM

PUTTING STOCKHOLM
ON THE MAP
10

THE HISTORY OF
STOCKHOLM *14*

STOCKHOLM THROUGH
THE YEAR *26*

STOCKHOLM AT A
GLANCE *30*

Kaknästornet, Stockholm's tallest
building at 155 m (508 ft)

STOCKHOLM AREA BY AREA

GAMLA STAN *44*

CITY *60*

BLASIEHOLMEN & SKEPPSHOLMEN *74*

DJURGÅRDEN *84*

MALMARNA & FURTHER AFIELD *100*

EXCURSIONS FROM STOCKHOLM *134*

Late winter walk along the shores of Kungsholmen

SURVIVAL GUIDE

PRACTICAL INFORMATION *182*

GETTING TO STOCKHOLM *190*

GETTING AROUND STOCKHOLM *192*

STOCKHOLM STREET FINDER *198*

GENERAL INDEX *212*

ACKNOWLEDGEMENTS *221*

PHRASE BOOK *223*

STOCKHOLM PUBLIC TRANSPORT MAP

Inside Back Cover

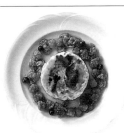

Cheesecake with cloudberries, a traditional Swedish dessert

The recently renovated Royal Chapel at the Royal Palace

TRAVELLERS' NEEDS

WHERE TO STAY *148*

RESTAURANTS, CAFÉS AND PUBS *154*

ENTERTAINMENT IN STOCKHOLM *166*

OUTDOOR ACTIVITIES *172*

SHOPPING IN STOCKHOLM *174*

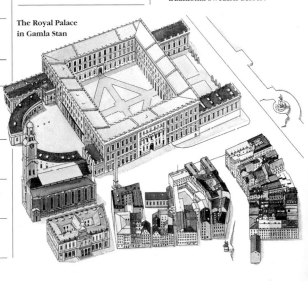

The Royal Palace in Gamla Stan

HOW TO USE THIS GUIDE

THIS DORLING KINDERSLEY travel guide will help you to get the most from your visit to Stockholm. *Introducing Stockholm*, the opening section, maps the city and sets it in its geographical and cultural context. *History of Stockholm* explains important events in Sweden's past and how they relate to the city. *Stockholm at a Glance* describes the main places of interest and lists events throughout the year. *Stockholm Area by Area* takes you to the most important sights in four different areas of the city centre

with the help of maps, photographs and illustrations. Sights outside the city centre are described in *Malmarna & Further Afield*. The section *Excursions from Stockholm* covers sights that can be visited on one- or two-day trips. Suggestions for hotels, restaurants, entertainment and shopping are covered in *Travellers' Needs*. The *Survival Guide* gives practical advice on everything from communications to personal safety. To help you find your way around, there are detailed *Street Finder* maps and, finally, an *Index*.

HOW TO USE THE SIGHTSEEING SECTION

Each geographical section begins with a map and an introduction that describes the area's history and character. The introductions to the city's four central sightseeing areas are each followed by a special *Street-by-Street* map which shows the most interesting parts of the

relevant area. The central areas have been colour-coded to make them easier to find. The five districts in the section *Malmarna & Further Afield* each begin with an overview map. All the sights are marked on the maps with the help of a simple numbering system.

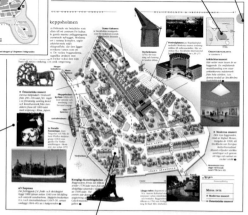

1 Area introduction
For easy reference the numbers have been quoted on an Area Map, which also shows underground stations and bus stops. Sights are divided into different categories.

Each area has a colour-coded thumb tab.

The pink-coloured section of the Area Map is shown in more detail on the *Street-by-Street* map.

A locator map refers to the *Street Finder* map.

A locator map shows where you are in relation to other parts of the city.

2 Street-by-Street map
This gives a bird's eye view of the most important parts of each sightseeing area, with illustrations of all the main buildings. The sights have the same number as shown on the Area Map, and are described in numerical order in more detail on the following pages.

Suggested route for a walk shown by dotted red line.

STOCKHOLM AREA BY AREA

THE COLOUR-CODED areas shown on this map *(inside front cover)* form the four central sightseeing districts into which the guide is divided, each having its own section in *Stockholm Area by Area (pp42–99)*. The same area colour coding is used on other maps in the guide, including the section *Stockholm at a Glance (pp30–39)*, where they can help you to locate the leading sights and venues for events.

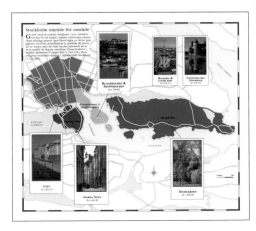

The number indicates the sight's position on the *Area Map* and the order in which it is described in the section.

Practical information with all the information you need to visit the sight, including a map reference to the *Street Finder (pp198–207)*.

3 Detailed information on each sight

All the more important sights are described in the same order as on the Area Map in the introduction to the relevant section. A key to the symbols used will be found on the back flap.

The Checklist gives all the practical information you need to plan your visit.

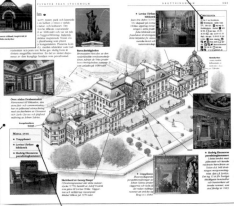

Fact boxes highlight the unique aspects or historical connections of a sight.

4 Stockholm's top sights

These take up two or more full pages. Buildings with specially interesting architecture are shown as cut-away diagrams, and museums have colour-coded floor plans so that you can easily find the various sections.

Stars indicate highlights of the sight which should not be missed.

INTRODUCING
STOCKHOLM

PUTTING STOCKHOLM ON THE MAP 10-13
THE HISTORY OF STOCKHOLM 14-25
STOCKHOLM THROUGH THE YEAR 26-29
STOCKHOLM AT A GLANCE 30-41

Putting Stockholm on the Map

Sweden is Europe's fourth largest country, covering 486,661 sq km (187,900 sq miles). Its southern-most point is on the same latitude as Edinburgh; its northern extremity is 280 km (174 miles) north of the Arctic Circle. Sweden borders Norway in the west and Finland in the east. Since 2000 it has been connected to Denmark in the south via a bridge over the Öresund strait. The capital, Stockholm, is in the south-east. It has around one million inhabitants. The city is built on islands which separate the Baltic Sea from Lake Mälaren *(see pp40–1)*.

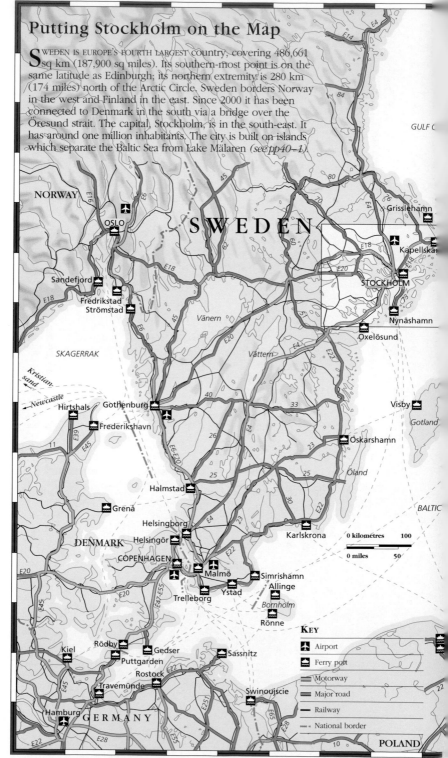

KEY

✈ Airport
⛴ Ferry port
— Motorway
— Major road
— Railway
–·– National border

0 kilometres   100
0 miles   50

◁ **View of Stockholm from Mosebacke, painted in 1787 by Elias Martin**

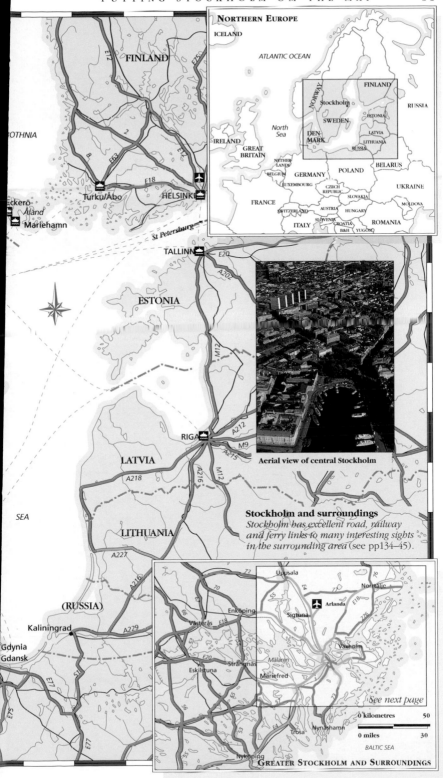

NORTHERN EUROPE

ICELAND

ATLANTIC OCEAN

FINLAND

NORWAY   Stockholm   RUSSIA

ESTONIA

North Sea   SWEDEN

IRELAND   DEN-MARK   LATVIA

GREAT BRITAIN   LITHUANIA

NETHER-LANDS   RUSSIA

BELGIUM   GERMANY   POLAND   BELARUS

LUXEMBOURG   CZECH REPUBLIC   UKRAINE

FRANCE   SLOVAKIA

SWITZERLAND   AUSTRIA   HUNGARY   MOLDOVA

SLOVENIA   ROMANIA

ITALY   CROATIA   YUGOSL

B&H

FINLAND

OTHNIA

Eckerö
Åland
Mariehamn

Turku/Åbo   HELSINKI

St Petersburg

TALLINN   E20

ESTONIA

RIGA   A212   M9

Aerial view of central Stockholm

LATVIA
A218

SEA

LITHUANIA
A227

(RUSSIA)

Kaliningrad

Gdynia
Gdansk

Stockholm and surroundings
*Stockholm has excellent road, railway
and ferry links to many interesting sights
in the surrounding area (see pp134–45).*

Uppsala

Norrtälje

Arlanda

Enköping   Sigtuna

Västerås   Vaxholm

Eskilstuna   Strängnäs   Mälaren
Mariefred

See next page

0 kilometres   50

0 miles   30

BALTIC SEA

Trosa   Nynäshamn

Nyköping   **GREATER STOCKHOLM AND SURROUNDINGS**

Stockholm and Surroundings

STOCKHOLM'S FIRST BUILDINGS were erected on a small island in the narrow Strömmen channel between the Baltic and Lake Mälaren. When the town started to expand, buildings sprang up on the "Malms", the areas on either side of Strömmen. Today Stockholm stretches over 14 islands, with high-rise suburbs sprawling almost all the way out to the royal country palaces. The network of underground and suburban trains, buses and ferry services offers easy transport to sights beyond the city centre (see pp134–45).

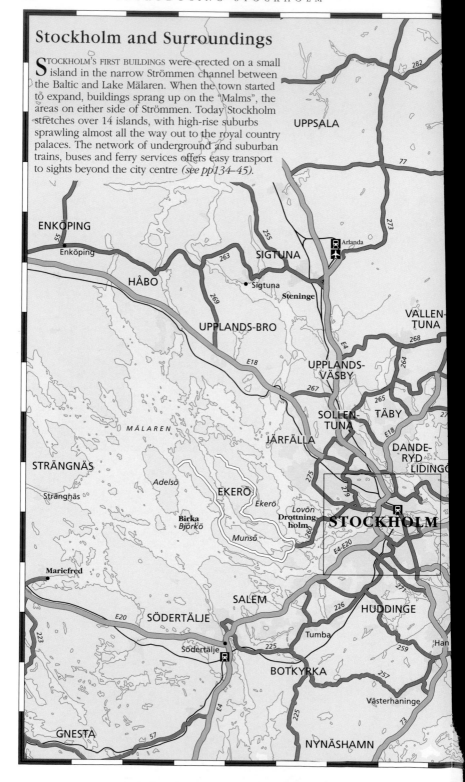

ENKÖPING

Enköping

UPPSALA

Arlanda

SIGTUNA

HÅBO

Sigtuna

Steninge

UPPLANDS-BRO

E18

VALLEN-TUNA

UPPLANDS-VÄSBY

SOLLEN-TUNA

TÄBY

MÄLAREN

JÄRFÄLLA

DANDE-RYD

LIDING

STRÄNGNÄS

Adelsö

EKERÖ

Ekerö

Lovön

Drottning-holm

STOCKHOLM

Stränghäs

Birka
Björkö

Munsö

E4-E20

Mariefred

SALEM

HUDDINGE

E20

SÖDERTÄLJE

Tumba

Södertälje

BOTKYRKA

Västerhaninge

GNESTA

NYNÄSHAMN

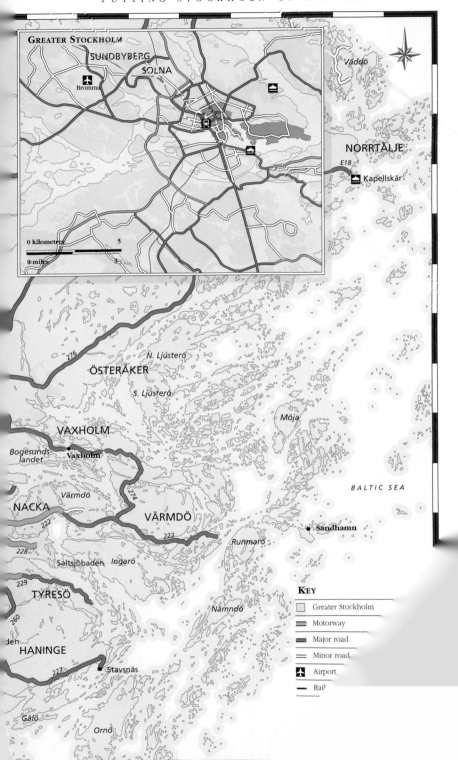

GREATER STOCKHOLM

SUNDBYBERG

SOLNA

Bromma

Väddö

NORRTÄLJE

E18

Kapellskär

0 kilometres 5

0 miles 3

276

N. Ljusterö

ÖSTERÅKER

S. Ljusterö

Möja

VAXHOLM

Bogesunds-
landet

Vaxholm

Värmdö

274

BALTIC SEA

NACKA

222

VÄRMDÖ

222

Sandhamn

228

Saltsjöbaden

Ingarö

Runmarö

229

TYRESÖ

260

Nämndö

den

HANINGE

227

Stavsnäs

Gålö

Ornö

KEY

Greater Stockholm

Motorway

Major road

Minor road

Airport

Rail

THE HISTORY OF STOCKHOLM

L EGENDS AND THEORIES *about Stockholm's origins have been many and varied, and sometimes even contradictory. But they have a common factor– control over the waterways. The generally accepted founder of Stockholm is the 13th-century regent Birger Jarl who, according to the medieval* Erik's Chronicle, *wanted to build a fortress to protect Lake Mälaren from marauding pirates.*

A thousand years ago the waters around the island now known as Gamla Stan were busy with warships, trading vessels and pirate ships using the narrow channel between the Baltic and Lake Mälaren. In those days boat was the quickest and safest method of travel.

Stockholm's oldest preserved city seal (1296)

In the first literary mention of what was to become Stockholm, the Icelandic poet and saga writer Snorre Sturlasson (1178–1241) described a barrier of piles across a waterway which he named Stocksundet, the present Norrström.The island formed by this piling became known as Stockholm. Excavations in the late 1970s revealed the remains of a large number of piles in the water dating from the 11th century. Snorre also mentioned a 12th- century castle tower which would have predated Birger Jarl's fortress, the predecessor of the present Royal Palace.

Documents show that Stockholm was already a city in 1252, four years after Birger Jarl became regent. Many towns in Sweden started to expand in the early 13th century. Stockholm was a late starter but soon caught up. A document from 1289 describes Stockholm as the biggest place in the kingdom. But it was not the capital city, because the king was always on the move. Birger Jarl's son, King Magnus Ladulås, did not regard Stockholm as his capital either. For a long time the city's importance lay in its role as a trading centre. It became an important port for the German-dominated Hanseatic League, which controlled Swedish overseas trade from the 13th century until the late 17th century.

The frontiers of the Nordic countries remained undefined for some time, but with a background of similar languages and cultures, Sweden, Norway and Denmark signed the Kalmar Union in 1397. Finland at that time was still part of Sweden. The era of union became one of conflict and violence. At the battle of Brunkeberg in Stockholm in 1471 the Danish king tried to take control of Sweden, but was defeated by the regent Sten Sture. A new Danish campaign in 1520 culminated in the notorious Stockholm Bloodbath at Stortorget *(see p54),* when more than 80 Swedish noblemen were executed.

TIMELINE

1000	1100	1200	1300	1400	15

1008 Olof Skötkonung converts to Christianity and is baptized in Västergötland

Birger Jarl, Stockholm's founder

c.**1250** Birger Jarl founds Stockholm

1350 Code of Magnus Eriksson replaces provincial laws

1364 Albrecht of Mecklenburg chosen as Sweden's King

1397 Kalmar Union links the Nordic countries

800–975 Vikings settle and trade at Birka *(see p138)*

1275 Magnus Ladulås chosen as Sweden's king at Mora

1101 Three Kings' Meeting fixes Scandinavian frontiers

1280 Ordinances of Alsnö give nobility freedom from taxation

1349–50 Plague ravages Sweden

1471 Sten Sture the Elder defeats the Danish King Kristian at Brunkeberg

1520 Sw nob exe St P

◁ **Painting in Storkyrkan (Stockholm's cathedral) depicting a remarkable light phenomenon seen**

The newly chosen king, Gustav Vasa, making his ceremonial entry into Stockholm, Midsummer Day 1523

THE VASA ERA

One of those who managed to avoid execution in the Stockholm Bloodbath was the young nobleman Gustav Eriksson. At the end of 1520 Gustav organized an army to oust the Danish King Kristian from Sweden. Gustav was successful and on 6 June 1523 – later to become Sweden's National Day – he was named king with the title Gustav Vasa.

When Gustav Vasa took the throne he discovered a nation in financial crisis. He called on Parliament to pass a controversial law transferring the property of the Church to the State, which then became the country's most important source of economic power. Another important result of this policy was the gradual separation from Catholicism and the adoption of the Lutheran State Church.

During his reign Gustav Vasa implemented tough economic policies in order to concentrate central power in Stockholm. This effective dictatorship also resulted in the Swedish

Portrait of Erik XIV (1561)

Parliament's decision in 1544 to make the monarchy hereditary.

Descendants of Gustav Vasa oversaw the rise of Sweden into one of Europe's great powers. During the reign of Gustav's son Erik XIV, there were wars against Denmark, Lübeck and Poland. His brothers dethroned him and he died in prison, probably of a pea soup poisoned by his brother Johan III. During the reign of Karl IX, the third son, Sweden waged war against Denmark and Russia.

GUSTAV II ADOLF AND KRISTINA

When the next king, Gustav II Adolf, came to power in 1611, Sweden was involved in wars against Russia, Poland and Denmark. Under his rule Sweden steadily increased its influence over the Baltic region. Stockholm started to develop into the country's political and administrative centre. In 1630 Gustav II Adolf, together with his influential chancellor Axel Oxenstierna, decided to intervene in the Thirty Years War on the

TIMELINE

Vasa dynasty's coat of arms

3 Gustav Vasa ~~s~~en as king in ~~g~~rängnäs and ~~m~~arches into Stockholm	**1542** Nils Dacke and supporters stage a peasant revolt in Småland	**1560** Gustav Vasa dies	**1568** Erik XIV imprisoned by his brothers at Gripsholms Slott **1577** Erik XIV dies, probably poisoned	**1611** Gustav II Adolf comes to power
	1525	**1550**	**1575**	**1600**
~~9~~ Reformation, ~~Par~~liament con-~~fisc~~ates Church property	**1544** Hereditary monarchy established for Gustav Vasa's male descendants	**1561** Eric XIV is crowned king and his brothers' powers curbed **1569** Johan III crowned in Stockholm	**1570** Nordic Seven Years War ends **1587** Johan III's son Sigismund chosen king of Poland	**1612** Axel Oxenstierna named State Chancellor

side of the Protestants, using religious motives as a pretext. Sweden had some notable military successes during the war, but paid a heavy price for winning the bloody battle at Lützen in 1632 as the king was killed in action.

Gustav II Adolf's only child, Kristina, came to the throne at the age of six. During her reign (1633–54), life at the court was influenced by the world of science and philosophy. Kristina corresponded with leading academics and invited the French philosopher René Descartes, who died in 1650 only a few months after arriving in Stockholm. The Tre Kronor castle became the permanent royal residence. Kristina's reluctance to marry resulted in her cousin, Karl Gustav, becoming Crown Prince. Kristina abdicated and left for Rome, where she converted to Catholicism.

Karl XII with the widowed queen on his arm leaving the burning Tre Kronor fortress

Queen Kristina, fascinated by science and corresponding with leading scientists

THE CAROLIAN ERA

Karl X Gustav (1654–60) was the first of three Karls to reign. At the height of Sweden's era as a great power and in one of the most audacious episodes in the history of war, he conquered Denmark by leading his army across the frozen waters of the Great Belt (*see p19*). Karl XI (1660–97) secured the southern Swedish provinces, and divided the land more evenly between the crown, nobility and peasants.

While the body of Karl XI lay in state at Tre Kronor in 1697 a fire broke out which destroyed most of the building. The new monarch was the teenage Karl XII (1697–1718). He faced awesome problems when Denmark, Poland and Russia formed an alliance in 1700 with the aim of crushing the power of Sweden. Karl XII set off to battle.

Denmark and Poland were soon forced to plead for peace, but Russia resisted. A bold push towards Moscow was unsuccessful and the Swedish army suffered a devastating defeat at Poltava in 1709. This marked the beginning of the end for Sweden as a great power.

Karl XII, the most controversial Swedish monarch, returned to Sweden in 1715 after an absence of 15 years. His plans to regain Sweden's position of dominance never came to pass and he was killed in Norway in 1718.

By now, Sweden was in crisis. Crop failures and epidemics had annihilated one-third of Stockholm's population and the state's finances were drained.

1617 Death penalty introduced for conversion to Catholicism

1632 Gustav II Adolf killed at battle of Lützen

1633 Six-year-old Kristina becomes queen; guardians rule

1654 Kristina abdicates and Karl X Gustav crowned king

1655 Kristina converts to Catholicism and is ceremonially greeted in Rome

1697 Tre Kronor castle destroyed by fire; 15-year-old Karl XII crowned

1625	1650	1675	1700

1618 Thirty Years War starts in Germany

Gustav II Adolf

1648 Peace of Westphalia gives Sweden new territories

1658 Swedish army crosses the Great Belt and acquires new territory under Peace of Roskilde

1680 Karl XI starts the era of Carolian autocracy and limits powers of the nobility

1709 Swedish army defeated by Peter the Great at Poltava

1718 Karl XII dies

Sweden's Era as a Great Power

FOR MORE THAN A CENTURY (1611–1721) Sweden was the dominant power in northern Europe, and the Baltic was effectively a Swedish inland sea. The country was at its most powerful after the Peace of Roskilde in 1658, when Sweden acquired seven new provinces from Denmark and Norway. Outside today's frontiers the Swedish Empire covered the whole of Finland, large parts of the Baltic, and important areas of northern Germany. Over 111 years as a great power Sweden spent 72 of them at war when many treasures were brought back to the new palaces. It was also an era of cultural development and efficient government.

SWEDISH EMPIRE

■ *Sweden's empire after the Peace of Roskilde, 1658*

The Tre Kronor Castle
Built as a defensive tower in the 1180s, the Tre Kronor castle was the seat of Swedish monarchs from the 1520s and became the administrative centre of the Swedish Empire. It was named after the three crowns on the spire which burned down in 1697.

The columns of troops
ride out over the shifting ice towards Danish Lolland.

THE THIRTY YEARS WAR

A major European war raged between 1618–48, largely on German soil. Sweden entered the war in 1631 in an alliance with France. Gustav II Adolf was a fine military leader and had modernized the Swedish army which immediately had major successes at the battles of Breitenfeld (1631) and Lützen (1632), where the king, however, was killed. Later the Swedes

The death of Gustav II Adolf at the Battle of Lützen in 1632

pressed into southern Germany and also captured and plundered Prague (1648). Some rich cultural treasures were brought back to Sweden from the war. In 1648 the Peace of Westphalia gave Sweden several important possessions in northern Germany.

Stockholm in 1640
The city's transformation from a small medieval town into a capital city can be seen in the network of straight streets, similar to the present layout.

Karl XI's Triumphs
The roof painting in Karl XI's gallery at the Royal Palace (1693) by the French artist Jacques Foucquet shows in allegoric form the king's victories at Halmstad, Lund and Landskrona.

Count Carl Gustaf Wrangel *(see p56).*

King Karl X Gustav himself leads the Swedish army of 17,000 men.

The Powerful Nobility
The nobility were very influential in the Empire era and many successful soldiers were ennobled. The Banér family coat of arms from 1651 is adorned by three helmets and barons' crowns.

Bondeska Palatset
One of the leading buildings of the era (1662–73), this palace was designed by Tessin the Elder and Jean de la Vallée for the State Treasurer Gustav Bonde (see p58).

CROSSING THE GREAT BELT
When Denmark declared war on Sweden in autumn 1657, the Swedish army was in Poland. Marching west, Karl X Gustav captured the Danish mainland, but without the navy, he could not continue to Copenhagen. However, unusually severe weather froze the sea, making it possible for the soldiers to cross the ice of the Great Belt, and the Danes had to surrender.

Karl XII's Pocket Watch
The warrior king's watch-case dates from 1700. It shows the state coat of arms, as well as those of the 49 provinces that belonged to Sweden at that time.

Karl XII's Last Journey
After being hit by a fatal bullet at Fredrikshald in Norway (1718), the king's body was taken first to Swedish territory then on to Uddevalla for embalming. Painting by Gustav Cederström (1878).

Gustav III with the white armband he wore when
mounting his *coup d'état* in 1772

THE AGE OF LIBERTY AND
THE GUSTAVIAN ERA

A new constitution came into force in
1719 which transferred power from the
monarch to parliament. As a result,
Sweden developed a system of parliamentary democracy similar to that of
Britain in the early 18th century.

The "Age of Liberty" coincided with
the Enlightenment, with dramatic
advances in culture, science and industry. The botanist Carl von Linné became
one of the most famous Swedes of his
time. Another was the scientist, philosopher and author Emanuel Swedenborg.
The production of textiles expanded in
Stockholm, and Sweden's first hospital
was constructed on Kungsholmen.

Changes in the balance of power
around 1770 gave the new king, Gustav
III, an opportunity to strike in an
attempt to regain his monarchical
powers. On 19 August 1772 Gustav
accompanied the guards' parade to the
Royal Palace where, in front of his life-
guards, he declared his intention to

mount a bloodless *coup d'état*. The
guards and other military units in Stockholm swore allegiance to the king, who
tied a white handkerchief round his arm
as a badge and rode out into the city to
be acclaimed by his people. Absolute
power had been restored.

Gustav III was influenced by the Age
of Enlightenment and by French culture, which had a great effect on
Swedish cultural life *(see pp22–3)*. But
over the years opposition grew to the
king's absolute powers, largely because
of his costly war against Russia. In 1792
he was murdered by a nobleman,
Captain Anckarström, during a masked
ball at the Opera House *(see p23)*.

Gustav III was succeeded by his son,
Gustav IV Adolf. During his reign
Sweden was dragged into the
Napoleonic wars. After a war against
Russia in 1808–9, Sweden lost its
sovereignty over Finland, which at the
time accounted for one-third of
Swedish territory. The king abdicated
and left Stockholm to flee the country.

THE ERA OF KARL JOHAN AND
BOURGEOIS LIBERALISM

By the early 19th century the absolute
powers of the monarch had been
removed for all time, and the privileges

Napoleon's former marshal, Jean-Baptiste Bernadotte,
as King Karl XIV Johan surrounded by his family

TIMELINE

1719 New constitution transfers power from the king to Parliament	1741 Carl von Linné appointed professor at Uppsala		1754 Royal family moves into Royal Palace		1790 Swedish defeat over Russia at battle of Svenskund
			1780s Immigrants are given wide religious freedom		1792 Gustav III murdered
1720	**1740**		**1760**	**1780**	**1800**
1738 Parliamentary power is established in the Age of Liberty as the "Hat" party wins elections		1772 Gustav III crowned and mounts *coup d'état* giving the king absolute power		1786 Swedish Academy founded	
Carl von Linné (1707–78)				1778 National costume decreed. Death penalty removed for some crimes	

Newspaper readers outside the *Aftonbladet* office in 1841

of the aristocracy were undermined even more in 1809 with a new constitution that divided power between the king, the government and parliament.

With a new class structure and the effect of the French Revolution, a new middle class emerged which also wanted to be more influential. One of the best-known newspapers founded around this time was the liberal mouthpiece, *Aftonbladet*.

Difficulties in finding a suitable new monarch led eventually to the choice of one of Napoleon's marshals, Jean-Baptiste Bernadotte, who took on the more authentic Swedish name of Karl Johan. Founder of the present royal dynasty, Karl XIV Johan continued to speak French and never fully learned the Swedish language. His French wife, Queen Desideria, found Stockholm a cultural backwater compared with Paris.

In 1813 a Swedish army with Karl Johan at its head became involved in a campaign against Napoleon. The Battle of Leipzig ended in defeat for France, but more significantly Denmark had to hand over Norway to Sweden. The

Stockholm's Eldkvarn mill, destroyed by fire in 1878

Norwegians were reluctant to unite with Sweden, but a union between the two countries was agreed which lasted from 1814 to 1905. A long era of peace began and with it came a dramatic increase in the country's population, which grew by 1 million to 3.5 million by 1850. Many Swedes were driven into poverty because there was not enough work to go round. Mass emigration followed. From the 1850s to the 1930s about 1.5 million people left Sweden. Most of the emigrants travelled to North America in search of a better life.

FOLK MOVEMENTS AND INDUSTRIALIZATION

As Sweden was transformed from an agricultural society into an industrialized country the problems posed by the population surplus were gradually tackled. Its industrial revolution started around 1850, gathering momentum in the late 19th century, and the textile, timber and iron industries provided the main sources of employment. In 1806 the nation's first steam-driven mill, Eldkvarn, was built on the site of the present-day City Hall in Stockholm. It continued production until destroyed by fire in 1878.

Folk movements sprang up in the 19th century which still play an important role in Swedish life. A temperance movement emerged against a background of alcohol abuse – in the 1820s annual consumption of spirits was 46 litres (80 pints) per person.

1809 Sweden loses Finland and Gustav IV Adolf abdicates

1810 Parliament chooses Jean-Baptiste Bernadotte as Crown Prince

1869 Emigration to North America increases due to crop failures

1842 Primary schools established by decree in every parish

1876 L M Ericsson starts manufacture of telephones

August Strindberg

1908 Royal Dramatic Theatre opens

1820	1840	1860	1880	1900

1818 Karl XIV Johan is crowned King of Sweden and Norway

1814 Sweden gains Norway in peace treaty with Denmark

1859 Sweden's first railway opens

1850 Sweden has 3.5 million population, 93,000 living in Stockholm

1879 August Strindberg's novel *The Red Room* is published

1905 Parliament dissolves union with Norway

The Era of Gustav III

GUSTAV III (1771–92) is one of the most colourful figures in Swedish history. The king's great interest in art, literature and the theatre made the late 18th century a golden age for Swedish culture, and several prestigious academies were founded at this time. After a bloodless revolution in 1772 Gustav III ruled with absolute power and initiated a wide-ranging programme of reform. But his attacks on the privileges of the nobility and his adventurous and costly foreign policy made him powerful enemies. In 1792 he was murdered during a masked ball at Stockholm's Opera House.

The Swedish Academy
The academy was founded by Gustav III in 1786 to preserve the Swedish language. Members received a token depicting the king's head at every meeting.

Gustav III's Coronation, 1772
The coronation of the all-powerful monarch in Stockholm's cathedral was a magnificent ceremony, portrayed here by C G Pilo (1782). Every detail was overseen by Gustav himself, who used his flair for the dramatic in politics as well.

A courtier entertains by reading aloud.

Gustav III studies architectural designs.

The Battle of Svenskund
Gustav III was not known as a successful warrior king, but in 1790 he led the Swedish fleet to its greatest victory ever, when it defeated Russia in a major maritime battle in the Gulf of Finland.

COURT LIFE AT DROTTNINGHOLM

Hilleström's painting (1779) gives an insight into court life at Drottningholm, where the king resided between June and November. In the present-day Blue Salon, Gustav III and Queen Sofia Magdalena socialized with their inner circle. Behaviour was modelled on the French court and etiquette was even stricter at Drottningholm than at Versailles.

Life in the Inns
The city abounded with inns, frequently visited by the 70,000 inhabitants. J T Sergel's sketch shows a convivial dinner party.

Murder at the Masked Ball

In 1792 Gustav III fell victim to a conspiracy at the Opera House. He was surrounded by masked men and shot by Captain Anckarström on the crowded stage. He died of his wounds 14 days later.

Gustav III's Mask and Cocked Hat

Despite his mask, Gustav III was easy to recognize since he was wearing the badges of two orders of chivalry. The drama intrigued the whole of Europe and inspired Verdi's opera Un Ballo in Maschera.

Flogging of the King's Murderer

Among the conspirators, only Anckarström was condemned to death. Before he was taken to his execution in Södermalm he was flogged on three successive days on the square in front of Riddarhuset.

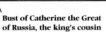

Bust of Catherine the Great of Russia, the king's cousin

Queen Sofia Magdalena does her needlework.

GUSTAVIAN STYLE

The mid-18th century saw the emergence of Neo-Classicism, with the focus on antiquities and Greek ideals. Gustav III embraced this trend with great enthusiasm and supported the country's talented artists and authors. He established his own Museum of Antiquities (*see pp52–3*) with marble sculptures which he brought home from Italy. In handicrafts, the sweeping lines of Rococo elegance were replaced by the stricter forms of what has become known as Gustavian Style. Rooms at the Royal Palace were renovated with decoration and furnishings adapted to suit this style.

Chair designed in Gustavian Style

Swedish Court Costume

In 1778 Gustav III introduced a costume based on French lines to restrain fashion excesses. This is the male court costume for daily wear.

UNIVERSAL SUFFRAGE

Sweden's population reached 5 million around 1900 despite mass emigration to America. Many people moved to the towns to work in industry, and by the early 20th century Stockholm's population was about 300,000, a fourfold increase since the year 1800.

Increasing social awareness and the rise of the Social Democrat and Liberal parties in the early 20th century gave impetus to the demands for universal suffrage. Radical authors like August Strindberg became involved. A political battle ensued which was not resolved until 1921 when universal suffrage was introduced for both sexes.

Another question which was hotly debated in the 19th century was the role of the king and the extent of his powers. In his "courtyard speech" at the Royal Palace in 1914 King Gustav V called for military rearmament. This led to a constitutional crisis and the resignation of the Liberal government. After the 1917 election the king was forced to accept a government which contained repub-

Branting and Gustav V in conversation, 1909

lican-friendly Social Democrats, including the future prime minister, Hjalmar Branting. By then it was parliament, not the king, that decided what sort of government Sweden should have.

THE GROWTH OF THE WELFARE STATE

In 1936 the Social Democrats and Farmers' Party formed a coalition which developed what was to become known as the welfare state. The Social Democrat prime minister, Per Albin Hansson (1885–1946), defined the welfare state as a socially conscious society with financial security for all. Reforms introduced under this policy included unemployment benefit, paid holidays and childcare. As a result, poverty in Sweden virtually disappeared during the 1930s and 1940s.

The right of everyone to good housing was also part of welfare state policy. Under the principle of "work-home-centre" a new Stockholm suburb, Vällingby, was planned and built in the early 1950s. The idea was to transform the dormitory suburbs into thriving communities where people would both live and work. The concept was unsuccessful. It soon became apparent that the people who lived there still worked somewhere else, and vice versa. The great shortage of housing in the 1960s led to the "million" programme, which involved the building of a million homes in an extremely short time. These areas soon became known as the "new slums" despite high standards of construction.

Calls for democratic reforms in June 1917 led to riots like this one outside the parliament building in Stockholm

TIMELINE

1914 Gustav V gives his "courtyard speech".	**1932** Suicide of industrial magnate Ivar Krueger is followed by stockmarket crash	**1940** Sweden–German agreement on transit of German military personnel	**1958** Women can be ordained as priests
1921 Universal suffrage for men and women			**1955** Obligatory national health insurance
1920		**1940**	**196**
Selma Lagerlöf, winner of the Nobel Prize for Literature	**1930** Rise of Functionalist style in architecture, stimulated by the Stockholm Exhibition	**1939** Sweden has coalition government and declares neutrality in World War II	**1950** First public TV broadcast in Sweden
			1952 Stockholm's first underground railway is inaugurated

THE WAR YEARS

Sweden declared its neutrality during both World War I and II. Its policy of continuing to trade with nations involved in the conflict during World War I provoked a number of countries into imposing a trade blockade on Sweden. The situation became so serious that hunger riots broke out in some towns.

World War II produced an even more difficult balancing exercise for Swedish neutrality, largely because its Nordic neighbours were at war. With a combination of luck and skill, Sweden remained outside the conflict, but the concessions it had to make were strongly criticized both nationally and internationally.

Neutrality stamp issued in 1942

THE POST-WAR ERA

Although the Social Democrats dominated government from the 1930s to the 1970s the socialist and non-socialist power blocs in Swedish politics have remained fairly evenly matched since World War II.

The policy of non-alignment has not proved an obstacle to Swedish involvement on the international scene, including the United Nations. The country has offered asylum to hundreds of thousands of refugees from wars and political oppression. Prime minister Olof Palme (1927–86), probably the best-known Swedish politician abroad, was deeply involved in questions of democracy and disarmament, as well as the problems of the Third World. He was renowned for condemning undemocratic acts by dictators. Palme's assassination on the streets of Stockholm in 1986 sent a shock wave across the world, but strangely the murder has still not been solved.

Important changes took place during the closing decades of the 20th century. These included a new constitution in 1974 which removed the monarch's political powers. In 1995 Sweden joined the European Union after a referendum approved entry by only the narrowest of majorities.

The start of the new millennium marked a change in the role of the church in Sweden, which severed its connections with the state after more than 400 years.

Sveavägen, the site of Palme's murder, 1986

As Stockholmers enter the third millennium, the country shows signs of economic crisis, even though most people still lead a good life. Rapid technical developments and globalization have provided Sweden both with new job opportunities and new inhabitants, as well as a leading international role in information technology.

The centre of Vällingby, which attracted attention among city planners worldwide in the 1950s

1964 Art exhibition at Moderna Museet shows works by Andy Warhol, Roy Lichtenstein and Claes Oldenburg

1967 Right-hand driving introduced

1974 The monarch loses all political powers

1974 ABBA pop group wins Eurovision Song Contest

1973 Gustav VI Adolf dies and is succeeded by grandson, Carl XVI Gustaf

1980 New constitution gives women the right of succession to the throne

1980

Crown Princess Victoria

1986 Prime minister Olof Palme murdered in Stockholm

2000 Öresund bridge opens between Denmark and Sweden

1995 Sweden joins European Union

200

STOCKHOLM THROUGH THE YEAR

STOCKHOLM'S HEART never misses a beat despite the vagaries of the climate. Although summer is a glorious time to visit the capital, the city shimmering in ice and snow is also an amazing experience, and numerous popular events take place throughout the year. Stockholm's countless sporting fixtures attract top-class international stars. Its many concerts, both pop and

Crocus, a sure sign of spring

classical, indoor and outdoor, feature performers from around the world. Sweden's national festivals are celebrated in the traditional way in Stockholm and are always popular attractions for both locals and visitors alike. The capital's proximity to the surrounding countryside and water provides an extensive range of opportunities for all kinds of outdoor activities throughout the year.

SPRING

AS IN ALL THE NORDIC countries, people long for spring after the dark days of winter, and it has a big impact on life in the capital. Sun-lovers sit on the steps of Konserthuset (Concert Hall) and Kungliga Dramatiska Teatern (Royal Dramatic Theatre); people work on their boats; football competes with ice hockey for attention; spring flowers come into bud in Kungsträdgården; and the traditional *semla* cream buns go on sale to break the Lenten fast.

Semla bun

MARCH

Stockholm International Boat Show *(early Mar)*. The spring's major boat exhibition at Stockholm International Fairs in Älvsjö.
Outdoors Fair *(Mar)*. Camping, tourism, and outdoor equipment fair at Sollentuna Exhibition Centre.

...thers at
...nsviken

Kuriosa *(early Mar)*. Fair for antiques and collectables at Sollentuna Exhibition Centre.
Sewing Festival *(early Mar)*. Needlework fair at Sollentuna Exhibition Centre.
Garden Fair *(Mar)*. Everything for the gardener on show at Sollentuna Exhibition Centre.
Stockholm Art Fair *(Mar)*. Works of art for sale at Sollentuna Exhibition Centre.
Spring Salon *(Mar)*. Annual art exhibition mainly featuring new artists at Liljevalchs Konsthall (gallery) on Djurgården.

APRIL

Gröna Lund *(last weekend in Apr)*. Djurgården's amusement park opens for the season.
Swedish Football Championship *(last weekend in Apr)*. Series starts at Råsunda and Söder stadiums.
Walpurgis Night at Skansen *(30 Apr)*. Traditional celebrations with massed standard bearers, folk dancing, torchlight procession, student choirs, bonfire and fireworks.
The King's Birthday *(30 Apr)*. The king is greeted at Kungliga Slottet (Royal Palace) with a military parade, and children hand over flowers and gifts.

MAY

Round Lidingö Race *(first Sat in May)*. Long-distance sailing race with hundreds of boats of all shapes and sizes.
Hat Parade *(mid-May)*. The parade starts at Nordiska Museet and finishes at

Walpurgis Night bonfire at Evert Taubes Terrass, Riddarholmen

Skansen, where the "hat of the year" is chosen.
Circus Princess *(May)*. A series of circus performances by female artists, the best of whom is chosen as the year's Circus Princess.
Archipelago Fair *(late May)*. Second-hand leisure boats for sale, purchase or exchange.
"Tjejtrampet" *(last weekend in May)*. 40-km (25-mile) cycling competition at Gärdet with 7,000 female cyclists.
Historical Festival *(last weekend in May)*. Wide range of programmes in Gamla Stan, and on Riddarholmen and Helgeandsholmen.
Elite Race *(last weekend in May)*. Trotting competition at Solvalla with top horses from all over the world.
Theatre in Hagaparken *(late May)*. Outdoor theatre in the old palace ruins.
Kungsträdgården *(late May)*. The programme of summer entertainment in the park starts on the main stage.
Popcorn *(late May)*. An eight-day film festival at cinemas in the city centre.

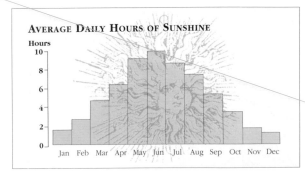

AVERAGE DAILY HOURS OF SUNSHINE

Hours: 10, 8, 6, 4, 2, 0

Jan Feb Mar Apr May Jun Jul Aug Sep Oct Nov Dec

Sunshine Chart
Stockholm's climate can vary markedly from hot, sunny days followed by a cooler rainy spell during the summer to winters with freezing temperatures and snow. From mid-June to mid-July it never really gets dark. Winter days are very short, although there can still be a strong sun at times.

SUMMER

STOCKHOLM SHOWS its best face at this time of year. Although May can be warm, summer does not really start until early June when the schools break up. In late June the sun shines almost round the clock, and with it comes a vibrant outdoor life with picnics and street festivals. The capital gets a bit emptier at peak holiday-time in July. When the schools go back in late August, Swedes celebrate the arrival of two annual culinary delights: crayfish and fermented Baltic herring.

Traditional Midsummer celebrations at Skansen, the open-air museum

JUNE

Stockholm Marathon *(first Sat in Jun).* One of the world's 10 biggest marathons with around 13,000 runners.
Gärdet Race *(early Jun).* Veteran cars in friendly competition at Gärdet.
Restaurant Festival *(early Jun).* Kungsträdgården becomes the world's largest outdoor restaurant.
American Festival *(early Jun).* American culture and food in Kungsträdgården.
Archipelago Boat Day *(first Wed in Jun).* Classic steamboats assemble at Strömkajen near the Grand Hôtel for a round trip to Vaxholm.
Riddardamen *(Jun).* Regatta for female sailors at Riddarfjärden.
Stockholm Grand Prix *(Jun).* Season's second-largest racing event at Täby racecourse with an international field.
National Day *(6 Jun).* Celebrations at Skansen in the presence of the royal family.

Midsummer Eve *(next to last Sat in Jun).* A major Swedish festival celebrated at Skansen over three days. It starts at 2pm on Midsummer Eve with the traditional raising of the maypole and ring dancing.
Music at the Palace *(Jun–Aug).* Summer concert season starts in the Hall of State and the Royal Chapel at Kungliga Slottet (Royal Palace).
Drottningholms Slottsteater *(Jun–Aug)* Season of concerts, opera and dance throughout the summer in the 18th-century court theatre.
Palace Gala *(mid-Jun)* Concerts with popular classics and modern music by international stars in the park at Ulriksdals Slott.

JULY

Round Gotland Race *(first week in Jul).* Major international sailing event, with start and finish at Sandhamn.
Boules Festival *(first weekend in Jul).* Boules enthusiasts gather in Kungsträdgården.

Stockholm International Jazz & Blues Festival *(third week in Jul).* Great artists play in a fantastic outdoor setting on Skeppsholmen.
DN Gala *(Jul).* Major international athletics competition at Stockholm Stadion.

AUGUST

Midnight Race *(early Aug).* Night-time running over 10 km (6 miles) in Söder with around 16,000 participants.
"Recykling" *(second week in Aug).* Environmentally-oriented event of 4,000 cyclists at Kungsträdgården.
Philharmonikerna i det Gröna *(2nd Sun in Aug).* Royal Philharmonic Orchestra performs free for picnicking music-lovers on the lawn by Sjöhistoriska Museet.
"Tjejmilen" *(last Sun in Aug).* About 25,000 female runners compete in a 10 (6-mile) event at Gärdet.
Crayfish Season *(last in Aug).* Swedes eat c and sing "schnapps s

Crayfish

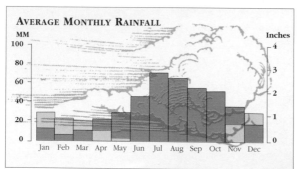

AVERAGE MONTHLY RAINFALL

MM / Inches

100 — 4
80
60 — 3
40 — 2
20 — 1
0 — 0

Jan Feb Mar Apr May Jun Jul Aug Sep Oct Nov Dec

Rainfall Chart
Some years Stockholm can have very rainy summers, but in other years the weather can be dry for several weeks at a time. Heavy snowfall in winter may lie until March, but some winters have been known to be virtually free of snow.

■ Rain (from the baseline)

▨ Snow (from the baseline)

AUTUMN

EARLY AUTUMN mornings can be crisp and clear, but summer often stages a successful and lengthy last-ditch stand, and the trees explode in a cascade of colours.

Globen and other indoor arenas draw increasingly large attendances, and cultural activities in theatres and art galleries get under way again, although many outdoor events continue well into the autumn, weather permitting.

Chanterelles

SEPTEMBER

NOW IS THE TIME to pick mushrooms in the forests, or apples, pears and plums in the garden. The summer cottages are shut and the boats are laid up for the winter, but there is still a lot going on in the capital.
Riddarfjärden Regatta *(first weekend in Sep)*. About 100 fine old wooden boats compete in this regatta.
Stockholm Cup *(first weekend in Sep)*. Horse race at Täby course with an international field.

Elite Series *(first weekend in Sep)*. The season's first ice-hockey matches at Globen.
Swedish Army Tattoo *(first weekend in Sep, even-numbered years)*. Military bands and display groups perform at Globen.
Stockholm Race *(last weekend in Sep)*. Fun-run round the city centre from Stadion.
Pet Fair *(last weekend in Sep)*. Pets on show at Stockholm International Fairs in Älvsjö.

OCTOBER

THIS IS A BUSY TIME for theatres, cinemas, restaurants and clubs. There are fewer outdoor events, instead people head for the parks and forests for autumn strolls.
Lidingö Race *(first weekend in Oct)*. The world's largest cross-country race with tens of thousands of competitors, including elite runners, senior citizens and children.

NOVEMBER

AS DARKNESS FALLS over the city, there is a wide selection of events to choose from.

Annual Stockholm International Horse Show at Globen

Autumn Antiques Fair *(mid-Nov)*. Notable antiques fair with a chance of some real finds at Wasahallen.
Scandinavian Sail and Motor Boat Show *(mid-Nov)*. Exhibition at Stockholm International Fairs with everything for large motor boats or yachts.
Det Goda Köket cookery exhibition *(mid-Nov)*. Food, wine and cooking equipment with participation by the country's leading chefs at Stockholm International Fairs.
Stockholm Open *(mid-Nov)*. ATP tennis tournament at Kungliga Tennishallen.
Skating Premiere *(mid-Nov)*. Skating with music starts on an artificial rink in Kungsträdgården.
Stockholm Film Festival *(mid-Nov)*. Ten-day event with public screenings and the presentation of awards.
Stockholm International Horse Show *(late Nov)*. World Cup competition in dressage and jumping plus entertainment at Globen.
Christmas displays *(late Nov)*. Shop windows and streets are decorated.

of autumn colours in Hagaparken

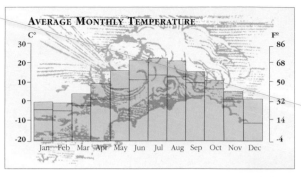

AVERAGE MONTHLY TEMPERATURE

C°		F°
30		86
20		68
10		50
0		32
-10		14
-20		-4

Jan Feb Mar Apr May Jun Jul Aug Sep Oct Nov Dec

Temperature Chart
Stockholm has a maritime climate and is much milder than might be expected. The summers are usually fairly cool, but sometimes there can be hot sunshine for several weeks running. Winter temperatures often fall below freezing, but it is rarely severely cold. The average maximum and minimum temperatures are shown.

WINTER

WINTER CAN VARY from temperatures a few degrees above freezing with slush on the streets to sparkling sunny days with the city under a dazzling white blanket of snow, ice-covered water and temperatures well below zero. Stockholmers get out their skis, skates, or toboggans, or go for long walks. There are also several cultural and sporting events.

DECEMBER

SOMETIMES THE eagerly awaited Christmas season seems a long way off, but there is no shortage of activities in early December, when some of the year's most important events are staged.
Handicraft and Arts Exhibition *(early Dec)*. Popular arts and crafts show at Sollentuna Exhibition Centre.
Nobel Day *(10 Dec)*. The year's Nobel Prize laureates are honoured in a ceremony at Konserthuset (Concert Hall). In the evening the royal family attends a banquet at Stadshuset (City Hall).

Lucia, the "Queen of Light", with her attendants at Skansen

Lucia Celebrations *(13 Dec)*. Sweden's white-clad Lucia, the "Queen of Light", with her girl attendants and "star boys", serves the Nobel laureates early morning coffee with saffron buns and performs traditional songs. In the evening a Lucia procession winds through the city to celebrations and fireworks at Skansen. Many Swedish homes, schools and workplaces have their own Lucia.
Christmas Markets *(from early Dec)*. Christmas goods on sale at traditional markets at Skansen, Rosendals Slott, Stortorget in Gamla Stan and Drottningholms Slott.
Christmas *(24–26 Dec)*. Filled with traditions, Christmas is the most important Swedish holiday. The main event is Christmas Eve, when an abundant *smörgåsbord* is followed by gifts, often delivered by a family member disguised as Father Christmas.
Christmas Sales *(first weekday after Christmas)* Shops start their sales.
Ice Sculptures *(late Dec)*. If the weather permits, Djurgården is the centre for this unusual art form.
New Year *(31 Dec–1 Jan)*. A major festival when many Stockholmers go out on the town. Traditional celebrations at Skansen include a reading of Tennyson's "*Ring out wild bells...*" on the stroke of midnight. Churches ring their bells, and there is a spectacular fireworks display.

Christmas market at Stortorget in Gamla Stan, a traditional prelude to the festive season

JANUARY

Antiques Fair *(early Jan)*. The year's first major fair is staged at Stockholm International Fairs, Älvsjö.

FEBRUARY

Sweden Hockey Games *(Feb)* Ice hockey tournament at Globen between Russia, the Czech Republic, Finland and the Swedish national team, Tre Kronor.
Globen Gala *(second half of Feb)*. International athletics stars converge on the Globen arena for one of the world's best indoor competitions.

PUBLIC HOLIDAYS

New Year's Day (1 Jan)
Epiphany (6 Jan)
Good Friday
Easter Monday
Ascension Day (6th Thu after Easter)
Labour Day (1 May)
Whit Monday (May/Jun)
Midsummer Eve (end Jun)
Christmas Day (25 Dec)
Boxing Day (26 Dec)

STOCKHOLM AT A GLANCE

THE OLD CONCEPTION of Stockholm as a small, rustic capital of a cold country far away to the north is no longer valid – the city has a rich cultural heritage and has become a dynamic Continental-style capital.

Stockholm is an unbelievably beautiful city, surrounded by clear water and unspoilt countryside which stretches right into the heart of the urban area. Stockholm's 750-year history has produced many beautiful buildings, as well as plenty of impressive cultural treasures which can be discovered in its fine museums.

To make your visit as rewarding as possible the following 10 pages give a quick guide to the best museums and palaces, the most distinguished architecture, and outstanding modern design. Activities along the city's quaysides and waterways are also described. Below is a selection of sights that should not be missed.

STOCKHOLM'S TOP TEN SIGHTS

Skansen
See pp96–7

Stadshuset
See pp114–15

Nordiska Museet
See pp90–91

Drottningholm
See pp140–43

Historiska Museet
See pp104–105

Moderna Museet
See pp80–81

Stockholm's Archipelago
See pp144–45

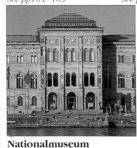

Nationalmuseum
See pp82–3

Royal Palace and its Guard
See pp50–53

Vasamuseet
See pp92–4

◁ Gamla Stan, and its romantic streets like Österlånggatan, is one of Stockholm's leading attractions

Stockholm's Best: Museums

STOCKHOLM HAS around 100 museums. Their remarkable collections cover every conceivable subject and interest. The "Top Ten" shown here are of particular note. Kungliga Slottet (the Royal Palace), for instance, is effectively four museums in one, while the most spectacular is the museum housing the *Vasa* warship, salvaged from the depths of Stockholm's harbour after 333 years and now an international attraction.

Hallwylska Palatset
Thanks to a methodical countess and her impeccable taste this lavishly decorated palace from the 1890s has become a magnificent museum with 67,000 exhibits displayed in an original setting.

VASASTADEN

Medeltidsmuseet
Parts of the city wall from the 1530s can be seen in this underground Museum of Medieval Stockholm, which focuses on the capital's origins. The wall's reconstruction shows medieval building techniques.

CITY

SÖDERMALM

Nationalmuseum
The National Museum of Fine Arts, Sweden's largest art museum, has fine collections of 17th- and 18th-century Swedish paintings and handicrafts, 18th-century French and 17th-century Dutch art. Rubens's Bacchanal on Andros *dates from the 1630s.*

The Royal Palace
In addition to its own attractions, the Royal Palace houses four specialist museums: the Treasury, featuring Erik XIV's State Orb (1561); the Royal Armoury; Gustav III's Museum of Antiquities; and the Tre Kronor Museum.

0 metres	500
0 yards	500

Historiska Museet

Behind the sculpted bronze gateways of the Museum of National Antiquities is a wealth of material, including a section on Viking life. The Gold Room shows priceless prehistoric finds, such as the Timboholm Treasure (400–450 BC).

Moderna Museet

Paradise *(1966) by Tinguely de Saint Phalle marks the way up to the Modern Museum with its superb collections of international and Swedish modern art.*

Sjöhistoriska Museet

The stern of the royal flagship Amphion, *dating from the late 18th century, is one of the many treasures on display in the National Maritime Museum, designed by Ragnar Östberg.*

ÖSTERMALM

Nordiska Museet

This colossal building from 1907 houses many different artifacts illustrating everyday Swedish life and customs, including this coat of Count Axel von Fersen (1780s).

SKEPPS-HOLMEN

 DJURGÅRDEN

Skansen

The world's first open-air museum, founded in 1891, shows the Sweden of bygone days with farms and manor houses, urban scenes and crafts people at work. Nordic fauna and flora are also on display.

Vasamuseet

A fatal capsizal in 1628 and a successful salvage operation 333 years later gave Stockholm its most popular museum. The warship Vasa *is now 95% intact after painstaking renovation.*

Exploring Stockholm's museums

STOCKHOLM'S WIDE RANGE of museums gives the visitor a chance to experience exhibitions covering a multitude of different interests. Many are housed in magnificent historic palaces or institutions with notable collections and the resources to bring each subject to life. In addition, there are numerous specialist museums, including the homes of highly regarded artists. Various important private collections are open to the public. This guide lists more than 50 of the best museums Stockholm has to offer.

Decorative Viking brooch, Historiska Museet

Karl XII's uniform, 1718, on show at Livrustkammaren

PALACE MUSEUMS

THE PERIOD WHEN Sweden was a great power (1611–1718) resulted in a number of beautiful buildings many of which are now museums. Foremost among these are the royal palaces in and around the city. **Kungliga Slottet** (Royal Palace, *pp50–53*) is a museum in itself. It also houses **Skattkammaren** (the Treasury) with Sweden's royal regalia, crowns and a large silver font for the baptism of royal children.

Also in the Royal Palace are **Gustav III's Antikmuseum**, containing the antique marble sculptures that Gustav III brought home from his Italian travels, and **Livrust-kammaren** (Royal Armoury, *p48*) where visitors can see a variety of items used at the court through the centuries. **Museum Tre Kronor** reflects the history of the earlier castle.

Other royal museums include **Rosendals Slott** (*p98*) on Djurgården, a pre-

fabricated building from the 1820s in Karl Johan (Empire) style. **Gustav III's Paviljong** (*pp122–3*) in Hagaparken has furnishings and decorations which are fine examples of the late 18th-century Gustavian style. **Ulriksdals Slott** (*p125*) has some interesting interiors, including a living room for King Gustav VI Adolf and Queen Louise.

In a class of its own is **Drottningholms Slott** (*pp140–43*), a UNESCO heritage site, which includes a notable theatre museum.

HISTORICAL MUSEUMS

SEVERAL OF Stockholm's museums focus on various historic aspects.

Historiska Museet (Museum of National Antiquities, *pp104–105*) has treasures from prehistoric times in its magnificent Gold Room, as well as a superb section on the Vikings. **Nordiska Museet** (*pp90–91*) and the open-air **Skansen** (*pp96–7*) show Swedish customs and traditions alongside traditional wooden homes. **Stockholms Stadsmuseum** (City Museum, *p127*) tells the story of Stockholm and its citizens. It also has a reference library.

The city's earliest history is highlighted at **Medeltidsmuseet** (Medieval Museum, *p59*).

Folkens Museum Etnografiska (National Museum of Ethnography, *p108*) features

anthropological artifacts from all around the world.

The culture and history of the Jewish people is the theme of **Judiska Museet** (*p118*).

Medelhavsmuseet (Museum of Mediterranean and Near Eastern Antiquities, *p65*) focuses on architecture and sculptures from the countries around the Mediterranean.

Östasiatiska Museet (Museum of Far Eastern Antiquities, *p78*) contains large collections of arts and crafts from China, Japan, Korea and India.

ART MUSEUMS

THE WIDE RANGE of collections at the **Nationalmuseum** (National Museum of Fine Arts, *pp82–3*) cover European and Swedish paintings up to the early 20th century, as well as Swedish handicrafts and design.

Moderna Museet (*pp80–81*) on Skeppsholmen has an outstanding collection of contemporary Swedish and international art. **Arkitekturmuseet** (Museum of Architecture, *p78*), highlights Swedish building techniques over the last 1,000 years and provides an overview of the wider international picture. Three magnificent art galleries are located in beautiful

Amor and Psyche by J T Sergel, Nationalmuseum

buildings on Djurgården.
Liljevalchs Konsthall *(p95)*
focuses on 20th-century
Swedish and international art,
while **Waldemarsudde** *(p99)*
and **Thielska Galleriet** *(p99)*
both specialize in Swedish
and Nordic art from the late
19th to the early 20th century.
Spökslottet (the Haunted
Palace, *p116)* shows
Stockholm University's
collection of classic Swedish
paintings, as well as artistic
Swedish glass.
Millesgården *(p144)* on
Lidingö is where the sculptor
Carl Milles lived and worked,
and where he is now buried.
Some of his best works are on
show in a beautiful outdoor
setting with a panoramic view
of Stockholm.

Drawing room in the lavishly decorated Hallwylska Palatset

MARINE MUSEUMS

A CITY LOCATED ON water
offers plenty of interest
for anyone interested in ships
and the sea.

One of the city's biggest
attractions, **Vasamuseet**
(pp92–4), shows the
magnificent and almost intact
warship *Vasa*, which sank in
Stockholm harbour after a
maiden voyage of only
1,300 m (1,400 yd). In
addition to the painstakingly
restored hull, there are other
exhibits which give an insight
into life on board a 17th-
century warship.

Close to *Vasa* are
Museifartygen (Museum
Ships *p89)*, including one of
the last Swedish lightships
Finngrundet (1903), and the
powerful ice-breaker *St Erik*
(1915) featuring Europe's
largest marine steam engine.

Nearby is **Aquaria** *(p95)*,
where visitors can see a
variety of animals and plants
in a living ecological system
of tropical rainforest, sea
and Nordic waters.

Sjöhistoriska Museet
(National Maritime Museum,
p106) features a fine
collection of model ships.

A short boat trip takes visitors to the **Fjäderholmarna**
islands, where there are two
boat museums, an angling
museum and a Baltic
aquarium *(p144)*.

MUSEUMS IN PRIVATE HOMES

O NE OF THE PEARLS among
Stockholm's museums,
Hallwylska Palatset *(p73)*, is
an opulent private residence
from the late 19th century,
complete with original
furnishings. The home of the
dramatist and author August
Strindberg, which became
**Strindbergsmuseet Blå
Tornet** (Strindberg's Blue
Tower Museum, *p69)*, gives
an insight into his life. A
statue of Strindberg by Carl
Eldh stands near **Carl Eldhs
Ateljémuseum** (Studio
Museum, *p121)*, the sculptor's
former residence.

MUSEUMS FOR SPECIAL INTERESTS

S TOCKHOLM HAS many
museums catering for
special interests. **Kungliga
Myntkabinettet** (Royal Coin
Cabinet, *p48)* shows coins

**Stage costume from *Les Ballets
Suédois* (1920s), Dansmuseet**

and other methods of pay-
ment dating back 1,000 years.
Junibacken *(p88)* is a
charming museum, bringing
to life the classic children's
books by Astrid Lindgren.

Leksaksmuseet (Toy
Museum, *p131)* is an
attraction for all ages with its
mechanical toys, models,
dolls and dolls' houses.

A traditional wine shop and
distillery can be seen at **Vin-
& Sprithistoriska Museet**
(Wine and Spirits Museum,
p120), housed in a former
wine warehouse. Another
human weakness, tobacco, is
documented at Skansen's
Tobaksmuseet (Tobacco
Museum, *pp96-7)*.

Postmuseum (Postal
Museum, *p55)* contains more
than 4 million stamps from
around the world.

Spårvägsmuseet
(Transport Museum, *p130)*
has some 40 original trams
and a large collection of
models. In the same area is
the delightful **Almgrens
Sidenväveri & Museum**
(Almgren's Silk-weaving Mill
& Museum, *p127)*.

The life of the 18th-century
troubadour Carl Michael Bellman *(p98)*, is portrayed at the
Bellmanmuseet *(p132)* on
Långholmen.

Dansmuseet (Dance
Museum, *p65)* reflects all
aspects of dance with a
superb international collection.

Musikmuseet (Music
Museum, *p72)* has some
6,000 instruments and the
country's biggest musical
archive, in which folk music
addicts can browse through
records covering 20,000
traditional ballads.

Stockholm's Best: Architecture

SWEDEN WAS SPARED THE ravages of World War II, so Stockholm has preserved a rich variety of architectural treasures. Gamla Stan was the city's first built-up area. The surrounding districts known as Malmarna *(see p101)* remained mainly rural until an intensive period of building begun in the second half of the 19th century. From 1930 the city started to expand further and this period is reflected in a band of Functionalist-style buildings. Suburbs like Farsta and Vällingby were built after 1945. In the 1990s, new buildings began appearing in the inner city on former industrial sites.

Stadsbiblioteket
(Erik Gunnar Asplund, 1920–28). The City Library is Stockholm's most admired example of the 1920s Neo-Classicist style. The book hall has a fascinating cylindrical shape and many fine interior details. (See p117.)

Kungliga Dramatiska Teatern
(Fredrik Liljekvist, 1901–1908). The Royal Dramatic Theatre is one of Stockholm's few monumental buildings in Jugendstil. The façades are of white marble, and inside the staircase and foyer are embellished with lavish gold decorative work. (See p72.)

VASASTADEN

CITY

KUNGSHOLMEN

GAMLA STAN

SÖDERMALM

The Royal Palace
(Nicodemus Tessin the Younger 1690–1704; completed under Carl Hårleman). Work on the Royal Palace, based on plans by Tessin the Younger, started after the fire in 1697. The façade exhibits influences of Roman palaces; the magnificent interiors are of French and Swedish design. (See pp50–53.)

Wrangelska Palatset
(Nicodemus Tessin the Elder 1652–70). This is one of several majestic palaces built on Riddarholmen in the imposing style popular during the 17th century. Original details include the gateway and the courtyard arcade. (See p56.)

Tessinparken
(Arvid Stille, 1930 city plan by Sture Frolén). Functionalist style on a large scale was tested on the three-storey buildings on pillars at Tessinparken. (See p110.)

THE TESSIN TRIO

Nicodemus Tessin the Younger (1654–1728), who designed the Royal Palace *(see pp50–53)*, can be regarded as Sweden's leading architect because he influenced not only building design but also city planning, landscape gardening and handicrafts. His father, Nicodemus Tessin the Elder (1615–81), designed several country mansions, with Drottningholm Palace being his master work *(see pp140–43)*. The third-generation Tessin, Carl Gustaf (1695–1770), along with Carl Hårleman, introduced the Rococo style to Sweden.

Etching of the Royal Palace, to which all three Tessins contributed

Nordiska Museet
(Isak Gustaf Clason, 1889–1907). This museum was conceived as a national monument for Nordic culture. The impressive building in a Scandinavian version of Renaissance style is only one-third of its planned size. (See pp90–91.)

ÖSTERMALM

Moderna Museet
(Rafael Moneo, 1995–8). The spacious Modern Museum was designed to be novel yet not to disturb the historically sensitive surroundings of the island of Skeppsholmen. (See pp80–81.)

SKEPPS-
HOLMEN

DJURGÅRDEN

Söder Cottages
Wooden cottages for port workers started to spring up from the early 18th century. Quite a few remain in the Söder area, for example at Åsöberget and on Fjällgatan. (See p129.)

0 metres 500
0 yards 500

STOCKHOLM'S SURROUNDING AREAS

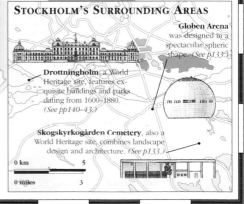

Globen Arena was designed in a spectacular spheric shape. *(See p133.)*

Drottningholm, a World Heritage site, features exquisite buildings and parks dating from 1600–1880. *(See pp140–43.)*

Skogskyrkogården Cemetery, also a World Heritage site, combines landscape design and architecture. *(See p133.)*

0 km 5
0 miles 3

Swedish Style

SWEDISH DESIGN FIRST attracted international attention at the 1925 World Exhibition in Paris, when glassware in particular took the world by storm and the concept of "Swedish Grace" was launched. The nation's design tradition is characterized by its simplicity and functionality with an emphasis on natural materials. Swedish designers and architects are renowned for creating simple, attractive "human" objects for everyday use. The 1990s marked the beginning of a new golden age in which contemporary Swedish design once more won worldwide acclaim.

Stoneware, Hans Hedberg
Swedish stoneware from the 1940s, 1950s and 1960s attracts worldwide attention, and collectors buy anything they can find.

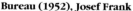

Armchair (1969), Bruno Mathsson
Bruno Mathsson, one of Sweden's most famous 20th-century furniture designers, is one of the creators of what came to be known as the "Swedish Modern" style. He designed the first version of the Pernilla armchair in 1942.

Pale wood and simplicity is the concept most closely associated with Swedish style.

Bureau (1952), Josef Frank
Frank was born in Austria but worked in Sweden and was another disciple of the "Swedish Modern" style. He is best known for his printed textiles for Svenskt Tenn (see p176), but also designed furniture.

Rag mats are an old Swedish weaving tradition taken up by Karin Larsson, whose skill as a textile designer is now widely recognized.

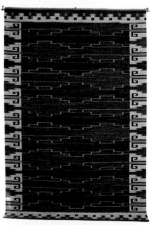

Carpet (1931), Märta Måås-Fjetterström
From 1919 Måås-Fjetterström wove her highly regarded carpets at her studio in southern Sweden. Her work was inspired by folklore and nature, and she created a design concept that was new but still deeply rooted in tradition.

Silver coffee pot (1953), Sigurd Persson

Persson had an unrivalled ability to handle metal. He made a big impact on the history of design with both his everyday industrial work and his exclusive artistic creations

Flowers and plants along a windowsill and no curtains typify the Larssons' ideas on interior decoration.

Chair (1981), Jonas Bohlin

The Concrete chair became the most remarkable piece of Swedish furniture design in the 1980s. A graduation project, it represented a completely new approach to furniture design.

Bookshelf (1989), John Kandell

Books are placed flat on the Pilaster bookshelf instead of stacking them in the usual way. The lines are simple and typically Scandinavian. The maker, Källemo, is one of Sweden's most unconventional furniture manufacturers.

Gustavian late 18th-century style elements have remained a strong feature in Swedish design through the centuries, and made a particular comeback in the 1990s.

CARL LARSSON'S SUNDBORN

The home created by the artist Carl Larsson (1853–1919) and his wife Karin, became an inspiration to the world when it featured in his watercolour series *A Home*. The mixture of old and new, pure colours, plants and windows without curtains was an expression of the "Beauty for All" movement.

Vase (1998), Ann Wåhlström

Wåhlström is one of the new young glass designers at Kosta Boda. Her vase, Cyklon, is a good example of contemporary Swedish glass.

WHERE TO SEE SWEDISH DESIGN

Asplund
Södra Blasieholmshamnen.
Map 3 E3.
Large range of 20th-century design.

Asplund
Sibyllegatan 31.
Map 3 E3.
Contemporary Swedish and international design.

Svenskt Tenn
Strandvägen 5. **Map** 3 E4
Josef Frank, etc.

Klara
Nytorgsgatan 36.
Map 9 E3.
Contemporary Swedish and international design.

Bo
Östgötagatan 2.
Map 9 D2.
Modern antiques.

Jacksons
Tyska Brinken 20.
Map 4 B3.
Modern antiques.

Stockholm, City on the Water

THE SWEDISH CAPITAL IS OFTEN called "The Venice of the North", built as it is on 14 islands surrounded by the clear waters of Lake Mälaren and Saltsjön, an inlet from the Baltic Sea. For most visitors "the green city on the water" is a remarkable experience. Stockholm's quaysides and waterways offer a whole range of activities not normally associated with a capital city, which are made possible only because of the pollution-free environment. The waterside location is Stockholm's most beautiful feature.

Canoe Slalom on Strömmen
Spectacular canoe slalom competitions are held every year in the rushing water of the Strömmen channel below Gustav Adolfs Torg.

Sailing Race on Riddarfjärden
The waters of Stockholm are always busy with sailing boats. The Riddarfjärden Regatta takes place annually in early September in front of Stadshuset (City Hall).

CITY

KUNGSHOLMEN

Strömmen

GAMLA STAN

Riddarfjärden

SK HO

Långholmen

SÖDERMALM

Swimming in the Heart of the City
During the summer months, swimmers bathe in the clean, warm water (about 20°C/68°F) in the city centre. Långholmen (see p132) has sandy beaches and smooth rocks offering an ideal setting for a refreshing dip.

Fishing for a Living
For 400 years fishermen have cast their nets from boats near Kungliga Slottet (Royal Palace). Today only four boats remain. Of the 30 species found here, smelt is the most commonly caught fish.

Exploring on Your Own

Kayaks, pedalos, rowing boats, motor boats, and sometimes sailing dinghies, can be hired near the Djurgården Bridge by visitors who want to explore the waters of Stockholm on their own.

Vintage Mahogany Boat

Lovingly renovated vintage motor boats with shining mahogany and brass fittings are often seen on the waterways of Stockholm, as well as the more exclusive Riva racing boats.

| 0 metres | 500 |
| 0 yards | 500 |

ÖSTERMALM

Djurgårdsbrunnsviken

DJURGÅRDEN

Fishing for Perch

The clean waters of the inner city are rich in edible fish. Anglers spin for sea trout, and here on Djurgårdsbrunn Canal bait-fishing for perch is popular, and fly-fishing in autumn.

Saltsjön

KEY

•••• Paved walking path

Open-air swimming

Cruise Ship Manoeuvres in Stockholm's Harbour

Cruise ships are an attractive sight when seen from the heights of Södermalm as they make their way through the narrow channel to their centrally located quay.

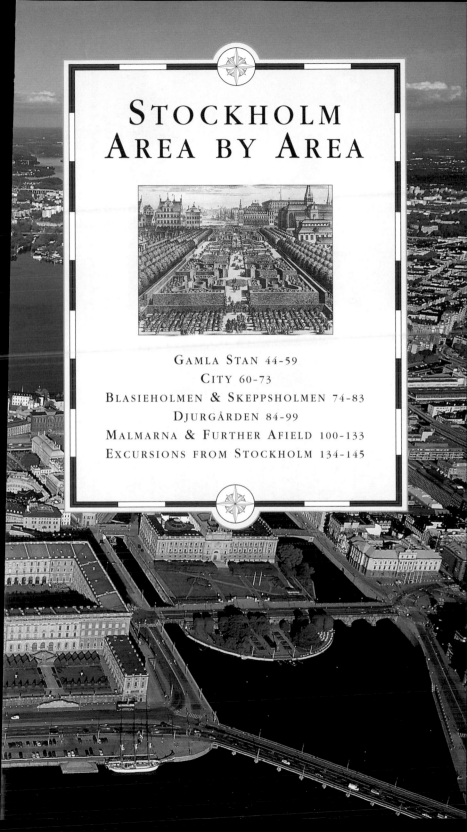

STOCKHOLM
AREA BY AREA

GAMLA STAN 44-59

CITY 60-73

BLASIEHOLMEN & SKEPPSHOLMEN 74-83

DJURGÅRDEN 84-99

MALMARNA & FURTHER AFIELD 100-133

EXCURSIONS FROM STOCKHOLM 134-145

GAMLA STAN

RELICS OF STOCKHOLM'S early history as a town in the 13th century can still be found on Stadsholmen, Gamla Stan's (Old Town) largest island. The whole island is one huge area of historical heritage, with the many sights just a few metres apart.

The Royal Palace is the symbol of Sweden's era as a great power in the 17th and early 18th centuries *(see pp18–19)*, and its magnificent state rooms, apartments and artifacts are well matched to the Roman Baroque-style exterior. The historic buildings standing majestically

Anchor point on the palace façade

around Slottsbacken, underline Stockholm's role as a capital city.

This area has a special atmosphere with much to offer: from the bustling streets of souvenir shops, bookstores and antique shops to elegant palaces, churches and museums. Many medieval cellars are now restaurants and cafés, while the narrow streets recall a bygone era.

Bridges lead to Riddarholmen, with its 17th-century palace and royal crypt, and to Helgeandsholmen for the newer splendours of Riksdagshuset (the Parliament building).

SIGHTS AT A GLANCE

Palaces and Museums
The Royal Palace pp50–53 ❶
Kungliga
Myntkabinettet ❸
Livrustkammaren ❷
Medeltidsmuseet ❶❾
Postmuseum ❿

Public Buildings
Bondeska Palatset ❶❼
Riddarhuset ❶❻
Riksdagshuset ❶❽
Stenbockska Palatset ❶❺

Historic Buildings
Birger Jarls Torn ❶❹

Tessinska Palatset ❹
Wrangelska Palatset ❶❷

Streets and Squares
Evert Taubes Terrass ❶❸
Mårten Trotzigs Gränd ❽
Stortorget ❻
Västerlånggatan ❾

Churches
Riddarholms-
kyrkan ❶❶
Storkyrkan ❺
Tyska Kyrkan ❼

KEY

▩	Street-by-Street map *See pp46–7*
🚢	Ferry landing point
Ⓣ	Tunnelbana station
🚌	Bus stop
P	Parking

0 metres　　　　250
0 yards　　　　　250

◁ **Prästgatan in Gamla Stan with its yellow ochre plastering typical of the 18th century**

Street-by-Street: Slottsbacken

SLOTTSBACKEN IS MUCH MORE than just a steep hill
linking Skeppsbron and the highest part of Gamla
Stan (Old Town). It also provides the background for
ceremonial processions and the daily changing-of-the-
guard, and is the route for visiting heads of state and
foreign ambassadors when they have an audience with
the king at the Royal Palace. Alongside Slottsbacken the
palace displays its most attractive façade, with the
entrance to the Treasury (Skattkammaren), State Room
(Rikssalen) and Palace Church (Slottskyrkan).
Nicodemus Tessin the Younger's ambition to make
Stockholm a leading European city in monumental terms
was realized in 1799 with the addition of the Obelisk.

The Olaus Petri statue by
Storkyrkan stands in front
of a tablet telling the
history of the
cathedral
since
1264.

**Axel Oxenstiernas
Palats** (1653) is, for
Stockholm, an
unusual example of
the style known as
Roman Mannerism.
For 30 years, Axel
Oxenstierna (1583–
1654) himself was a
dominant figure in
Swedish power
politics.

**Outer
Courtyard**

The Obelisk by
Louis Jean Desprez
was erected in 1799
to thank the citizens
for their support of
Gustav III's Russian
war in 1788–90.

Stock Exchange
(See p54)

**STOR–
TORGET**

★ **Storkyrkan**
*An impressive cathedral
with a late Gothic interior,
it is full of treasures from
many different eras* ❺

Stortorget
*This square is the heart of
the "city between the
bridges", with a well
dating from 1778. It was
the scene of the Stockholm
Bloodbath in 1520* ❻

STAR SIGHTS

★ **The Royal Palace**

★ **Livrustkammaren**

★ **Storkyrkan**

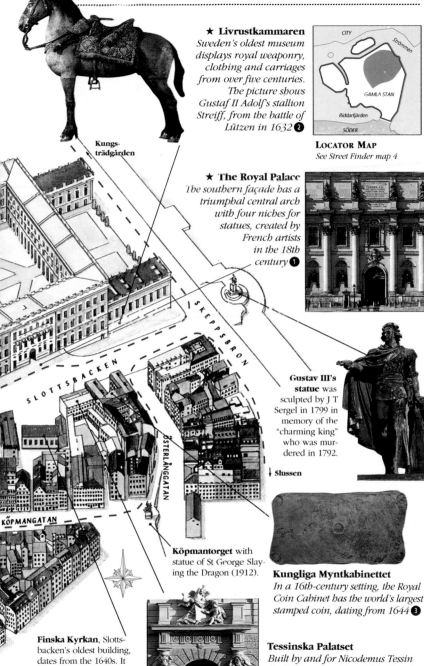

★ **Livrustkammaren**
Sweden's oldest museum displays royal weaponry, clothing and carriages from over five centuries. The picture shows Gustaf II Adolf's stallion Streiff, from the battle of Lützen in 1632 ❷

LOCATOR MAP
See Street Finder map 4

Kungs-
trädgården

★ **The Royal Palace**
The southern façade has a triumphal central arch with four niches for statues, created by French artists in the 18th century ❶

SKEPPSBRON

SLOTTSBACKEN

ÖSTERLÅNGATAN

KÖPMANGATAN

Gustav III's statue was sculpted by J T Sergel in 1799 in memory of the "charming king" who was murdered in 1792.

↓ **Slussen**

Köpmantorget with statue of St George Slaying the Dragon (1912).

Kungliga Myntkabinettet
In a 16th-century setting, the Royal Coin Cabinet has the world's largest stamped coin, dating from 1644 ❸

Finska Kyrkan, Slottsbacken's oldest building, dates from the 1640s. It was originally a royal ballgames court for the palace, but since 1725 it has been the religious centre for the Finnish community.

Tessinska Palatset
Built by and for Nicodemus Tessin the Younger, architect of the Royal Palace, in 1694–7, this palace has been the residence of the Governor of Stockholm County since 1968 ❹

0 metres   100
0 yards   100

KEY
- - - Suggested route

The Royal Palace **❶**

See pp50–53.

Livrust-kammaren **❷**

Slottsbacken 3. **Map** 4 C2.
C 519 555 00. **T** Gamla Stan.
🚌 43, 46, 55, 59, 76. **○** May–Aug:
10am–4pm daily; Sep–Apr: 11am–
5pm Tue–Sun (Thu also 5–8pm). **✦**
Eng: Jul–Aug. **○ 🎥 ✗ 👶 🅿**
W www.lsh.se

SWEDEN'S OLDEST museum, Livrustkammaren (the Royal Armoury) was founded in 1633 and is full of *objets d'art* and everyday items used by the Royal Family over the past five centuries. The oldest exhibit is Gustav Vasa's crested helmet dating from 1548. The museum also houses a variety of royal items which illustrate events in Swedish history. Among them are Gustav II Adolf's stuffed stallion, Streiff, which he rode at the Battle of Lützen in 1632; Gustaf III's costume from the notorious masked ball at which he was murdered in 1792; and Karl XII's blue uniform with the still muddy boots he had on when he died at the siege of Frerikshald in Norway in 1718.

Coronation ceremonies are illustrated by costumes such as those worn by King Adolf Fredrik and Queen Lovisa Ulrika in 1751. The King's attire alone was adorned with some 2 kg (4 lb) of silver. The coronation carriage, originally

Sweden's first coin, struck in about AD 995

built in the 17th century, was modernized for this event. Its renovation in the 1970s took eight years and cost 700,000 kronor. The cellar vault, once used for firewood, is skilfully lit, providing an imaginative setting for the exhibits.

Kungliga Myntkabinettet **❸**

Slottsbacken 6. **Map** 4 C3.
C 519 553 00. **T** Gamla Stan.
🚌 43, 46, 55, 59, 76. **○** 10am–
4pm Tue–Sun. **✦** by arrangement.
🎥 👶 🍴 🛒 🅿
W www.myntkabinettet.se

THE ROYAL COIN CABINET is a museum highlighting the history of money from the 10th century to the present day – from the little cowrie shell via the drachma and denarius to the cash card of today. The museum also gives an insight into the art of medal design over the past 600 years and shows both traditional portrait medals and more modern examples like those that have been awarded to Nobel laureates. Visitors can also see the first Swedish coin, struck in the late 10th century by King Olof Skötkonung. Other rarities include Queen Kristina's coin from 1644, weighing 19.7 kg (43 lb) and reckoned to be the world's heaviest coin. From the island of Yap in Micronesia the museum has acquired the world's largest means of payment, a so-called "rai-stone" which greets visitors in the foyer.

The many sections in the museum include "The World's Money", "State Finance" and "Saving in a Piggy Bank and Bank". "Summa Summarum" is a section designed for children and illustrates the use of money in play and real life.

The elegant Baroque garden in Tessinska Palatset's courtyard

Tessinska Palatset **❹**

Slottsbacken 4. **Map** 4 C3.
T Gamla Stan. **🚌** 43, 46, 55, 59, 76. **●** to the public.

THE TESSIN PALACE at Slottsbacken is considered by many to be the most beautiful private residence north of Paris. It is the best-preserved palace from Sweden's era as a great power in the 17th century and was designed by and for Tessin the Younger (1654–1728), the nation's most renowned architect.

Completed in 1697, the building is located on a narrow site which widens out towards a courtyard with a delightful Baroque garden. The relatively discreet façade with its beautiful porch was inspired by the exterior design of Roman palaces. The decor and garden were influenced by Tessin's time in Paris and Versailles.

Tessin, who became a count and State Councillor, spent large sums on the building's ornamentation. Sculptures and paintings were provided by the same French masters whose work had graced the Royal Palace. Later, however, his son, Carl Gustaf, had to sell the palace for financial reasons.

The building was acquired by the City of Stockholm as a residence for its Governor in 1773. In 1968 it became the residence of the Governor of the County of Stockholm.

The coronation carriage of King Adolf Fredrik and Queen Lovisa Ulrika in Livrustkammaren

Storkyrkan ❺

Trångsund 1. **Map** 4 B3.
📞 723 30 16. 🚇 Gamla Stan.
🚌 43, 46, 55, 59, 76. ⏰ May–Aug:
9am–6pm daily; Sep–Apr: 9am–4pm
daily. ✝ 11am Sat & Sun.
🎧 Eng: Jul–Aug: 1pm (tour of the
tower 2pm). ♿ 📷

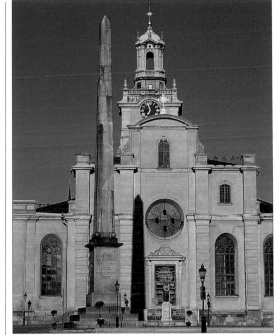

Storkyrkan's façade in Italian Baroque style, seen from Slottsbacken

STOCKHOLM'S 700-year-old cathedral is of great national religious importance. It was from here that the Swedish reformer Olaus Petri (1493–1552) spread his Lutheran message around the kingdom. It is also used for royal ceremonies.

Originally, a small village church was built on this site in the 13th century, probably by the city's founder Birger Jarl. It was replaced in 1306 by a much bigger basilica, St Nicholas, which was altered over the centuries.

The Gothic character of the interior, acquired in the 15th century, was revealed in 1908 when, during restoration work, plaster was removed from the pillars, exposing the characteristic red tiling. The late Baroque period provided the so-called "royal chairs" and the pulpit, while the façade was adapted to bring it into keeping with the rest of the area around the Royal Palace. The 66-m (216-ft) high tower, added in 1743, has four bells, the largest of which weighs about 6 tons.

The cathedral houses some priceless artistic treasures, including *St George and the Dragon*, regarded as one of the finest late Gothic works of art in Northern Europe. The sculpture, situated to the left of the altar, was carved from oak and elk horn by Lübeck sculptor Bernt Notke. Unveiled in 1489, it commemorates Sten Sture the Elder's victory over the Danes in 1471 (*see p15*).

The Last Judgment (1696) is a massive Baroque painting by David Klöcker von Ehrenstrahl. The 3.7-m (12-ft) high bronze candelabra before the altar, likely to be German, has adorned the cathedral for some 600 years. One of the cathedral's most prized treasures is the silver altar, which gave the interior a completely new appearance in the 1650s. It was a gift from the diplomat Johan Adler Salvius.

The pews nearest to the chancel, the "royal chairs", were designed by Nicodemus Tessin the Younger in 1684 to be used by royalty on special occasions. In 1705, the pulpit was installed above the grave of Olaus Petri.

On 20 April 1535, a light phenomenon was observed over Stockholm – six rings with sparkling solar halos. *The Parhelion Painting*, recalling the event *(see p14)*, hangs in Storkyrkan and is thought to be the oldest portrayal of the capital. It shows the modest skyline dominated by the cathedral, at that time still the basilica of St Nicholas.

The sculpture *St George and the Dragon* by Bernt Notke (1489) in Storkyrkan

Storkyrkan's silver altar (detail)

The Royal Palace (Kungliga Slottet) ➊

Royal Sceptre

DEFENSIVE INSTALLATIONS or castles have stood on the island of Stadsholmen ever since the 10th century. The Tre Kronor (Three Crowns) fortress was completed in the mid-13th century, but during the following century it became a royal residence. The Vasa kings turned the fortress into a Renaissance palace which burned to the ground in 1697. In its place the architect Nicodemus Tessin the Younger created a new palace in Roman style with an Italianate exterior and a French interior toned down by Swedish influences. The palace's 608 rooms were decorated by Europe's foremost artists and craftsmen. King Adolf Fredrik was the first king to move into the palace, in 1754. It is no longer the king's residence, but remains one of the city's leading sights.

★ **Changing of the Guard**
Stockholm's most popular tourist event is the daily changing of the guard at midday in the Outer Courtyard.

Entrance to the State Apartments

The Western Staircase
Tessin was especially proud of the two stair-cases, made from Swedish marble and porphyry. On the western staircase stands a bust of the gifted architect.

★ **The Hall of State**
This opulent hall has an atmosphere of ceremonial splendour and forms an ideal setting for Queen Kristina's silver throne, probably the palace's most famous treasure.

The Guest Apartments

Entrance to Treasury and Royal Chapel

A ROYAL WORKPLACE

The king and queen have their offices at the palace, where they hold audiences with visiting dignitaries, and official ceremonies. They travel around the country attending special events, official openings and anniversaries, and they make regular State visits abroad. The king is well known for his interest in the environment while the queen is heavily involved with her work for children, especially the disabled.

King Carl XVI Gustav and Queen Silvia

The Royal Chapel
This delightful little church has a rich interior decorated by many different artists. The pulpit is the work of J P Bouchardon.

Gustav III's State Bedchamber
Sergel's bust of Gustav III (1779) stands in the room where the king died after being shot at the Opera House. The decor by J E Rehn dates from the 1770s.

The Bernadotte Apartments are situated on the floor below Karl XI's Gallery.

Tre Kronor Museum entrance from Lejonbacken.

★ Karl XI's Gallery
One of the most magnificent rooms in the palace, this fine example of Swedish Late Baroque is used for banquets hosted by the king and queen. In the cabinet is this priceless salt-cellar dating from 1627–8.

Carl Hårleman played an important role in the design of the palace. His bust adorns this niche.

Livrustkammaren *(see p48)*

Logården is the terrace between the palace's east wings.

Gustav III's Museum of Antiquities
The museum's collection includes antique statues brought home by Gustav III from his journey to Rome.

Exploring the Royal Palace

THE PUBLIC AREAS of the Royal Palace allow you to walk through grand rooms of sumptuous furnishings and priceless works of art and craftsmanship. The Hall of State and the Royal Chapel are both characterized by their magnificent lavish decor and Gustav III's Museum of Antiquities contains ancient marble sculptures from the king's journey to Italy. The palace also houses the Treasury with the State regalia; the new Tre Kronor Museum, which depicts the palace before the 1697 fire; and the Livrustkammaren *(see p48)*.

The Pillar Hall in the Bernadotte Apartments with original decor

Karl XI's Gallery, the finest example of the Late Baroque period in Sweden

THE STATE APARTMENTS

THE ROYAL FAMILY has lived at Drottningholm Palace *(see pp140–43)* since 1982, but official functions still take place in the State Apartments, including banquets hosted by the king during visits by foreign heads of state. Other official dinners are staged here, as well as the festivities held every year to honour the Nobel laureates.

These meals are served in Karl XI's Gallery, the finest example of Swedish Late Baroque, modelled on the Hall of Mirrors at Versailles. Each window is matched with a niche on the inner wall where some of the palace's priceless works of arts and crafts are exhibited. Most remarkable is the salt-cellar made from ivory and gilded silver designed by the Flemish painter Rubens (1577–1640). The room known as "The

King Karl XIV Johan's egg cup

White Sea" serves as a drawing room. Gustav III's State Bedchamber, where the king died after being shot at the Opera House in 1792 *(see pp22–3)*, is the height of Gustavian elegance. Along with Queen Sofia Magdalena's State Bedchamber, it was designed by the architect Jean Eric Rehn. The lintels on the doors to the Don Quixote Room, named after the theme of its tapestries, were made by François Boucher and are among the palace's most treasured pieces.

THE GUEST APARTMENTS

AN IMPOSING part of the palace, these apartments are where visiting heads of state stay. The beautiful rooms include the Meleager Salon, where official gifts and decorations are exchanged, and a large bedroom with a sculpted and gilded bed. Other impressive rooms are the Inner Salon, whose decor was inspired by the excavations in Pompeii, and the Margareta Room, named after the present king's grandmother, which displays some pictures painted by her.

The apartments contain remarkable works of craftsmanship by such 18th-century masters as Georg Haupt, Ephraim Ståhle and Jean Baptiste Masreliez.

THE BERNADOTTE APARTMENTS

THIS MAGNIFICENT suite has earned its name from the gallery displaying portraits of the Bernadotte dynasty. The apartments have some notable ceiling paintings and mid-18th-century chandeliers, and are used for many a ceremonial occasion. The elegant Pillar Hall is the venue for investitures, and the East Octagonal Cabinet with probably the palace's best Rococo decor, is where the king receives foreign ambassadors. Along with the western cabinet, its interior has remained just as it was planned by Carl Hårleman more than 250 years ago.

Oscar II's very masculine Writing Room, dating from the 1870s, also still looks much as it did in his day. However, it is clear the palace was kept up to date with technical advances. Electricity was installed in 1883, and the telephone only one year later.

THE HALL OF STATE

ROCOCO AND Classicism were brought together in perfect harmony by the architects Nicodemus Tessin the Younger and Carl Hårleman when they designed the two-storey Hall of State. It provides a worthy framework for Queen Kristina's silver throne, a gift for the coronation in 1650 and one of the most valuable treasures in the palace. The throne was given to the Queen by Magnus Gabriel de la Gardie and was made in Augsburg by the goldsmith Abraham Drentwett. The

canopy was added 100 years later for the coronation of King Adolf Fredrik and was designed by Jean Eric Rehn.

The decor of the Hall of State is lavish. The throne is flanked by colossal sculptures of Karl XIV Johan and Gustav II Adolf, while those on the cornice symbolize Peace, Strength, Religion and Justice.

Until 1975 the Hall of State was the scene of the ceremonial opening of the Swedish Parliament (Riksdagen) which included a march past of the royal bodyguard in full regalia. It is now used more for other official occasions and, like the Royal Chapel, is a venue for summer concerts *(see pp168–9)*.

The Hall of State, the most important ceremonial room in the palace

THE ROYAL CHAPEL

I T TOOK 50 YEARS to build the Royal Palace, and a lot of effort went into the interior decoration of the Royal Chapel. The work was carried out largely by Carl Hårleman under the supervision of Tessin. As with the Hall of State, the co-operation between the two produced a magnificent result, enhanced by the contributions of several foreign artists.

A number of remarkable artifacts have been added over the centuries. The most recent was a group of six 17th-century-style bronze crowns, as well as two crystal crowns, given by the Court to King Carl XVI Gustaf and Queen Silvia to mark their marriage in 1976.

It also has some rare relics of the original Tre Kronor

fortress: new benches that had been ordered by Tessin. They had been rescued during the palace fire in 1697 and preserved but not put in the chapel until the 19th century. The benches were made by Georg Haupt, grandfather of the Georg Haupt who was to create some of the palace's most prized furnishings *(see p82)*.

GUSTAV III's MUSEUM OF ANTIQUITIES

O PENED IN 1794 in memory of the murdered king, the Museum of Antiquities initially housed more than 200 exhibits, mainly acquired during Gustav's Italian journey in 1783–4 and then supplemented with more purchases later.

In 1866 the museum's collection was moved to the city's National Museum *(see pp82–3)*. During the 1950s the main gallery was renovated, followed by the smaller galleries 30 years later, which enabled the collection to be returned to its original setting.

The most prized exhibits are in the main gallery, the best known being the sculpture of Endymion, the eternally sleeping young shepherd and lover of the Moon Goddess Selene. The 18th-century sculptor Johan Tobias Sergel is represented by *The Priestess*, ranked as the collection's second most important piece. She is flanked by two large candelabras.

THE TREASURY

A T THE BOTTOM of 56 well-worn steps, below the Hall of State on the south side of the palace, is the entrance to the Treasury (Skattkammaren) where the State regalia, the most potent symbols of the monarchy, are kept.

On the rare occasions that King Erik XIV's crown, sceptre, orb and the keys of the kingdom are taken out of their showcase, they are placed beside the uncrowned

Erik XIV's crown, made by Cornelis ver Weiden in Stockholm in 1561

King Carl XVI Gustaf. The 1-m (3-ft) high silver baptismal font, which took the French silversmith Jean François Cousinet 11 years to make, is 200 years old and is still used for royal baptisms. Hanging in the Treasury is the only undamaged tapestry among six dating from the 1560s, salvaged from the 1697 fire.

TRE KRONOR MUSEUM

T HE NEWEST attraction at the Royal Palace is the Tre Kronor (Three Crowns) Museum, which is housed in the oldest parts of the ruined Tre Kronor fortress, preserved under the north side of the palace. About half of a massive 12th-century defensive wall and brick vaults from the 16th and 17th centuries provide a unique setting for the museum which illustrates the palace's history of almost 1,000 years.

Two models of the Tre Kronor fortress show changes made during the second half of the 17th century and how it looked by the time of the fire. Among items rescued from the ashes are a schnapps glass, amber pots and bowls made from mountain crystal.

A glass bowl in the Tre Kronor Museum, saved from the 1697 fire

The imposing Stock Exchange on the north side of Stortorget

Stortorget ❻

Map 4 B3. Ⓣ *Gamla Stan.* 🚌 *3, 43, 46, 53, 55, 59, 76.*

IT WAS NOT until 1778, when the Stock Exchange (Börsen) was completed, that Stortorget, the square in the heart of the Old Town, acquired a more uniform appearance. Its northern side had previously been taken up by several buildings that served as a town hall. Since the early Middle Ages the square had been a natural meeting point with a well and marketplace, lined with wooden stalls on market days.

A pillory belonging to the jail, which was once sited on nearby Kåkbrinken, used to stand on the square. It is now in the Town Hall on Kungsholmen *(see p112).*

The medieval layout is clear on Stortorget's west side, where the red Schantzska Huset (No. 20) and the narrow Seyfridtska Huset were built in around 1650. The Schantzska Huset

remains unchanged and has a lovely limestone porch adorned with figures of recumbent Roman warriors. The artist Johan Wendelstam was responsible for most of the notable porches in the Old Town. The 17th-century gable on the Grilska Huset (No. 3) is also worth closer study. Today there are cafés and restaurants in some of the medieval vaulted cellars.

The decision to construct the Stock Exchange was taken in 1667 but the many wars delayed the start of the building by 100 years. The architect was the young and talented Erik Palmstedt (1741–1803), who also created the decorative cover for the old well. However, 200 years of trading on the floor of the Stock Exchange came to an end in 1990. On the upper floor, the Swedish Academy still holds its ceremonial gatherings, a tradition maintained since Gustav III gave his famous inauguration speech here on 5 April 1786.

Radiating from Stortorget, the three main streets of Köpmangatan, Svartmangatan and Skomakargatan have been laid out with the prescribed wider measure of 8 ells (about 4.80 m/16 ft) wide to allow for the horse-drawn carts.

Tyska Kyrkan ❼

Svartmangatan 16. **Map** 4 B3. Ⓒ *411 11 88.* Ⓣ *Gamla Stan.* 🚌 *3, 43, 46, 53, 55, 59, 76.* ⏰ *May–Aug: noon–4pm daily; Sep–Apr: noon–4pm Sat & Sun.* ⛪ *11am Sun, German.* 🎧 *by appt in Swedish & German.* ♿

THE GERMAN CHURCH is an impressive reminder of the almost total influence that Germany had over Stockholm during the 18th century. The Hanseatic League trading organization was in control of the Baltic and its ports, which explains why the basic layout of Gamla Stan resembled that of Lübeck. Germany's political influence was only broken after the Stockholm Bloodbath and Gustav Vasa's accession to the throne in 1523 *(see p16),* but its cultural and mercantile influence remained strong as German merchants and craftsmen settled in the city.

The church's parish assembly, which today has some 2,000 members, was founded in 1571. The present twin-nave church was built in 1638–42, as an extension of a smaller church which the parish had used since 1576.

In German Late Renaissance and Baroque style, the interior has a royal gallery, added in 1672 for German members of

---

THE STOCKHOLM BLOODBATH

Detail of a painting of the Bloodbath (1524)

Stortorget is intimately linked with the Stockholm Bloodbath of November 1520. The Danish King Kristian II besieged the Swedish Regent, Sten Sture the Younger, until he capitulated and the Swedes chose Kristian as their king. He promised an amnesty and ordered a three-day feast at Tre Kronor Fortress. Near the end of the festivities, the revellers were suddenly shut in and arrested for heresy. The next day more than 80 noblemen and Stockholm citizens were beheaded in the square.

The royal gallery in the 17th-century Tyska Kyrkan

the royal household. The pulpit (1660) in ebony and alabaster is unique in Sweden and the altar, from the 1640s, is covered with beautiful paintings surrounded by sculptures of the apostles and evangelists.

The sculptures on the south porch by Jobst Hennen date from 1643 and show Jesus, Moses and three figures portraying Faith, Hope and Love.

Mårten Trotzigs Gränd, the narrowest street in the city

Mårten Trotzigs Gränd ❽

Map 4 C4. Ⓣ *Gamla Stan.* 🚌 *3, 43, 46, 53, 55, 59, 76.*

A T ONLY 90 CM (3 ft) wide, Mårten Trotzigs Gränd is the city's narrowest street, and climbing up the 36 steps gives a good idea of how different parts of the Old Town vary so much in height and how tightly packed together the houses are.

Mårten Trotzigs Gränd is named after a German merchant called Traubzich, who owned two houses here at the end of the 16th century. After being fenced off at both ends for 100 years, the street was reopened in 1945.

Västerlånggatan ❾

Map 4 B3. Ⓣ *Gamla Stan.* 🚌 *3, 43, 46, 53, 55, 59, 76.*

O NCE A MAIN ROAD outside the city proper, built along parts of the original town wall, Västerlånggatan now runs through the heart

of the Old Town, and is usually thronging with people – tourists and locals – shopping or strolling. Starting at Mynttorget in the north, where the Chancery Office (Kanslihuset) and Lejonbacken are, the lively and atmospheric street finishes at Järntorget in the south, where the export of iron was once controlled. Alongside is Bancohuset, which served as the headquarters of the State Bank from 1680 to 1906.

The building at No. 7 has been used by the Swedish Parliament since the mid-1990s. Its late 19th-century façade has a distinctive southern European influence.

No. 27 was built by and for Erik Palmstedt, who also designed the Stock Exchange and the well at Stortorget. No. 29 is a really venerable building, dating from the early 15th century. The original pointed Gothic arches were revealed during restoration in the 1940s.

No. 33 is a good example of how new materials and techniques in the late 19th century made it possible to fit large shop windows into old houses. The cast iron columns which can be seen in many other places also date from this period.

No. 68, Von der Lindeska House, has a majestic 17th-century façade and a beautiful porch with sculptures of Neptune and Mercury.

Postmuseum ❿

Lilla Nygatan 6. **Map** 4 B3. 🔲 *781 17 55.* Ⓣ *Gamla Stan.* 🚌 *3, 53.* 🕐 *11am–4pm Tue–Sun, Sep–Apr also Wed 4pm–7pm.* 🎫 *by arrangement.* ♿ 🚻 🛍 🆆 *www.posten.se/museum*

A N ATTRACTION in itself, the Postmuseum building takes up a whole area bought by the Swedish Post Office in 1720. About 100 years later

Västerlånggatan, Gamla Stan's most popular shopping street

the majestic-looking Post Office was built, incorporating parts of the 17th-century buildings already there. Stockholm's only Post Office until 1869, it was turned into the Postal Museum in 1906.

Letters have been sent in Sweden since 1636, and the museum's permanent exhibits include a portrayal of early "peasant postmen" fighting the angry Åland Sea in their boat *Simpan*. Also on display is the first post bus which ran in northern Sweden in the early 1920s and a stagecoach used in eastern Sweden.

Mauritian stamp in the Postmuseum

The collection includes Sweden's first stamp-printing press and no less than four million stamps among which are the first Swedish stamps, produced in 1855. Also on display is the "Penny Black", the world's first stamp dating from 1840, and some stamps issued by Mauritius in 1847.

The reference section has a philatelic library holding 51,000 volumes and stamp collections, as well as computers and multimedia equipment for research purposes.

There is a special exhibition for children in the basement.

Riddarholms-kyrkan ⑪

Birger Jarls Torg. **Map** 4 A3.
(402 61 30. **T** Gamla Stan. **3**,
53. **◯** May–Aug: 10am–4pm daily,
Sep: noon–3pm Sat & Sun. **✱** Eng:
every hour. **⬛ ⊘ ⬛**

THIS CHURCH ON the island of Riddarholmen is best known as a place for royal burials. Its interior is full of ornate sarcophagi and worn gravestones, and in front of the altar are the tombs of the medieval kings Karl Knutsson and Magnus Ladulås.

Built on the site of the late 13th-century Greyfriars abbey, founded by Magnus Ladulås, the majestic brick church was gradually enlarged over the centuries. After a serious fire in 1835, the church acquired its present lattice-work, cast-iron tower.

The church is surrounded by ornate burial vaults which date back as far as the 16th century. The coffins rest on a lower level with space for a memorial above. The most recent was built in 1858–60 for the Bernadotte dynasty.

The vaults contain the remains of all the Swedish monarchs from Gustav II Adolf in the 17th century to the present day with two exceptions: Queen Kristina was buried at St Peter's in Rome in 1654 and Gustav VI Adolf, who died in 1973, was interred at Haga (see pp122–3). The most magnificent sarcophagus is that of the 19th-century king, Karl XIV Johan, which had to be towed here by sledge from his porphyry work-

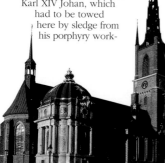

Riddarholmskyrkan with the external burial vault by Tessin and Hårleman

Wrangelska Palatset, a royal residence after the Tre Kronor fire of 1697

shops in the Älvdalen region in northern Sweden.

Particularly moving are the graves of royal children who met an early death, including the many small tin coffins that surround the last resting place of Gustav II Adolf and his queen, Maria Eleonora.

Wrangelska Palatset ⑫

Birger Jarls Torg 16. **Map** 4 A3.
T Gamla Stan. **3**, 53. **●** to the public.

ONLY TWO PARTS of the fortification work which Gustav Vasa undertook around 1530 still remain – Birger Jarl's Tower and the southernmost tower of what became the Wrangel Palace. Built as a residence for the nobleman Lars Sparre in 1652–70, it was extensively rebuilt only a few decades later. The owner by then was Carl Gustaf Wrangel, a field marshal during the Thirty Years War, who chose Nicodemus Tessin the Elder as his architect. The result was Stockholm's largest palace in private hands.

In 1694 Wrangel lost many valuable possessions in a major fire, and three years later his palace became a royal residence when the Royal Family moved to Riddarholmen after the Tre Kronor fortress (see pp50–53) was ravaged by another fire. The palace then became

known as the King's House, and it was here in 1697 that the 15-year-old Karl XII took the oath of office after the death of his father. Three years later the young king left his palace to go to war; he would never return to Stockholm. Gustav III was born here, eight years before the Royal Family moved back to the new Royal Palace in 1754.

The Court of Appeal now uses the whole building, where in 1792 the assassin of Gustav III was manacled in the dungeons during his trial.

The court also rents the Rosenhane Palace (Birger Jarls Torg 10) and the Hessenstein House (Birger Jarls Torg 2), which was built in 1630 by Bengt Bengtsson Oxenstierna. It was named after Fredrik Wilhelm von Hessenstein, the son of Fredrik I and his lover Hedvig Taube. Later it was occupied by Carl Gustav Tessin, son of the Royal Palace architect and a leading personality in the world of culture.

The city founder Birger Jarl's statue on the square that bears his name

Evert Taubes Terrass ⓭

Norra Riddarholmshamnen. **Map** 4 A3.
Ⓣ Gamla Stan. 🚌 3, 53.

A STATUE OF Evert Taube (1890–1976), the much-loved troubadour and ballad writer, stands on the terrace below Wrangelska Palatset looking out over the waters of Riddarfjärden. In an ideal position, given the poet's close links to the sea, the bronze sculpture was created by Willy Gordon in 1990. Close by, Christer Berg's *Solbåten* (the Sun Boat), an elegant sculpture in granite, was unveiled in 1966. Inspired by the shape of a shell, from some angles it looks like a sail.

Evert Taube (1890–1976)

Birger Jarls Torn ⓮

Norra Riddarholmshamnen. **Map** 4 A3
Ⓣ Gamla Stan. 🚌 3, 53. ● to the public.

WHEN THE ST KLARA convent on Norrmalm was pulled down in 1527 following the Reformation, Gustav Vasa used some of its stonework to build a defensive installation on Riddarholmen. The north-ernmost of the two towers came to be known as Birger Jarls Torn in the 19th century when some thought it had been erected 600 years earlier. The tower has been linked with one of the legends that surround the founding of Stockholm by Birger Jarl. The story goes that the inhabitants of the town of Sigtuna floated a log on Lake Mälaren after a fire in 1187. It drifted on to the shore where the tower now stands, and it was this log – or "stock" in Swedish – that gave the capital its name. A famous picture in Storkyrkan (*see p14*) dating from 1535, shows the waves break-ing over the rocks beneath the tower.

The 16th-century Birger Jarls Torn

Stenbockska Palatset ⓯

Birger Jarls Torg 4. **Map** 4 A3.
Ⓣ Gamla Stan. 🚌 3, 53. ● to the public.

BOTH EXTERNALLY and inter-nally the Stenbock Palace is the best-preserved building on Riddarholmen. Built in the 1640s by the State Councillor

Stenbockska Palatset, the best-preserved nobleman's residence on Riddarholmen

Fredrik Stenbock and his wife Katarina de la Gardie, the family's coat of arms can be seen above the porch. The palace underwent major extension work in 1805 when it was taken over by the State Archives. Then in 1969–71 was restored as the head-quarters of the Supreme Court.

Many leading Swedish and foreign architects and artists have all played their part in enhancing the palace's outstanding appearance. The roof beams and flooring are from the Stenbock period, and the staircase was designed by Nicodemus Tessin the Elder.

Several beautiful ceilings are the work of the master of stucco, Carlo Carove from Italy (d. 1697), and there is a cabinet created by Rococo architect Carl Hårleman.

TIMELINE: RIDDARHOLMEN

1250s The island, then called Kidskär, is a cattle-grazing area outside the settlement	**1527** Following the Reformation, the monks are evicted from the island	**Late 17th century** The prosperity of the nobility starts to diminish. Palaces are replaced by government offices	**1697–1754** The royal family takes over Wrangelska Palatset after Tre Kronor fortress is destroyed by fire	**1865–66** The Par-liament building and Hebbe House are rebuilt for new two-chamber Parliament	

1200	1300	1400	1500	1600	1700	1800	1900

| **1270–85** The Greyfriars' abbey is founded. Kidskär is renamed Gråmunke-holmen. The abbey church is used for royal burials | **1625–35** Land is do-nated to noblemen and distinguished officers. The name is changed to Riddarholmen *Wrangelska Palatset* | | **1830s** Fleming House used for Parliament by priests, burghers and peasants. Noblemen stay in Riddarhuset | **1905** Parliament moves to new build-ing on Helgeands-holmen |

Riddarhuset in lavish Dutch Baroque style, built in the 17th century

Riddarhuset ⑯

Riddarhustorget 10. **Map** 4 A3.
【 723 39 90. Ⓣ *Gamla Stan.*
📠 3, 53. ◐ 11:30am–12:30pm
Mon–Fri. 📷 ✂ *by arrangement.*
ⓦ www.riddarhuset.se

OFTEN REGARDED as one of Stockholm's most beautiful buildings, Riddarhuset (House of Nobility) stands on Riddarhustorget, which as late as the mid-19th century was still the city's centre.

Built in 1641–7 on the initiative of the State Chancellor, it was designed by the architects Simon and Jean de la Vallée, Heinrich Wilhelm and Justus Vingboons. The nobility, whose privileges were granted in 1280, then had a base for meetings and events.

The building is a supreme example of Dutch Baroque design and colouring. Over the entrance on the northern façade is the nobility's motto *Arte et Marte* (Art and War) with Minerva, Goddess of Art and Science, and Mars, God of War, on either side.

The sculptures on the vaulted roof symbolize the knightly virtues. On the south side is *Nobilitas* (Nobility) holding a small Minerva and spear. She is flanked by *Studium* (Diligence) and *Valor* (Bravery). Facing the north is the male equivalent, *Honor*, flanked by *Prudentia* (Prudence) and *Fortitudo* (Strength).

The interior is equally impressive. The lower hall is dominated by a magnificent double staircase which leads

The motto at Riddarhuset

up to the Knights' Room. This has a masterly ceiling painting by David Klöcker Ehrenstrahl (1628–98) and Riddarhuset's foremost treasure, a sculpted ebony chair that dates from 1623. The walls are covered by some 2,320 coats of arms.

Bondeska Palatset ⑰

Riddarhustorget 8. **Map** 4 B3.
Ⓣ *Gamla Stan.* 📠 3, 53. ◐ *to the public.*

THE SEAT OF the Supreme Court since 1949, the Bonde Palace was created in 1662–73 by popular architect Nicodemus Tessin the Elder in the style of a French town house. The year previously, the State Treasurer Gustav Bonde had bought the site opposite Riddarhuset to build a palace with the idea of renting out most of it.

Since then the Bonde Palace has had several owners and was damaged by fires in 1710

Bondeska Palatset, now the seat of the Supreme Court

and 1753. In 1730 the building became the property of the city and served as the City Hall until 1915. After that, there was little interest taken in the palace until renovation planned by the architect Ivar Tengbom was begun in the late 1940s. It had even been suggested that the building should be destroyed, but public opinion ensured that it remained intact.

Riksdagshuset ⑱

Riksgatan 3 A. **Map** 4 B2. 【 020–34 99 00. Ⓣ *Kungsträdgården.* 📠 3, 43, 53, 62. ◐ *tours & meetings in the Chamber.* ✂ *ring for details on tours of the building & art works.* ♿ ⓘ
ⓦ www.riksdagen.se

THE PARLIAMENT building (Riksdagshuset) and State Bank (Riksbank) on Helgeandsholmen were inaugurated in 1905 and 1906 respectively. Since 1983, when Parliament returned after 12 years at Sergels Torg, the two buildings have been combined and enlarged. Parliament also occupies five premises in Gamla Stan, as well as an information office at Västerlånggatan 1. All the buildings are connected by underground passages and together amount to 130,000 sq m (1,400,000 sq ft), with a staff force of about 600, plus 250 in the political parties' offices.

Parliamentary debates can be watched from the public gallery, which holds up to 500 visitors. There are guided tours of the buildings every day during the summer and only at weekends in winter. Visitors should use the public entrance at Riksgatan 3A.

From the gallery level is a striking view from as far as Gustav Adolfs Torg to Riddarholmen. The main chamber has benches of Swedish birch and wall panelling in Finnish birch, carved in Norway. A large tapestry, *Memory of a Landscape* (1983), by Elisabeth Hasselberg-Olsson, covers 54 sq m (581 sq ft) of wall, weighs 100 kg (220 lb) and took 3,500 hours to make.

The old two-chamber Parliament's beautifully renovated rooms are now used for meetings of the majority party. The former Upper House has three paintings by Otte Sköld (1894–1958), and in the other chamber there are works by Axel Törneman and Georg Pauli, who realized Törneman's sketches after his death. Between the chambers is a 45-m (148-ft) long hall with an elegant display of coats of arms, paintings and chandeliers. The Finance Committee meets in the old oak-panelled library surrounded by old prints and Jugendstil lamps.

Facing the old entrance at Norrbro, the magnificent stairwell still retains its colouring from 1905. Other impressive survivors from opulent days include eight columns, a floor, steps and balusters all in various types of marble. The

The chamber where the 349 Members of Parliament meet

present entrance was the State Bank's main hall until 1976. It has magnificent columns, too, made from polished granite, and some outstanding paintings from the Parliamentary collection of 3,000 works.

Medeltidsmuseet  ⑲

Strömparterren, Norrbro. **Map** 4 B2.
☎ 508 317 90. ⓣ Kungsträdgården.
🚌 43, 62. ⭕ Jul & Aug: 11am–6pm Tue–Thu, 11am–4pm Fri–Mon; Sep–Jun: 11am–4pm Tue–Sun, (also 4–6pm Wed). 🎫 ♿ 📷 🚫 📷
ⓦ www.medeltidsmuseet.stockholm.se

THIS FASCINATING museum of medieval Stockholm is built around the capital's archaeological remains, mainly parts of the city wall that date from the 1530s. They were found during intensive archaeological research in 1978–80 which unearthed a number of remarkable finds from Stockholm's medieval history.

Completely underground, the museum also includes artifacts from other parts of the city. Among them is the 22-m (72-ft) long Riddarholm ship which was discovered off Riddarholmen in 1930 and dates from the 1520s.

The museum provides a good picture of Stockholm's early days. From the entrance, a 350-year-old tunnel leads into a reconstructed medieval world. There is a pillory in the square and the gallows hill with the tools of the executioner's grisly trade. The old harbour has been rebuilt, complete with quayside, jetties, boathouses and warehouses, as well as authentic nautical smells. The spruce wreath hanging outside the wine cellar shows that supplies of wine and beer have arrived from the Continent. The large house is built from 6,000 original bricks.

The new Parliament building, with the older building behind

PARLIAMENTARY WANDERINGS

Sweden's first Parliament was opened in the 1860s on Riddarholmen in the combined properties of Fleming House and Hebbe House. From 1835–65, commoners – priests, burghers and farmers – met in Fleming House, which became known as the "House of Commons", while the noblemen sat in nearby Riddarhuset. Situated behind Riddarholmskyrkan at Birger Jarls Torg 5, Fleming House was constructed on the site of the Greyfriars abbey after the monks were forced to flee due to the Reformation in the 17th century (see p57), and remains of the huge abbey can still be seen in the cellar.

A new base for Parliament, adapted for the needs of a two-chamber legislature, was inaugurated on Helgeandsholmen in 1905. When a single chamber was established in 1971, a lack of space meant that Parliament had to move to the newly built Kulturhuset (see p67) on Sergels Torg. It returned to Helgeandsholmen in 1983 into an extended and reconstructed Parliament building.

"Mother Svea" above the old Parliament building

Medieval carved stone head of Birger Jarl at Medeltidsmuseet

CITY

THE AREA KNOWN AS City today was where, in the mid-18th century, the first stone-built houses and palaces outside Gamla Stan started to appear for the burghers and nobility. After World War II, the run-down buildings around Hötorget were demolished to form what is now Sergels Torg; many homes were replaced by rather dreary office blocks.

In recent years, though, the area has been livening up after dark and become the true heart and commercial centre of Stockholm. A hub for public transport and banking, City is the place for the best department stores and shopping malls, exclusive boutiques and nightspots. The centre also has some beautiful parks and pleasant squares serving as popular meeting places. The unique landscape surrounding Stockholm permeates even City here and there appear unexpected glimpses of the water with its bustling boat life and a string of anglers along the embankments.

Street light near Kungliga Operan

SIGHTS AT A GLANCE

Museums
Armémuseum **25**
Dansmuseet **5**
Hallwylska Palatset **29**
Medelhavsmuseet **6**
Musikmuseet **26**
Strindbergmuseet **11**

Squares
Hötorget **13**
Kungsträdgården **2**
Sergels Torg **12**
Stureplan **21**

Public Buildings
Arvfurstens Palats **7**
Centralbadet **16**
Hovstallet **27**
Konstakademien **9**
Kulturhuset and Stadsteatern **11**
Kungstornen **15**
Kungliga Biblioteket **20**
Rosenbad **8**
Sweden House **1**

Theatres and Musical Stages
Dansens Hus **17**
Konserthuset **14**
Kungliga Dramatiska Teatern **18**
Kungliga Operan **4**

Churches
Adolf Fredriks Kyrka **19**
Hedvig Eleonora Kyrka **24**

Jacobs Kyrka **3**
Klara Kyrka **10**

Markets & Malls
Sturegallerian and Sturebadet **22**
Östermalmshallen **23**

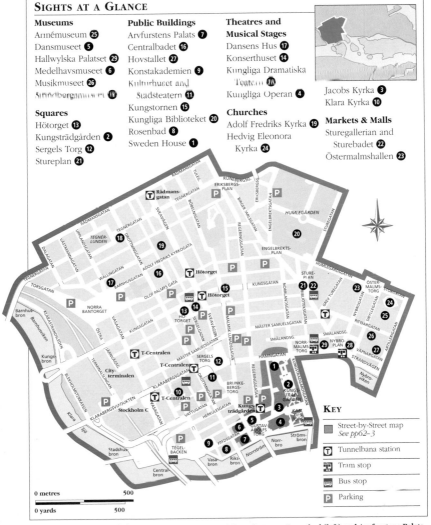

KEY

	Street-by-Street map See pp62–3
T	Tunnelbana station
	Tram stop
	Bus stop
P	Parking

0 metres   500
0 yards   500

◁ **Sagerska Palatset, official residence of the Prime Minister, between Rosenbad (left) and Arvfurstens Palats**

Street-by-Street: Around Kungsträdgården

WITH A HISTORY GOING back to the 15th century, the King's Garden (Kungsträdgården) has long been the city's most popular meeting place and recreational centre. Both visitors and Stockholmers gather here for summer concerts and festivals, or just to enjoy a stroll among the lime trees. Close by is Sweden House where the tourist office is based, and around the park is a wealth of shops, boutiques, churches, museums and restaurants. A short walk takes you to Gustav Adolfs Torg, flanked by the Royal Opera House and other stately buildings, including the Swedish Foreign Office.

Dansmuseet
Anything connected with dance such as costumes, stage set sketches and posters for the famous Les Ballets Suédois, can be seen here ⑤

★ Medelhavsmuseet
This museum near Gustav Adolfs Torg has vast collections from prehistoric cultures around the Mediterranean ⑥

Gustav II Adolf's equestrian statue, designed by L'Archevêques, was unveiled in 1796.

Sagerska Palatset

FREDSGATAN

REGERINGSGATAN

STRÖMGATAN

GUSTAV ADOLFS TORG

STRÖMGATAN

NORRBRO

NORRSTRÖM

Arvfurstens Palats
The Swedish Foreign Office is based in this palace, built for Gustav III's sister Sofia Albertina in 1794 ⑦

KEY

– – – Suggested route

Opera-källaren
(see p160)

★ Kungliga Operan
Built in 1898 with a magnificently ornate auditorium, the Royal Opera House replaced an earlier one from the time of Gustav III ④

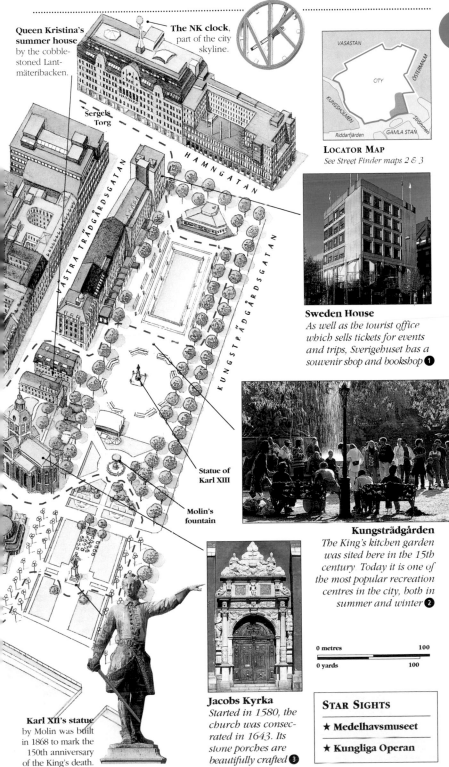

Queen Kristina's summer house by the cobble-stoned Lant-mäteribacken.

The NK clock, part of the city skyline.

Sergels Torg

HAMNGATAN

VÄSTRA TRÄDGÅRDSGATAN

KUNGSTRÄDGÅRDSGATAN

Statue of Karl XIII

Molin's fountain

Karl XII's statue by Molin was built in 1868 to mark the 150th anniversary of the King's death.

LOCATOR MAP
See Street Finder maps 2 & 3

Sweden House
As well as the tourist office which sells tickets for events and trips, Sverigehuset has a souvenir shop and bookshop ①

Kungsträdgården
The King's kitchen garden was sited here in the 15th century Today it is one of the most popular recreation centres in the city, both in summer and winter ②

0 metres		100
0 yards		100

Jacobs Kyrka
Started in 1580, the church was consec-rated in 1643. Its stone porches are beautifully crafted ③

STAR SIGHTS

★ **Medelhavsmuseet**

★ **Kungliga Operan**

Sweden House ●

Hamngatan 27. **Map** 3 D4. 🛈 789 24 00. 🚇 Kungsträdgården. 🚌 46, 47, 55, 59, 62, 76. **Tourist Office** 🕐 Jun–Aug: 8am–7pm Mon–Fri, 9am–5pm Sat & Sun; Sep–May: 9am–6pm Mon–Fri; Apr–May & Sep also 10am–3pm Sat & Sun. ♿ 🚻
Ⓦ www.stockholmtown.com

SWEDEN HOUSE (Sverigehuset) is strategically placed on Hamngatan, close to the hustle and bustle of Kungsträdgården and opposite the NK department store. It is the home of the Swedish Institute, which promotes cultural exchanges with other countries and gives information on Sweden from its offices abroad. One floor up is the Sweden Bookshop.

Also based here on the ground floor is the Stockholm Information Service, run by the City and County Councils and visited by about 700,000 people a year. Information on the capital and region is available in several languages, along with more limited information on the rest of the country. There is an accommodation booking centre, and tickets can be bought for excursions and events. The shop sells high-quality Swedish souvenirs.

Kungsträdgården ●

Map 4 B1. 🚇 Kungsträdgården. 🚌 46, 47, 55, 59, 62, 65, 76.

ONCE THE ROYAL KITCHEN garden in the 15th century, the "King's Garden" today is a popular meeting place for Stockholmers where there is

something going on for everyone all year round. The park, encircled by avenues, is the city's oldest and at the Strömgatan end has a square: Karl XII's Torg with J P Molin's statue of the warrior king, unveiled in 1868, in the centre. In Kungsträdgården itself there is a statue of Karl XIII (1809–18) by Erik Göthe. During the summer concerts of all kinds, food festivals, dancing and live street theatre take place here. In winter, the central skating rink attracts children and grown-ups alike. Also here is Molin's famous fountain, made from gypsum in 1866 and cast in bronze seven years later. During Erik XIV's reign in the 16th century, the kitchen garden was transformed into a formal Renaissance garden and Queen Kristina had a stone summer house built in it. The beautiful 17th-century house still stands at Västra Trädgårdsgatan 2 by the cobble-stoned Lantmäteribacken.

Molin's fountain

Jacobs Kyrka ●

Jakobs Torg 5. **Map** 4 B1. 🛈 723 30 38. 🚇 Kungsträdgården. 🚌 46, 55, 59, 62, 65, 76. 🕐 11am–3pm daily, Thu also 4:30–6:30pm. ✝ 12:10pm Mon–Fri, 10am Sun, 12pm Sun in Eng,12:10 & 5:30pm Thu. **Concerts** 3pm Sat. 📷 by arrangement. ♿

EVEN IN MEDIEVAL times there was a small chapel where Kungsträdgården now lies. Dedicated to St Jacob, the patron saint of wayfarers, the chapel and another modest-sized church in the area were destroyed by King Gustav Vasa

in the 16th century. Johan III wanted to provide two new churches in Norra Malmen, as the area was then called, and work to build the churches of St Jacob and St Klara (see p66) started in 1580. St Jacob's was consecrated first, in 1643. It has been restored several times since then, in some cases rather clumsily. However, several valuable items have been preserved, including a baptismal font from 1634 and some church silver, as well as porches by stonemasons Henrik Blom and Hans Hebel.

The organ's façade was created by the architect Carl Hårleman and the large painting on the west wall of the southern nave is by Fredrik Westin, Sweden's most distinguished historical painter in the early 19th century.

Altar in Jacobs Kyrka, partly dating from the 17th century

Kungliga Operan ●

Gustav Adolfs Torg. **Map** 4 B1. 🛈 791 43 00. 🚇 Kungsträdgården. 🚌 43, 62, 65. **Ticket Office** 🕐 12–6pm Mon–Fri, 12–3pm Sat. 📷 by arrangement. ♿ 🖥 🚻
Ⓦ www.kungliga operan.se

OPERA HAS BEEN performed in Sweden since 18 January 1773, when a performance took place at Bollhuset at Slottsbacken. Kungliga Operan (The Royal Opera House) on Gustav Adolfs Torg was inaugurated on 30 September 1782, but by the late 19th century it had become a fire hazard. The architect Axel Anderberg was commissioned to design a new opera house which was

View of Kungsträdgården, towards Hamngatan

The 28-m (92-ft) long gold foyer at Kungliga Operan

transferred to the State in 1898 from a consortium founded by the financier K A Wallenberg.

The colouring of the building in late Renaissance style is in keeping with the Royal Palace and Parliament building, and some details of the architecture are common to all three. The beautiful staircase with ceiling paintings by Axel Jungstedt was inspired by the Paris Opera. The same artist's portrait of Oscar II hangs in the 28-m (92-ft) long gold foyer, where Carl Larsson was responsible for the decorative paintings. The wings at either side of the stage have been kept, as has the width of the proscenium arch (11.4 m/37 ft). Also saved was J T Sergel's group of angels, holding the national coat of arms, above the stage. An angel in Vicke Andrén's ceiling painting is holding a sketch of the Opera House.

Gold ceiling in Kungliga Operan

Dansmuseet **❺**

Gustav Adolfs Torg 22–24. **Map** 4 B1.
 441 76 50. Kungsträdgården.
 43, 62, 65. 11am–8pm Tue, 11am–4pm Wed–Fri, 12–5pm Sat & Sun.
 www.dansmuseet.se

IN 1999 THE Dance Museum moved into new premises on Gustav Adolfs Torg, in the former bank building opposite the Norrbro bridge. The museum was originally founded in Paris in 1953 by the Swedish aristocrat Rolf de Maré (1888–1964). He was a noted art collector who founded the world-renowned Les Ballets Suédois.

The museum reflects all aspects of dance – costumes and masks, scenery sketches, art and posters, books and documents – and includes an archive on popular dance. Apart from the exhibition hall, there is also a data bank in the form of the Rolf de Maré Study Centre, with video facilities, a library and archives. The museum shop has Sweden's largest collection of dance videos for sale.

Medelhavs- museet **❻**

Fredsgatan 2. **Map** 4 B1.
 519 553 80. Kungsträdgården.
 43, 62, 65. 11am–8pm Tue, 11am–4pm Wed–Fri, 12–5pm Sat & Sun.
 www.medelhavsmuseet.se

GODS AND PEOPLE from prehistoric cultures around the Mediterranean rub shoulders in Medelhavsmuseet (Museum of Mediterranean and Near East Antiquities). Its many treasures include a large group of terracotta figures discovered on Cyprus in the 1930s. Models made of unusual materials like cork show how houses were once constructed, and the museum also has a fascinating gold room. The Islamic collections are complemented by temporary exhibitions.

The museum is housed in a former bank, originally built in the 17th century for Gustav Horn, a general in the Thirty Years War. The stairwell, dating from 1905, and the peristyles and colonnade around the upper part of the hall are worth a visit in themselves.

Arvfurstens Palats **❼**

Gustav Adolfs Torg 1. **Map** 4 B1.
 Kungsträdgården. 43, 62, 65.
 to the public.

OPPOSITE THE Royal Opera House, on the other side of Gustav Adolfs Torg, stands Arvfurstens Palats (Prince's Palace), built for Gustav III's sister Sofia Albertina and inaugurated in 1794. She commissioned the architect Erik Palmstedt to carry out the work. He was a pupil of Carl Fredrik Adelcrantz, designer of the original opera house.

The palace and its decor are shining examples of the Gustavian style, thanks to the contributions of artists and craftsmen like Louis Masreliez and Georg Haupt and their pupils Gustaf Adolf Ditzinger, Johan Tobias Sergel and Gottlieb Iwersson. In 1906 the building was taken over by the Swedish Foreign Office.

Nearby is the elegant Sagerska Palatset (1894) in French Renaissance style, which is used by the Prime Minister as an official residence.

Arvfurstens Palats (1794), now the Swedish Foreign Office

Rosenbad, home of the Government and City Council committees

Rosenbad ●

Rosenbad 4. **Map** 4 A2.
Ⓣ *Kungsträdgården.* 🚌 *3, 53, 62, 65.*
● *to the public.*

SINCE 1981, the Rosenbad complex – a collection of palatial buildings overlooking the Strömmen channel – has housed the Swedish Government and the Prime Minister's private office in three internally linked sites.

Three of the late 19th century's most notable architects were commissioned to design these buildings. The Venetian-style palace along Strömgatan was the last one to be added, in 1904. Designed by Ferdinand Boberg (1860–1916), it used to house private apartments, a bank and a popular restaurant, traces of which survive in the ornamentation of the open loggia facing the water.

Gustav Wickman (1858–1916) designed the pink sandstone house on the corner of Fredsgatan and Drottninggatan in exuberant, almost baroque, Jugendstil. The Skåne Bank moved into this building in 1900.

The Florentine-style house on Fredsgatan facing Rödbodtorget is three years older. It was designed by Aron Johansson (1860–1936), architect of the old Parliament building on Helgeandsholmen.

Rosenbad got its name from a former 17th-century bathhouse which offered bathers a choice of a lily bath, a chamomile bath or a rose bath – *rosenbad* in Swedish.

Konstakademien ●

Fredsgatan 12. **Map** 4 A2.
📞 *23 29 45.* Ⓣ *T-centralen.* 🚌 *3, 53, 62, 65.* ◯ *11am–5pm Tue–Fri, 12–4pm Sat & Sun.* ♿ *entrance Jakobsgatan 27.* 📷

THE ART COLLECTIONS of Konstakademien (Royal Academy of the Arts) reflect more than 250 years of paintings and sculptures, mostly by past and present members. Today the Royal Academy has around 120 members.

Between Fredsgatan and Jakobsgatan, the imposing corner house was designed by Tessin the Elder in the early 1670s. The Royal Academy moved in while under the patronage of Gustav III in the late 18th century. It has been rebuilt several times, the latest in 1897 by the architect Erik Lallerstedt. Its present look ties in with the Royal Opera House *(see p62)* and the Royal Palace *(see pp50–53),* whose architect Tessin the Younger

The Fredsgatan entrance of Konstakademien

had a vision of this area as an extension of his work.

Traces of the older buildings can still be seen. The interior of the small meeting room was designed by Carl Fredrik Adelcrantz around 1780 and two tiled stoves from the same period have been preserved, along with the main porch facing Jakobsgatan. The four allegorical female figures which were once at the entrance have been recast in cement and placed on the roof.

Interior of Klara Kyrka with decor by Olle Hjortzberg

Klara Kyrka ●

Klara Östra Kyrkogata. **Map** 2 C4.
📞 *723 30 31.* Ⓣ *T-centralen* 🚌 *47, 52, 59, 65.* ◯ *10am–5pm daily.* ✝ *10:30am Tue, 8am Thu, 11am, 2pm (Swahili) Sun.* ♿ 📷

THE CONVENT OF St Klara stood on the site of the present church and cemetery until 1527, when it was pulled down on the orders of Gustav Vasa. Later, his son Johan III commissioned a new church, completed in 1590.

The church was ravaged by fire in 1751 and its reconstruction was planned by the period's two outstanding architects, first Carl Hårleman and later C F Adelcrantz. The pulpit was made in 1753 to Hårleman's design, and J T Sergel *(see p83)* created the angelic figures in the northern gallery. A pair of identical angels adorn the exquisite chancel, based on the sculptor's gypsum originals.

In the 1880s, the 116-m (380-ft) tower was added and for many years could be seen from all over the city. The 20th-century church artist, Olle Hjortzberg, created the vault paintings, dating from 1904.

Edvin Öhrström's glass obelisk in Sergels Torg, with Kulturhuset behind to the left

Kulturhuset and Stadsteatern ⓫

Sergels Torg 3. **Map** 2 C4. **Kulturhuset**
[508 315 08. **Stadsteatern**
[506 202 00. **[T]** T-centralen. 🚌
47, 52, 59, 65, 69. ⏰ 11am–6pm
Mon, 10am–7pm Tue–Sun, 🎞 some
parts. ♿ 🍴 🛗 🏛
[W] www.kulturhuset.stockholm.se

A QUARTER OF a century after
it was opened in 1974,
Kulturhuset (Cultural Centre)
was renovated to meet the
needs of the new millennium.
Typical of its era, the creation
of the architect Peter Celsing
blends well with surrounding
Sergels Torg and has become
a symbol of Swedish Modern-
ism. The building, which was
the winner of a Nordic design
competition, has a façade of
glass all along the southern
side of the square.

Kulturhuset offers some-
thing for everybody: three
galleries hold regularly changing exhibitions suitable for all

tastes, and the auditorium
presents varied programmes
of music, dance, drama and
lectures. "Kilen" is the centre
for an artform which is a cross
between drama, stand-up,
installations and dance.

The Children's Room gives
youngsters an opportunity to
read books, draw pictures,
listen to stories or watch a
film. "Lava" is a meeting place
for young people and for
nationwide youth culture.

The centre is also home to
Sweden's only library for fans
of strip cartoons, along with
reading rooms which provide
international newspapers and
magazines, as well as newly
published Swedish literature.
Visitors can borrow anything
from books to CD-ROMs.
Café Panorama offers food
for mind and body, and Café
Access is for surfing the
Internet. Several shops sell
items of Swedish design.
Kulturhuset also houses
Stadsteatern (City Theatre),

whose main auditorium was
finally inaugurated in 1990.
This section had been
occupied by Parliament while
its usual meeting place on
Helgeandsholmen was being
rebuilt *(see p59)*.

The ambitions of the theatre's
architects Lars Fahlsten and
Per Ahrbom were eventually
realized when the six stages
of varying size and style were
all united under one roof; from
the main auditorium seating
700 to the tiny Dolls' Theatre
with space for about 70. Every
year the theatre holds around
1,400 performances for audiences totalling about 225,000.

Sergels Torg ⓬

Map 2 C4. **[T]** T-centralen. 🚌 47,
52, 59, 65, 69.

A S PART OF THE city centre's
transformation, around
1930 there was a strong lobby
in favour of extending
Sveavägen through to Gustav
Adolfs Torg. But in 1945 it
was decided to end the road
at the junction with Klarabergsgatan and Hamngatan to form
a new square, Sveaplan. In
1957 a two-level square was
proposed – a lower level for
pedestrians and an upper
level for traffic. The plan was
finalized in 1960 and the
name changed to Sergels Torg.

In 1972 the sculptor Edvin
Öhrström's glass obelisk,
*Crystal Vertical Accent in Glass
and Steel* was erected in the
centre and now shimmers at
night due to improved lighting.

CITY'S TRANSFORMATION

During the 20th century Stockholm's population grew from
250,000 to more than 1.6 million. By the 1920s it was obvi-

**The first steps towards a
new Hötorg City, 1958**

ous that the old heart of the city
did not meet the future needs of
business, public administration
and the growth in traffic. In
1951 a controversial 30-year programme to transform the lower
Norrmalm city centre was
launched. Slums on 335 of the
600 sites were pulled down and
78 new houses were built. Two-
thirds of the area's buildings
were added during this period.

Fresh produce on sale at Hötorget, a marketplace since the 17th century

Hötorget ⑬

Map 2 C4. 🇹 *Hötorget.* 🚌 *1, 52, 56.* 🚆 *7:30am–6pm Mon–Fri, 7:30am–4pm Sat, 10am–5pm Sun.*

TRADITION IS STILL going strong on Hötorget (Hay Market). Formerly belonging to St Klara convent, in the 1640s the square evolved into an important place for trading in animal fodder, milk, vegetables and meat. Today it is still a lively market for fresh produce.

The buildings around the square are relatively new. The most recent is the glass-fronted cinema complex opened in 1995, while the PUB department store was added in 1916 and Konserthuset in 1926. On nearby Sergelgatan, where the five high-rises of Hötorgs City were constructed in 1952–6, there is a reminder of the old

city centre. A tablet marks where the renowned sculptor Johan Tobias Sergel (1740–1814) had his studio. A later sculptor, Carl Milles (see p144), created the well-noted fountain, *Orpheus*, that stands in front of Konserthuset.

Konserthuset ⑭

Hötorget. **Map** 2 C4. 📞 *786 02 00.* 🇹 *Hötorget.* 🚌 *1, 52, 56.* **Ticket Office** 🕐 *noon–6am Mon–Fri, 11am–3pm Sat, and 2 hours before a concert.* 🎫 ♿ 🖥 🚻 🌐 *www.konserthuset.se*

A NORDIC VERSION of a Greek temple, Konserthuset (the Concert Hall) is a masterpiece of the architect Ivar Tengbom (1878–1968) and is an outstanding example of the 1920s' Neo-Classical style. Tengbom's tradition has been carried on by his son Anders (b. 1911), who was in charge of its renovation in 1970–71, and his grandson Svante

(b. 1942), who had a similar task in 1993–6.

Constructed in 1923–6, the main hall at the outset matched Ivar Tengbom's original concept. However, acoustical problems led to major reconstruction work and modernization. Its internal decor is rather frugal, but the Grünewald Hall, by the artist Isaac Grünewald (1889–1946), is more lavish in the style of an Italian Renaissance palace. The four marble statues in the main foyer are by Carl Milles, creator of the *Orpheus* sculpture group outside. Other artists who have contributed to the decor are Einar Forseth, Simon Gate, Edward Hald and Carl Malmsten.

The Concert Hall has been the home of the Swedish Royal Philharmonic Orchestra since it opened. The orchestra gives some 70 concerts every year and international star soloists perform here regularly. It is also the venue for the Nobel Prize presentations.

Kungstornen ⑮

Kungsgatan 30 and 33. **Map** 3 D4. 🇹 *Hötorget.* 🚌 *1, 43, 56.* ⬤ *to the public.*

IN 1915 THE YOUNG architect Sven Wallander submitted a sketch showing how Stockholm could be given a modern, USA-inspired main street. His plans were accepted during the 1920s, when a

The *Orpheus* sculpture group by Carl Milles at Konserthuset

THE NOBEL PRIZES

Alfred Nobel (1833–96) was an outstanding chemist and inventor, and the prestigious Nobel Prizes – consisting of a monetary award and a medal – have been presented every year since 1901 on 10 December, the date of his death. The ceremony takes place in Konserthuset, where prizes are presented for physics, chemistry, physiology or medicine, and literature. Since 1969 the Bank of Sweden has also given a prize for economic sciences in Nobel's memory. The Nobel Peace Prize is presented in Oslo's City Hall on the same day. In 1901 each prize was worth 150,000 kr, while in 1999 it had increased to 7.9 million kr.

The Nobel Medal, awarded annually

new road was excavated through the Brunkeberg hill linking Hötorget with Sture-plan. A bridge was built over what is now Kungsgatan, and a few years later the twin Kungstornen (King's Towers) were added.

Designed in Neo-Classical style by Wallander, the northern tower was originally owned by the sugar company Sockerbolaget. The southern tower was designed by Ivar Callmander and owned by L M Ericsson. Apart from a period when restaurants occupied the top of each one, the towers have been used only as offices. Both 16 floors high, the northern tower, covering an area of 7,000 sq m (75,320 sq ft), is referred to as the "male", with his more graceful, slightly larger twin, as the "female". At the entrance of the northern tower are some beautiful granite sculptures created by Eric Grate.

The "male" and "female" Kungstornen on Kungsgatan

Centralbadet ⑯

Drottninggatan 88. **Map** 4 C4.
[24 24 03. ⓣ Hötorget. 🚌 52.
○ 6am–8:30pm Mon–Fri, 8am–8:30pm Sat, 10am–8:30pm Sun; Jun–Aug: 7am–8:30pm Mon–Fri, noon–8:30pm Sat 📷 🍴 🛗

D ESIGNED BY the architect Wilhelm Klemming in Jugendstil, Centralbadet swimming and fitness centre was completed in 1904. Since then, it has been rebuilt and extended but the façade remains the same, while the Jugendstil influence continues into the main pool and restaurant.

A protected cultural heritage building, the classic swimming

Centralbadet's characteristic Jugenstil façade

centre has a 23-m (25-yd) long pool, a children's section, bubble and treatment pools, three saunas and skin-care and massage departments.

The garden between Drottninggatan and Centralbadet was originally designed by the prolific 18th-century architect Carl Hårleman. A few of the trees growing there are thought to date from his era. The garden is a delightful oasis set round an ornamental pool and fountain, and there is a sculpture showing a Triton riding a dolphin, created by Greta Klemming in the 1920s.

Dansens Hus ⑰

Barnhusgatan 12–14. **Map** 2 C3.
[796 49 10. ⓣ T-centralen.
🚌 47, 53, 69. **Ticket Office** ○ noon–6pm Mon–Sat. 📷 🛗 🖥 🛗
🅦 www.dansenshus.se

T HE "HOUSE OF DANCE" has been Stockholm's main permanent stage for modern dance since 1991 when it took over this site from the City Theatre which moved to Kulturhuset in 1990 (see p67). Dansens Hus has two auditoriums: one for audiences of more than 800, and Blå Lådan (the Blue Box) for experimental performances seating 150.

The theatre does not have a resident ensemble but during the season it presents a dozen national and international guest performances, usually staying for three to five days. Exhibitions are staged in the foyer,

designed by Sven Markelius (1889–1972). Seminars and lectures are also held here and it is the base for the Dance Production Service (DPS), a choreographers' organization.

Strindbergsmuseet Blå Tornet ⑱

Drottninggatan 85. **Map** 2 C3.
[411 53 54. ⓘ Rådmansgatan.
🚌 52, 69. ○ noon–7pm Tue, noon–4pm Wed–Sun; Jun–Aug: noon–4pm Tue–Sun. 📷 2:30pm Thu, 1pm Sat. 🛗 📷 🛗
🅦 www.strindbergsmuseet.se

T HE WORLD-FAMOUS dramatist August Strindberg (1849–1912) had 24 different addresses in Stockholm over the years. He moved to the last of these in 1908, and gave it the name Blå Tornet (The Blue Tower). By then he had gained international recognition.

The house, now the Strindbergsmuseet, was newly built with central heating, toilet and lift, but lacked a kitchen. Instead he relied on Falkner's Pension, in the same building, for food and other services. On his last few birthdays the great man would stand on his balcony and watch his admirers stage a torchlight procession in his honour.

Opened in 1973, the museum includes reconstructions of the author's home with his bedroom, dining room and study, as well as 3,000 books and archives for photographs, press cuttings and posters. In the adjoining premises, a permanent exhibition portrays Strindberg as author, theatrical director, artist and photographer. Temporary exhibitions and other activities are often held here.

Strindberg's desk and writing materials in his study

Adolf Fredriks Kyrka ⑲

Holländargatan. **Map** 2 C3.
📞 20 70 76. 🚇 Hötorget. 🚌 52.
🕐 1–8pm Mon, 10am–4pm Tue–Sat,
10:30am–4pm Sun; later in summer.
🕐 7pm Mon, 12:15pm Wed & Thu,
8am Fri, 11am Sun. 🎫 by appointment. ♿ 🅿 🎁

KING ADOLF FREDERIK laid the
foundation stone of this
church in 1768 on the site of
an earlier chapel dedicated to
St Olof. Designed by Carl
Fredrik Adelcrantz, in Neo-
Classical style with traces of
Rococo, the church has been
built in the shape of a Greek
cross and has a central dome.
The interior has undergone
a number of changes, but
both the altar and
pulpit have remained
intact. The sculptor
Johan Tobias Sergel
created the altarpiece,
which is probably
his most important
religious work. The
memorial to French
philosopher
Descartes (see
p17) is also
Sergel's work.
The paintings
on the dome
were added in
1899–1900 by
Julius Kron-
berg. More
recent items
of value include altar silverware by Sigurd Persson.
The cemetery is the resting
place of the assassinated Prime
Minister Olof Palme, as well
as the politician Hjalmar
Branting, a key figure of the
Social Democratic movement.
J T Sergel is also buried here.

**Memorial to
Descartes**

**The "Devil's Bible" from the early 13th century,
one of Kungliga Biblioteket's foremost rarities**

Kungliga Biblioteket ⑳

Humlegården. **Map** 3 D3.
📞 463 40 00. 🚇 Östermalmstorg.
🚌 1, 46, 55, 56, 91, 96. 🕐 9am–
8pm Mon–Thu, 9am–7pm Fri,
10am–5pm Sat, noon–5pm Sun;
21 Jun–8 Aug: 9am–6pm Mon–Thu,
9am–5pm Fri, 11am–3pm Sat.
🎫 by appointment. ♿ 🅿
W www.kb.se

THIS IS SWEDEN'S national
library and an autonomous
Government department in its
own right. Ever since 1661,
when there were only nine
printing presses in Sweden,
copies of every piece of
printed matter have had to
be lodged with Kungliga
Biblioteket (Royal Library).
Since 1993 this requirement
has also applied to electronic
documents. As there are now
some 3,000 printers and publishers in Sweden the volume
of material is expanding
rapidly. The stock of books is
increasing at the rate of 35,000
volumes a year, not to mention
40,000 magazine issues.
The library's shelving space
is increasing by 1,300 m
(4,265 ft) per year and the
collection now covers more
than 3 million books and
magazines, more than 500,000
posters, 300,000 maps, 750,000

portraits and 500,000
pictures of varying
types. The imposing
original building,
dating from 1865–
78, had to be
expanded in the
1920s, and again in
the 1990s. This
major extension pro-
vided an auditorium
for 120 people, an
exhibition area and, most
importantly, two underground
book storage areas covering
an area in total of 18,000 sq m
(193,680 sq ft). The first of
these is already fully utilized
despite its 843 mobile shelves.
Altogether the library's shelves
cover 137 km (85 miles).
The library is in a beautiful
setting in Humlegården,
created by Gustav II Adolf in
1619 to grow hops for the
royal household. Ever since
the 18th century, the park has
been a favourite recreation
area for Stockholmers.

Stureplan ㉑

Map 3 D4. 🚇 Östermalmstorg.
🚌 1, 46, 55, 56, 91.

A NEW TOWN PLAN for Stockholm towards the end of
the 19th century recommended that the Stureplan area
should become the capital's
new centre. The proposal was
accepted and the area around
Svampen (The Mushroom)

**Stureplan and Svampen, one of the
city's most popular meeting places**

THE MURDERED PRIME MINISTER

On 28 February 1986 the Swedish Prime
Minister Olof Palme was killed in a
Stockholm street on his way home from
a cinema without a bodyguard. The murder happened at the corner of Sveavägen
and Tunnelgatan, whose western section
was renamed Olof Palmes Gata. A
memorial tablet has been placed there.
The murder provoked strong reactions
but was still unsolved at the beginning
of the new millennium. His grave is in
the nearby Adolf Fredrik cemetery.

**Olof Palme
(1927–86)**

rain shelter became a popular meeting place, as more and more shops and restaurants opened. However, a new street layout after the introduction of right-hand driving in Sweden in 1967 brought its halcyon days to a close.

But now Stureplan has staged a phoenix-like comeback out of the ashes of a major fire at the Sturebadet swimming pool in 1985. Plans to revamp the area were made: the pool was modernized and the Sturegallerian shopping mall was built, revitalizing the whole eastern part of the city. Once again Stureplan became one of the capital's most popular meeting places.

Sturegallerian and Sturebadet ㉒

Stureplan 4. **Map** 3 D4. **T** *Östermalmstorg.* **E** *1, 46, 55, 56, 91.* **Shopping mall** ◯ *10am–7pm Mon–Fri, 10am–5pm Sat, noon–5pm Sun.* **Pool** **C** *545 015 00.* ◯ *10am–3pm Mon–Fri; other times by appointment & members only.* ▣ ▥

THE ORIGINAL Sturebadet swimming pool, inaugurated in 1885, was sited within the present-day StureCompagniet complex. Rebuilt on its present site in 1902, it was ahead of its time – even in the 1930s it was offering exercise facilities.

After a disastrous fire in 1985 some 600 million kr was invested, partly on reconstructing the pool according to its original design and partly on developing Sturegallerian, a world-class shopping mall. The architects managed to link the late 19th-century exterior with interiors of modern design using marble, granite, steel, copper, cedar and mahogany.

Indoor streets and squares with some 50 retail outlets have been created, including restaurants, cafés and various services. Today's swimming pool is now the most traditional part of the complex, which also includes offices.

Opened in 1989, the development won an international award in 1990 for its excellent design.

Painstakingly restored Jugendstil decor at Sturebadet

Östermalms-hallen ㉓

Humlegårdsgatan 1–3. **Map** 3 E4. **T** *Östermalmstorg.* **E** *56, 62.* ◯ *9:30am–6pm Mon–Thu, 9:30am–6:30pm Fri, 9:30am–4pm Sat, 9:30am–2pm Sat in Summer.* ▤ ▥

THE TEMPLE OF gastronomy, this market hall on Östermalmstorg is as far removed from a fast-food outlet as you could imagine. Nowhere else in the city is there such a range of high quality delicacies under one roof. But it was certainly an example of fast building. Taking only eight months to erect, the hall was opened by King Oscar II in 1888. It is regarded as a fine example of the city's late 19th-century architectural heritage. Construction of a brick building around a cast-iron shell was a novelty in Sweden, and the architects Gustaf Clason and Kasper Sahlin won acclaim for their design, inspired by the arcades of Mediterranean markets. Renovation in 1999 has preserved the delightful atmosphere. In the early days there were 153 stalls, and today there are 13 larger specialist shops and some popular lunch spots.

Hedvig Eleonora Kyrka ㉔

Storgatan 2. **Map** 3 E4. **C** *663 04 30.* **T** *Östermalmstorg.* **E** *62.* ◯ *10am–4pm Mon & Thu–Sat 10am–6pm Tue, Wed & Sun.* ✝ *12:15pm Tue & Thu, 7pm Wed, 11am Sun.* ▦ *by appt.* ▥ ▯

FOUNDED IN 1669 to give the Swedish Navy its own place for religious services, the church was not officially opened until 1737. The first plans were drawn up by Jean de la Vallée, but the work was completed with Göran Josuae Adelcrantz as architect. The dome was added in 1866–8. The main bell was cast in Helsingør, Denmark, in 1639 and hung in Kronborg Castle before being seized as a war trophy by General Carl Gustaf Wrangel (*see p50*).

The church has many valuable artifacts. The altarpiece *Jesus on the Cross* was painted in 1738 by Engelhard Schröder. The designer of the majestic pulpit in Neo-Classical style was Jean Eric Rehn, who saw his work unveiled on Christmas Day in 1784.

The new organ was built in the mid-1970s, but Carl Fredrik Adelcrantz's 1762 organ façade is still in its original state. Included in the silverware is a Baroque chalice from 1650 and a ciborium dated 1685. The 1678 font is now housed in the baptismal chapel which was added at the time of the church's restoration in 1944.

Östermalmshallen, a culinary temple inspired by markets in southern Europe

Armémuseum, with the dome of Hedvig Eleonora Kyrka in the background

Armémuseum ㉕

Riddargatan 13. **Map** 3 E4.
📞 788 95 60. Ⓣ Östermalmstorg.
🚌 62. 🕐 11am–4pm Tue–Sun.
🎫🎦🚫♿🅿️

THE OLD ARMOURY on
Artillerigården has been
the home of the Armémuseum
(Royal Army Museum) since
1879. During the 1990s the
250-year-old building and its
exhibits underwent extensive
renovation. After reopening in
2000 it is now one of the
capital's best-planned and
most interesting museums.
It puts Sweden's history in a
1,000-year perspective, present-
ing exciting information in a
more comprehensive way.
The march of history is
illustrated by life-size settings,
and visitors can see many
unique objects from the
collection of 80,000 exhibits.
Processions for royal visits
in the city start from the
museum, and during the
summer guardsmen march
from here to the Royal Palace
at 11.45am every day for the
changing of the guard.

Musikmuseet ㉖

Riddargatan/Sibyllegatan. **Map** 3 E4.
📞 519 554 50. Ⓣ Östermalmstorg.
🚌 62. 🕐 11am–4pm Tue–Sun.
🎫🎦🚫♿🅿️
[W] www.musikmuseet.se

AFTER BEING HOUSED on nine
different sites, the Museum
of Music finally moved into
this former royal bakery in
1979. It is the capital's oldest
preserved industrial building,
right in the city centre. Bread
was baked here for military
personnel in Stockholm from
1640 right up to 1958. Today
the museum's collection

includes about 6,000 instruments, and it also holds
Sweden's national musical
archive. With some 20,000
manuscripts, it is a gold
mine for anyone
interested in Swedish
folk music. The archive
is open to visitors by
arrangement, and
there is a regular
programme of
temporary
exhibitions.

**A so-called *hummel*
instrument once
owned by the troub-
adour C M Bellman**

Hovstallet ㉗

Väpnargatan 1. **Map** 3 E4.
📞 402 61 06. Ⓣ Östermalmstorg.
🚌 47, 62, 69, 76. 🕐 for guided
tours. 🎫 2pm Sat & Sun;
Jul–Aug: 2pm Mon–Fri. 🎦 🅿️

FORMERLY ON Helgeands-
holmen, Hovstallet (the
Royal Mews) was moved here
in 1893 when the new Parliament building was being
constructed. Together with
the Museum of Music, it now
occupies a large site next to
the Royal Dramatic Theatre.
The Mews arranges the transport for the Royal Family and

**Coach and four, with riders on the
left-hand horses, at Hovstallet**

the Royal Household. It
maintains about 40 carriages,
a dozen cars and carriage
horses, and a few horses used
for riding. The royal horses
are Swedish half-breeds.
There are many treasures
among the carriages, such as
the State coach with glass
panelling known as a
"Berliner" made in Sweden at
the Adolf Freyschuss carriage
works. It was first seen at
Oscar II's silver jubilee in
1897 and is still used on
ceremonial occasions.
Incoming foreign ambassa-
dors travel to the Royal Palace
for their formal audience with
the monarch in Karl XV's
coupé. Open carriages from
the mid-19th century drawn
by two horses are normally
used for processions.

Kungliga Drama-tiska Teatern ㉘

Nybroplan. **Map** 3 E4. 📞 667 06 80.
Ⓣ Östermalmstorg. 🚌 47, 62, 69,
76. **Ticket Office** 🕐 noon–6pm Mon,
noon–7pm Tue–Sat, 2–4pm Sun. 🎫
🚫♿🍴[W] www.dramaten.se

WHEN PLANS WERE drawn up
in the early 20th century
to build the present Kungliga
Dramatiska Teatern (Royal
Dramatic Theatre) at Nybroplan, the State refused to give
financial aid, so it was funded
by lotteries instead. The results
exceeded all expectations,
giving the architect Fredrik
Lilljekvist generous resources
which he used to the full.
The new theatre, known as
Dramaten, was opened in 1908
after six years' construction
work, and its fittings and decor
were remarkable for their era.
The Jugendstil façade
inspired by Viennese architecture is in costly white

marble. Christian Ericsson provided the powerful relief frieze, Carl Milles the centre section and John Börjesson the bronze statues *Poetry* and *Drama*. These are complemented in the foyer by *Tragedy* and *Comedy* by Börjesson and Theodor Lundberg respectively.

The lavish design continues inside, both in the choice of materials and in the contributions by leading Swedish artists. The ceiling in the foyer is by Carl Larsson, while the upper lobby's back wall was painted by Oscar Björk, and the auditorium's ceiling and stage lintel by Julius Kronberg. Gustav Cederström provided the central painting in the marble foyer, which also has some fantastic sculptures and busts.

Georg Pauli gave his name to a café where visitors can see his paintings and enjoy a meal without necessarily attending a performance.

The 805-seat auditorium and revolving stage with a diameter of 15 m (49 ft) have a classic beauty. When Gustav III founded the Royal Dramatic Theatre in 1788 it performed in a building on Slottsbacken. The probable colour scheme there – blue, white and gold – was chosen for the new national stage but was changed to the traditional "theatre red" in the 1930s. The auditorium was returned to its original colouring during renovation in 1988.

About 100 contracted actors give some 1,200 performances every year on the theatre's five stages to audiences totalling about 300,000.

The Hallwylska Palatset courtyard, seen through the gateway arch

Hallwylska Palatset ㉙

Hamngatan 4. **Map** 3 D4.
☎ 519 555 99. **Ⓣ** *Östermalmstorg.*
🚌 46, 47, 55, 62, 69, 76. **🕐** *noon–3pm every hour Tue–Sun, also 6pm Wed, 1pm Sun (Eng). 26 Jun–15 Aug: 11am–4pm daily every hour.*
📷 🚫 ♿ W www.lsh.se/hallwyl

THE IMPRESSIVE façade of Hamngatan 4 is nothing in comparison with what is concealed by the heavy gates. The Hallwyl Palace was built from 1892–7 as a residence for the immeasurably rich Count and Countess Walther and Wilhelmina von Hallwyl. They decided quite early that the house should eventually become a museum. When the Countess died in 1930 the State was left a fantastic gift: an

The Steinway grand piano in Hallwylska Palatset

unbelievably lavish private palace whose chatelaine had amassed a priceless collection of *objets d'art* over many decades. Eight years later the doors opened on a new museum with 67,000 catalogued items.

Wilhelmina left nothing to chance. The architect Isac Gustav Clason (1856–1930) had no worries about cost and nor did Julius Kronberg, who was a decorative painter and artistic adviser. Everything had to be perfect down to the smallest detail. A typical example is the billiards room which has gilt-leather wallpaper and walnut panelling, with billiard balls sculpted into the marble fireplace.

The paintings in the gallery, mostly 16th- and 17th-century Flemish, were bought over a period of only two years. Adjoining the gallery, the family skittles alley has become a showcase for top-class glazed earthenware. Visitors can also see a rich variety of household objects which could well form a separate exhibition.

Various styles were chosen for the different rooms. The main salon in late Baroque style is built around four grandiose Gobelin tapestries and is finished in 24-carat gold leaf, clearly influenced by Hårleman's work at the Royal Palace *(see pp50–53)*. It is difficult to believe that this was once a room in a private residence.

The most remarkable artifact is a Steinway grand piano, dating from 1896, adapted to fit into its majestic setting with a "casing" of hardwood and inlaid wood. In 1990 it was flown to New York in two sections, weighing a total of 900 kg (1,980 lb), for a renovation lasting several months. Visitors strolling through the salon can listen to a recording of music played on this magnificent piano.

Kungliga Dramatiska Teatern's Jugendstil façade in white marble

BLASIEHOLMEN & SKEPPSHOLMEN

OPPOSITE THE Royal Palace on the eastern side of the Strömmen channel lies Blasieholmen, a natural springboard to the islands of Skeppsholmen and Kastellholmen.

Several elegant palaces were built at Blasieholmen during Sweden's era as a great power in the 17th and early 18th centuries. But the area's present appearance was acquired in the period between the mid-19th century, when buildings like Nationalmuseum were erected, until just before World War I. In the early 1900s, stately residences such as Bååtska Palatset became overshadowed by prestigious hotels, lavish banks and

Porthole in wooden boat

entertainment venues. Blasieholmen is also the place for auction houses, art galleries, antique shops and second-hand bookshops. And the quayside is the departure point for sightseeing and archipelago boats.

Skeppsholmen is reached by a wrought-iron bridge with old wooden boats moored next to it. In the middle of the 17th century the island became the base for the Swedish Navy and many of its old buildings were designed as barracks and stores. Today they house some of the city's major museums and cultural institutions, juxtaposed with the avant-garde construction of the Moderna Museet.

SIGHTS AT A GLANCE

Museums
Arkitekturmuseet ③
Moderna Museet pp80–81 ②
Nationalmuseum pp82–3 ⑦
Östasiatiska Museet ①

Public Buildings
Konsthögskolan ⑤

Islands and Squares
Blasieholmstorg ⑨
Kastellholmen ⑥
Raoul Wallenbergs Torg ⑫

Synagogues
Synagogan ⑩

Hotels and Restaurants
af Chapman ④
Berns' Salonger ⑪
Grand Hôtel ⑧

Concert Halls
Nybrokajen 11 ⑬

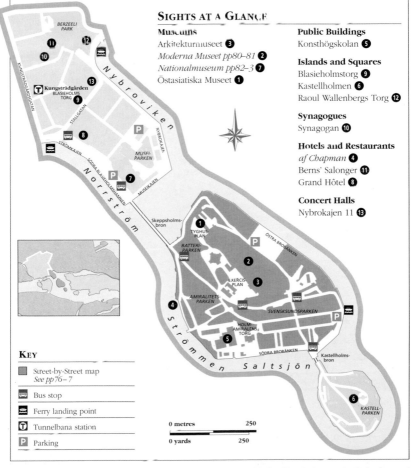

KEY

▨	Street-by-Street map *See pp76–7*
▦	Bus stop
▦	Ferry landing point
Ⓣ	Tunnelbana station
Ⓟ	Parking

0 metres 250
0 yards 250

◁ **Skeppsholmsbron linking Blasieholmen and Skeppsholmen, with the ship *af Chapman* in the background**

Street-by-Street: Skeppsholmen

Sᴋᴇᴘᴘꜱʜᴏʟᴍᴇɴ ʜᴀꜱ ʟᴏɴɢ ꜱɪɴᴄᴇ lost its importance as a naval base and has been transformed into a centre for culture. Many of the naval buildings have been restored and traditional wooden boats are moored here, but pride of place now goes to the exciting new Moderna Museet.

The island is ideal for a full-day visit, with its location between the waters of Strömmen and Nybroviken acting as a breathing space in the centre of Stockholm. The attractive buildings, the richly wooded English-style park and the view towards Skeppsbron and Strandvägen also make Skeppsholmen an ideal place for those who would just prefer to have a quiet stroll.

Teater Galeasen is Stockholm's avant-garde theatre for new Swedish and international drama.

Skepps-holmsbron

Blasie-holmen

★ **Östasiatiska Museet**
This belt plaquette in Ordos style from the 1st or 2nd century BC is included in a remarkable collection of arts and crafts from China, Japan, Korea and India, covering the period from the Stone Age to the 19th century ❶

Skeppsholmen Church (1824–42) in well-preserved Empire style.

Salute battery

Admiralty House

Paradise (1963), a sculpture group by Jean Tinguelys and Niki de Saint Phalles for Montreal's World Exposition, has stood outside the site of the Moderna Museet since 1972.

Youth Hostel

Swedish Society of Crafts & Design

Kungliga Konsthögskolan
The first part of the Royal College of Fine Arts was completed in the 1770s, but it acquired its present appearance in the mid-1990s. This cast-iron boar stands at the entrance ❺

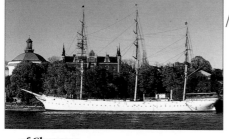

af Chapman
Built in 1888, the full-rigged former freighter and school ship has served as a popular youth hostel since 1949. Skeppsholmen Church (left) and the Admiralty House (1647–50, rebuilt 1844–6) are in the background ❹

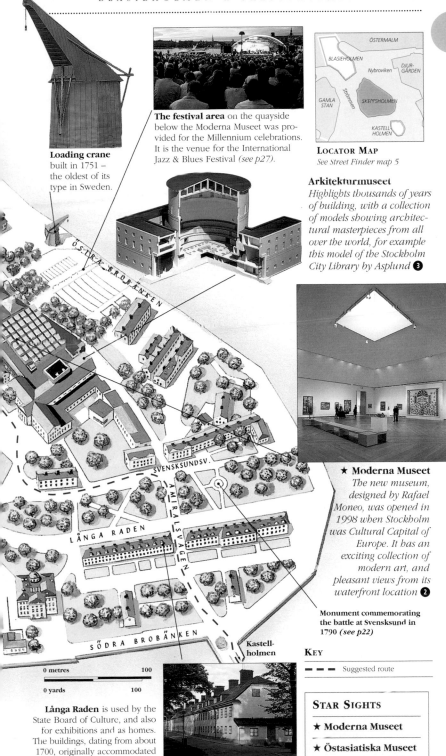

Loading crane built in 1751 – the oldest of its type in Sweden.

The festival area on the quayside below the Moderna Museet was provided for the Millennium celebrations. It is the venue for the International Jazz & Blues Festival *(see p27)*.

LOCATOR MAP
See Street Finder map 5

Arkitekturmuseet
Highlights thousands of years of building, with a collection of models showing architectural masterpieces from all over the world, for example this model of the Stockholm City Library by Asplund ❸

★ **Moderna Museet**
The new museum, designed by Rafael Moneo, was opened in 1998 when Stockholm was Cultural Capital of Europe. It has an exciting collection of modern art, and pleasant views from its waterfront location ❷

Monument commemorating the battle at Svensksund in 1790 *(see p22)*

Långa Raden is used by the State Board of Culture, and also for exhibitions and as homes. The buildings, dating from about 1700, originally accommodated King Karl XII's bodyguard.

Kastell-holmen

0 metres   100
0 yards   100

KEY

– – – Suggested route

STAR SIGHTS

★ Moderna Museet

★ Östasiatiska Museet

Arkitekturmuseet, housed in the Neo-Classical former naval drill hall

Östasiatiska Museet ❶

Tyghusplan. **Map** 5 D2.
🎫 *519 557 70*. Ⓣ *Kungsträdgården.*
🚌 *65.* 🚢 *Djurgårdsfärja.* ◯ *noon–8pm Tue, noon–5pm Wed–Sun.*
📷 🚫 ♿ 🏪 Ⓦ *www.mfea.se*

IT IS NOT UNUSUAL for Western capitals to have a museum devoted to art and archaeo-logy from China, Japan, Korea and India. But it is not every Museum of Far Eastern Antiquities that, like Öst-asiatiska Museet, can claim one of the world's foremost collections of Chinese art outside Asia.

On a visit to the Yellow River valley in China in the early 1920s, the Swedish geologist Johan Gunnar Andersson discovered hitherto unknown dwellings and graves containing objects dating from the New Stone Age.

He was allowed to take a rich selection of finds back to Sweden, and these formed the basis for the museum, founded in 1926. A key figure in its development was the then Crown Prince, later to become King Gustaf VI Adolf,

who was both interested in and knowledgeable about archaeology. He eventually bequeathed to the museum his own large collection of ancient Chinese arts and crafts.

The museum has been on Skeppsholmen since 1963, when it was moved into a restored house which had been built in 1699–1700 as a depot for Karl XII's bodyguard.

Moderna Museet ❷

See pp80–81.

Arkitektur-museet ❸

Exercisplan. **Map** 5 E3.
🎫 *587 270 00*. Ⓣ *Kungsträd-gården.* 🚌 *65.* 🚢 *Djurgårdsfärja.*
◯ *11am–8pm Tue–Thu, 11am– 6pm Fri–Sun.* 🎫 *2pm Sat & Sun (in Eng: summer only).* 📷 🚫 ♿ 🍴 🏪 🏪
Ⓦ *www.arkitekturmuseet.se*

THE SWEDISH Museum of Architecture shares an entrance hall and restaurant with the new Moderna Museet. It has also taken over

its earlier home, the one-time naval drill hall.

In the permanent exhibi-tion, over a hundred models guide visitors through a thousand years of building. These cover categories from the oldest and simplest of wooden houses to the highly varied building techniques and architectural styles of the present day.

It is fascinating to switch from an almost 2,000-year-old longhouse to a Konsum supermarket, in between examples of architecture in Gothenburg dating from the 17th century to the 1930s and the new Årsta bridge situated to the south of Stockholm.

Models of historic architec-tural works worldwide, from 2000 BC up to the present day, are also on show.

The museum offers an ambitious programme – albeit only in Swedish – alongside the permanent and temporary exhibitions, including lectures, study days, city walks, guided tours, school visits and family events on Sunday afternoons which involves model-building.

Chinese Bodhisattva in limestone from about AD 530

THE SKEPPSHOLMEN CANNONS

A salute battery of four 57-mm rapid-fire cannons is sited on Skeppsholmen and are still in use. Salutes are fired to mark national and royal special occasions at 12 noon on weekdays and 1pm at weekends:
28 January – the King's name day; 30 April – the King's birthday; 6 June – Sweden's National Day; 14 July – Crown Princess Victoria's birthday; 8 August – the Queen's name day; 23 December – the Queen's birthday.

The salute battery on Skeppsholmen

af Chapman ❹

Västra Brobänken. **Map** 5 D3.
[463 22 66 **T]** Kungsträdgården.
🚌 65. **🚢** Djurgårdsfärja. **🅿** See
Where to stay p149.

THE SAILING SHIP *af Chapman* is one of Sweden's most attractive and unusual youth hostels and has 136 beds. The hostel also includes the 152-bed building facing the ship's gangway.

Visitors staying in more conventional accommodation can still go on board and enjoy *af Chapman*'s special atmosphere. The three-masted ship was built in 1888 at the English port of Whitehaven and used as a freight vessel. She came to Sweden in 1915 and saw service as a school ship until 1934. The City of Stockholm bought the ship after World War II and she has been berthed here since 1949. She is named after Fredrik Henrik af Chapman, a master shipbuilder who was born in Gothenburg in 1721.

Kungliga Konsthögskolan ❺

Flaggmansvägen 1. **Map** 5 E3.
[614 40 00. **T]** Kungsträdgården.
🚌 65. **🚢** Djurgårdsfärja. **◯** to the
public for special events. **♿ 🅿**

A STROLL AROUND Skeppsholmen provides an opportunity to have a closer look at the beautifully restored 18th-century naval barracks which now houses Kungliga Konsthögskolan (the Royal College of Fine Arts). At the entrance there are two statues depicting a lion and a boar. "In like a lion and out like a pig" is an old saying among the lecturers and the 200 or so students at this college, rich in tradition.

The college started out in 1735 as an academy for painting and sculpture for the decorators working on Tessin's new Royal Palace. Gustaf III granted it a royal charter in 1773. Before it moved here in 1995, the college was located on Fredsgatan as part of Konstakademien (*see p66*), although since 1978 it had

been run independently with departments for painting, sculpture, graphics, computing and video, as well as offering courses for architects.

The college is not normally open to the public, apart from an "open house" once a year. Then visitors can enjoy the beautiful interiors, especially the vaulted 18th-century cellars.

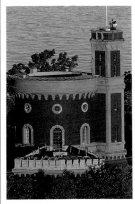

The medieval-style castle on Kastellholmen, built in 1846–8

Kastellholmen ❻

Map 5 F4. **T]** Kungsträdgården.
🚌 65. **🚢** Djurgårdsfärja.

RIGHT IN THE middle of Stockholm, Kastellholmen is a typical archipelago island with granite rocks and steep cliffs. From Skeppsholmen it is reached by a bridge built in 1880. Every morning since 1640 a sailor has hoisted the three-tailed Swedish war flag at the castle. Whenever a visiting naval vessel arrives, the battery's four cannons

fire a welcoming salute from the castle terrace.

The charming brick pavilion by the bridge was built in 1882 for the Royal Skating Club, which used the water between the two islands when it froze.

Nationalmuseum ❼

See pp80–81.

Grand Hôtel ❽

Södra Blasieholmshamnen 8. **Map** 4
C1. **[** 679 35 00. **T]** Kungsträdgården. **🚌** 46, 55, 59, 62, 65, 76.
See **Where to stay** p151 and **Where
to eat** p161.

OSCAR II's head chef, Régis Cadier, founded the Grand Hôtel, Sweden's only five-star hotel, in 1874. And since 1901, the hotel has accommodated the Nobel Prize winners every year.

Traditional Swedish delicacies are served in an abundant *smörgåsbord* in the elegant Grands Veranda, while Franska Matsalen is a stylish gourmet restaurant. The Cadier Bar is named after the hotel's founder.

The hotel has 19 banqueting and meeting suites, the best known of which is the *Vinterträdgården* (Winter Garden) with a ceiling height of 20 m (66 ft) and space for more than 800 people. The *Spegelsalen* (Hall of Mirrors) is a copy of the one at Versailles and was where the Nobel Prize banquet was held until 1929, when the event became too big and was moved to the City Hall (*see p114*).

Grand Hôtel on Blasieholmen, Sweden's only five-star hotel

Moderna Museet ⊙

AFTER THREE DECADES in a former naval drill hall, the Museum of Modern Art was moved into its airy new building, designed by the Catalan architect Rafael Moneo, in 1998. Now the museum has both the space and a setting worthy of its top-class collections of international and Swedish modern art, as well as photography and film. Built partly underground, the museum includes a cinema and auditorium; the photographic library is the most comprehensive collection of its type in northern Europe. A wide choice of books on art, photography, film and architecture can be found in the bookshop and the Restaurant Kantin Moneo has attractive views over the water.

Breakfast Outdoors (1962)
This sculpture group by Picasso, executed in sandblasted concrete by Carl Nesjar, stands in the museum garden near the entrance.

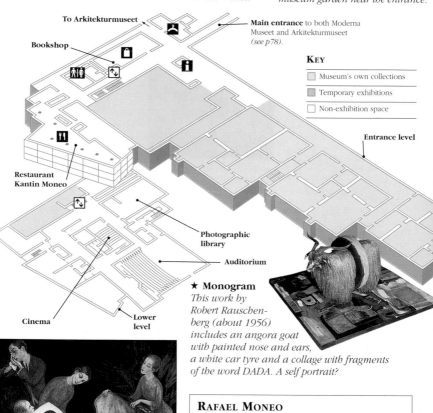

To Arkitekturmuseet

Bookshop

Restaurant
Kantin Moneo

Cinema

Lower
level

Photographic
library

Auditorium

Main entrance to both Moderna Museet and Arkitekturmuseet (see p78).

KEY

- Museum's own collections
- Temporary exhibitions
- Non-exhibition space

Entrance level

★ **Monogram**
This work by Robert Rauschenberg (about 1956) includes an angora goat with painted nose and ears, a white car tyre and a collage with fragments of the word DADA. A self portrait?

★ **The Dying Dandy** (1918)
The cosmopolitan artist Nils Dardel (1888–1943) produced this Expressionistic painting when he was about to marry. It can be interpreted as a farewell to his misspent youth.

RAFAEL MONEO

Rafael Moneo (b. 1937) is one of the leading contemporary architects. As a young architect Moneo took part in the project to build the Sydney Opera House. His flair for adapting building design to sensitive surroundings was recognized in 1989 when he was chosen out of 211 entries as the winner of the competition to design the new Moderna Museet.

Moderna Museet's northern façade

GALLERY GUIDE

*The large room on the
entrance level is used for
temporary exhibitions. Three
rooms on the same level have
an alternating selection of the
museum's collections from
three eras: 1900–45, 1946–
70, and 1971 to the present
day. The lower level has an
auditorium, cinema and
photographic library.*

★ **The Child's Brain** (1914)
*The surrealist Giorgio de
Chirico gave his work the
title* The Ghost *but Louis
Aragon renamed it in a
pamphlet about the artist's
1927 retrospective exhibition.*

STAR FEATURES

★ **The Dying Dandy
by Dardel**

★ **Monogram
by Rauschenberg**

★ **The Child's Brain
by de Chirico**

Blasieholmstorg 9

Map 4 C1. Kungsträdgården.
46, 55, 59, 62, 65, 76.

Two of the city's oldest
palaces are located in this
square, flanked by two bronze
horses. The palace at No. 8
was built in the mid-17th
century by Field Marshal
Gustaf Horn. It was rebuilt
100 years later, when it
acquired the character of an
18th-century French palace.
Foreign ambassadors and
ministers started to lodge here
when they visited
the capital, so it
became known
as the Ministers'
Palace. Later it
became a base for
overseas admin-
istration and soon
earned its present
name of Utrikes-
ministerhotellet
(Foreign Ministry
Hotel). Parts of the
building are now used as
offices by the Musical Academy
and the Swedish Institute.
Bååtska Palatset stands
nearby at No. 6. Its newly
restored exterior dates from
1669 and was designed by ·
Tessin the Elder. In 1876–7 it
was partly rebuilt by F W
Scholander for the Free-
masons, who still have their
lodge here.
Another interesting complex
of buildings can be found on
the square at No. 10. The
façade which faces on to
Nybrokajen, along the water's
edge, is an attractive example
of the Neo-Renaissance style
of the 1870s and 1880s.

**Bronze horse on
Blasieholmstorg**

Synagogan 10

Warendorfgatan 3. **Map** 4 C1.
679 29 00. Kungsträdgården.
46, 55, 59, 62, 65, 76.
5:30pm Mon, Thu, Fri; 9:15 Sat;
Hebrew, partly Swedish. Summer
and on request.

It took most of the 1860s
to build the Conservative
Jewish community's syna-
gogue on what was once the
seabed. When it was inaugurated in 1870, the synagogue
was standing on 1,300 piles

**Monument to the victims of the
Holocaust during World War II**

which had been driven down
to a depth of 15 m (50 ft). It
is built in what the architect,
F W Scholander, called
"ancient Eastern style".
Alongside this
synagogue, which
can be visited on
guided tours during
the summer, is the
congregation's
assembly room and
library. Outside is a
monument erected
in 1998 to the mem-
ory of 8,000 victims
of the Holocaust whose
relations had been rescued
and taken to Sweden during
World War II.
There is also an Orthodox
synagogue in the city centre,
reached through the Jewish
Centre (Judiska Centret) on
Nybrogatan at No. 19.

Berns' Salonger 11

Berzelii Park. **Map** 3 D4.
566 322 00. Kungsträdgården,
Östermalmstorg. 46, 55, 59, 62,
65, 76. **Where to eat** p160.

This has been one of Stockholm's most legendary
restaurants and entertainment
venues since 1863. Both
salons, with their stately
galleries, magnificent crystal
chandeliers and elegant
mirrors, have recently been
restored to their original
splendour by the British
designer Terence Conran to
mark the new millennium.
The new-look Berns' is one
of Stockholm's biggest
restaurants with seating for
400 diners. The gallery level,
with its beautifully decorated
dining rooms, was made
famous by August Strindberg's
novel *The Red Room* (1879).

Nationalmuseum 🄬

THE NATIONAL MUSEUM is a landmark on the southern side of Blasieholmen. The location by the Strömmen channel inspired the 19th-century German architect August Stüler to design a building in the Venetian and Florentine Renaissance styles.

Completed in 1866, the museum houses Sweden's largest art collection, with some 16,000 classic paintings and sculptures. Drawings and graphics from the 15th century up to the early 20th century bring the total up to 500,000. The handicrafts section has 30,000 works spanning five centuries, including a 500-year-old tapestry, Scandinavia's largest collection of porcelain, exquisite works in glass and silver, as well as examples of work by master furnishers, such as Georg Haupt, and of modern Swedish design.

The Love Lesson (1716–17)
Antoine Watteau's speciality was the so-called fêtes galantes, *depicting young couples in playful mood.*

★ **The Conspiracy of the Batavians under Claudius Civilis**
(1661–62)
Originally intended for Amsterdam, Rembrandt's painting shows the Batavians' journey to Rome, symbolizing the Dutch liberation campaign against Spain.

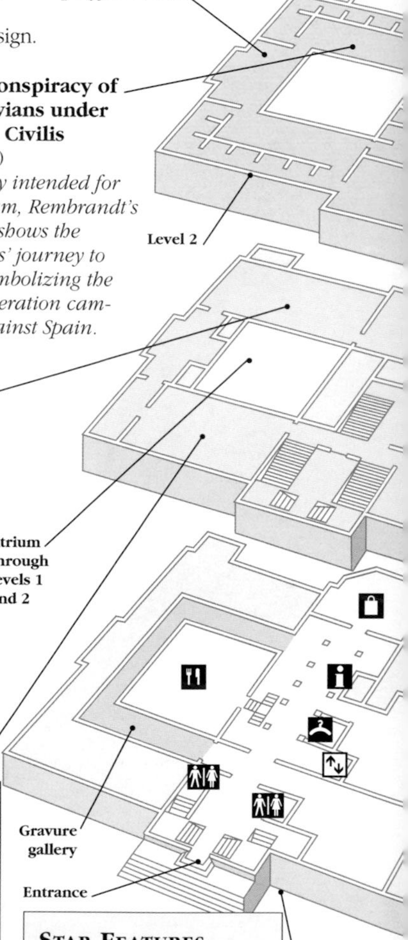

Level 2

Atrium through levels 1 and 2

Chest of Drawers (1780)
This impressive piece of furniture was created by Georg Haupt, who was one of the foremost Swedish cabinet-makers of the 18th century.

Gravure gallery

Entrance

David and Bathsheba (1490)
This tapestry from Brussels is created in the decorative medieval style, with pomegranates, faces and hands forming an exquisite work.

STAR FEATURES

★ **The Lady with the Veil by Roslin**

★ **The Conspiracy of the Batavians by Rembrandt**

Entry for wheelchairs

★ **The Lady with the Veil**
Alexander Roslin's elegant portrait (1769) is often considered a symbol for 18th-century Sweden.

VISITORS' CHECKLIST

Södra Blasieholmshamnen.
Map 5 D2. 📞 *519 543 00.*
🚇 *Kungsträdgården.* 🚌 *65; or 46, 55, 59, 62, 76 to Karl XII:s Torg.* ⏰ *11am–8pm Tue, 11am–5pm Wed–Sun.* ● *24, 25 & 31 Dec, 1 Jan, 25 Jun.* 📷 *Eng: tours twice a week in summer.* 🖼 📷 ♿
♟ 🍴 📷
Ⓦ *www.nationalmuseum.se*

The upper staircase
At the back is Carl Larsson's monumental mural The Entry of King Gustav Vasa of Sweden in Stockholm 1523. *On the opposite wall is his* Midwinter Sacrifice.

The Faun (1774)
Johan Tobias Sergel was the foremost sculptor of the Gustavian era. This piece is regarded as his most triumphant work.

Level 1

Auditorium

Entrance level

KEY

- ☐ Painting and sculpture
- ☐ Handicraft and design
- ☐ Temporary exhibitions
- ☐ Non-exhibition space
- ☐ No admission

GALLERY GUIDE

Level 2 is devoted to painting and sculpture. The accent is on Swedish 18th- to early 20th-century art, but the 17th-century Dutch and Flemish, and 18th-century French schools are also represented. Exhibits may change. Level 1 shows mainly Swedish handicrafts, particularly furniture, porcelain, silver and glass from the 15th century up to modern Swedish design. To the left of the main entrance is the Gravure Gallery with temporary exhibitions of graphics etc.

Raoul Wallenbergs Torg ⑫

Map 3 E4. 🚇 *Östermalmstorg.* 🚌 *46, 55, 59, 62, 65, 76.*

THIS SQUARE IS dedicated to Raoul Wallenberg (1912–unknown), who during World War II worked as a diplomat at the Swedish Embassy in Budapest. By using Swedish "protective passports" he helped a large number of Hungarian Jews to escape deportation to the Nazi concentration camps.

In 1945, when Budapest was liberated, he was imprisoned by the Soviets and according to Soviet sources he died in Moscow's Lubianka prison in 1947. His fate, however, has never been satisfactorily explained.

The small square adjoins Berzelii Park and Nybroplan and faces the Nybrokajen waterfront. The definitive design of the square has been hotly debated because it is set in a sensitive architectural environment, but great efforts have been made to ensure that it remains a worthy memorial to Raoul Wallenberg.

Nybrokajen 11 ⑬

Nybrokajen 11. **Map** 4 C1.
📞 *401 17 00.* 🚇 *Kungsträdgården, Östermalmstorg.* 🚌 *47, 62, 69, 76.* 🚢 *Djurgårdsfärja.* ⏰ *for concerts (phone for details).* ♿

CONSTRUCTED IN the 1870s, this building facing the waters of Nybroviken once housed the Musical Academy. Its concert hall, opened in 1878, was the first in the country, and was used for the first presentations of the Nobel Prize in 1901. Designed in Neo-Renaissance style with cast-iron pillars, the hall has a royal box and galleries, and can seat up to 600 people.

After extensive restoration work, it is now run by the state musical organization Rikskonserter which has provided Stockholmers with a much-needed concert stage for chamber, choral, jazz and folk music (see p169).

DJURGÅRDEN

ONCE A ROYAL hunting ground, Djurgården is an island right in the centre of Stockholm covered by a natural park. It has very few buildings with only around 800 permanent residents and forms part of the Stockholm National City Park, the only one of its type in the world *(see p121)*.

From 1580 parts of Djurgården were a royal animal reserve where Johan III kept reindeer, red deer and elk. A century later the area was fenced off by Karl XI to be used for hunting. It developed into a popular

Museum tram

recreational park during the 18th century, and in the time of troubador Carl Bellman *(see p98)* many inns appeared. The Gröna Lund funfair was established just a few decades before Artur Hazelius founded the fascinating outdoor museum of Skansen and Nordiska Museet in around 1900. Today, there is a wealth of museums on Djurgården offering a mixture of nature, culture and entertainment. A royal connection survives in the beautiful Rosendal Palace which has magnificent Empire-style decor.

SIGHTS AT A GLANCE

Museums
Aquaria ⑧
Biologiska Museet ⑦
Junibacken ②
Liljevalchs Konsthall ⑨
Museifartygen ⑥
Nordiska Museet pp90–91 ③
Waldemarsudde ⑭
Skansen pp96–7 ⑫
Thielska Galleriet ⑮
Vasamuseet pp92–3 ⑤

Amusement Parks
Gröna Lund ⑩

Historic Areas
Djurgårdsstaden & Beckholmen ⑪
Rosendals Slott & Trädgårdar ⑬

Memorials
Estoniaminnesvården ④

Bridges
Djurgårds-bron ①

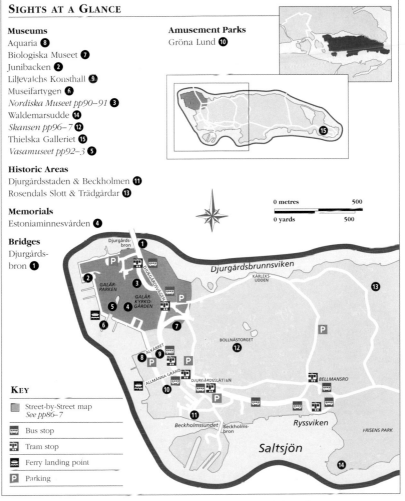

KEY

▢	Street-by-Street map See pp86–7
🚌	Bus stop
🚋	Tram stop
⛴	Ferry landing point
P	Parking

◁ Some of the 300-year-old oaks in Royal Djurgården, part of the National City Park

Street-by-Street: Around Lejonslätten

LIONS WERE KEPT FOR animal-baiting up to 1792 on the spot where Nordiska Museet now stands, hence the name of this area – Lejonslätten (The Lion Plain). Today visitors can safely stroll along the waterfront, look at the boats, and take in the panorama across to Nybroviken, Skeppsholmen and the heights of Södermalm.

This area also offers several sights of cultural interest. The majestic Nordiska Museet, built in Neo-Renaissance style, reflects Swedish cultural history over almost 500 years. In Vasamuseet lies the beautifully restored 17th-century warship and two more vintage ships are moored outside. Nearby, Junibacken brings Pippi Longstocking and other favourite children's book characters imaginatively to life.

Junibacken
A fun place for children, dedicated to the author Astrid Lindgren. It also features characters from stories by other authors ❷

★ **Vasamuseet**
The royal warship Vasa was salvaged after 300 years in the depths of Stockholm's harbour. It is now housed in Stockholm's most popular museum ❺

Museifartygen
Alongside Vasamuseet are two faithful vessels: the icebreaker Sankt Erik and the lightship Finngrundet ❻

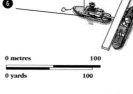

| 0 metres | 100 |
| 0 yards | 100 |

STAR SIGHTS

★ **Vasamuseet**

★ **Nordiska Museet**

Estoniaminnesvården
Near the Galär cemetery, a national memorial has been erected to the 852 people who lost their lives in the Estonia ferry disaster on the night of 27–28 September 1994. The ferry sank on its way from Tallinn to Stockholm ❹

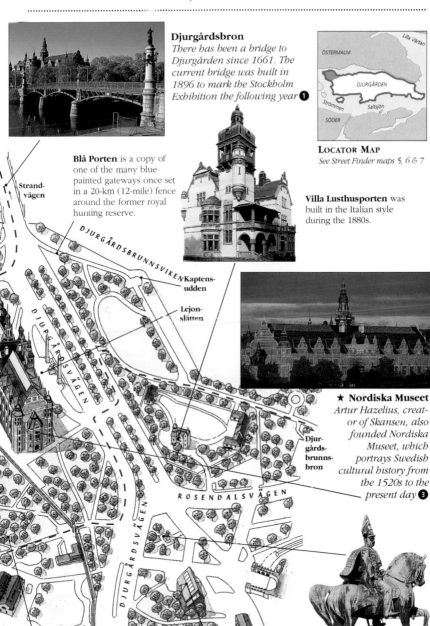

Djurgårdsbron
There has been a bridge to Djurgården since 1661. The current bridge was built in 1896 to mark the Stockholm Exhibition the following year ❶

LOCATOR MAP
See Street Finder maps 5, 6 & 7

Blå Porten is a copy of one of the many blue-painted gateways once set in a 20-km (12-mile) fence around the former royal hunting reserve.

Villa Lusthusporten was built in the Italian style during the 1880s.

Strand-vägen

Kaptens-udden

Lejon-slätten

Djur-gårds-brunns-bron

★ Nordiska Museet
Artur Hazelius, creator of Skansen, also founded Nordiska Museet, which portrays Swedish cultural history from the 1520s to the present day ❸

ROSENDALSVÄGEN

DJURGÅRDSVÄGEN

Karl XV's equestrian statue by Charles Friberg was erected in 1909. The king (1826–72) was a great patron of the arts.

Galärkyrkogården (cemetery)

Biologiska Museet
Swedish fauna is shown in realistic natural settings in this charming old museum ❼

KEY

– – – Suggested route

One of the beautifully decorated pillars supporting Djurgårdsbron

Djurgårdsbron ❶

Map 3 F4. 🚌 44, 47, 69, 76. 🚊 7.
🚢 Djurgårdsfärja.

THE DJURGÅRDEN Bridge came into use a few days before the major Art and Industrial Exhibition opened in Stockholm in May 1897. Made at the Bergsund plant in Södermalm, the bridge is richly ornamented with cast-iron railings in the form of stylized water plants. At that time Sweden was in union with Norway, and King Oscar II's monogram and motto "The sister nations' wellbeing" can be seen on the central span. The capital's patron saint, St Erik, is depicted on the pillar supports among sea gods and water lilies.

Wrought-iron lamps and sculptures portraying mytho-logical gods, created by Rolf Adlersparre, adorn the four granite pillars at either end. On the Strandvägen side, the pillars show Heimdal, the watchman, and Frigga, the wife of Oden. On the opposite side is Thor, with his hammer, and Freja, goddess of love and fertility.

The gate of Blå Porten, just to the left on the Djurgården side, recalls the time when the island was a royal hunting ground during the 17th century, and the surrounding fence was punctuated by blue-painted wooden gate-ways. This gate, decorated with Oscar I's monogram, was made from cast iron in 1849.

Junibacken ❷

Galärvarvsvägen. Map 5 F1.
📞 587 230 00. 🚌 44, 47. 🚊 7.
🚢 Djurgårdsfärja. ⭕ Jun–Aug:
9am–6pm daily, Sep–May: 10am–
5pm Tue–Sun. 🎦 ⭐ 🚻 🛍 🍴
Ⓦ www.junibacken.se

YOU CAN FIND them all here – Pippi Longstocking, Mardie, Karlsson on the Roof, Emil, Nils Karlsson Pyssling, Ronja the robber's daughter, the Lionheart Brothers and many more favourite characters from Astrid Lindgren's children's books. In accordance with the popular novelist's wishes, visitors can also meet the creations of other Swedish children's authors. When she heard about Staffan Götesam's project for a children's cultural centre she was adamant it should not be just an Astrid Lindgren museum.

Nevertheless Junibacken is still something of a tribute to the much-loved author. It was officially opened by the Royal Family in the summer of 1996 and has become one of the city's most popular tourist attractions. A mini-train takes

A colourful scene from one of Astrid Lindgren's stories seen from the mini-train

visitors from a mock-up of the station at Vimmerby (the author's home town) to meet some of her characters, finishing with a visit to Pippi's home in Villekulla Cottage, where children can play in the different rooms. There is also a well-stocked children's bookshop and a restaurant.

Nordiska Museet ❸

See pp90–91.

Estoniaminnes-vården ❹

Galärkyrkogården. Map 5 F2.
🚌 44, 47. 🚢 Djurgårdsfärja.

ON THE NIGHT of 27–28 September 1994 the ferry MS *Estonia* sank in the Baltic on its journey from Tallinn to Stockholm with the loss of 852 lives. They came from many countries including Sweden, Estonia, Latvia, Russia, Finland, Norway, Denmark, Germany, Lithuania, Morocco, the Netherlands, France, the United Kingdom, Canada, Belarus, Ukraine and Nigeria. Their names and their fate will never be forgotten.

So reads the inscription on the national memorial to the victims of the *Estonia* disaster adjoining the cemetery of Galärkyrkogården. It was designed by the Polish artist Miroslaw Balka (b. 1958), who created it together

ASTRID LINDGREN AND PIPPI LONGSTOCKING

Astrid Lindgren has written around 100 children's books which have been translated into 74 languages, making her one of the world's most-read child-ren's authors. Publishers turned down her first book about Pippi Longstocking but she went on to win a children's book competition two years later, in 1945. Her headstrong and tough character Pippi soon won the hearts of children worldwide.

Born on 14 November 1907 in Vimmerby in the south, Astrid stopped writing books at 85, but her characters live on at Junibacken.

Astrid Lindgren

Museifartygen: the lightship *Finngrundet* and ice-breaker *Sankt Erik* outside Vasamuseet

with the two landscape architects Anders Jönsson and Thomas Andersson.

Unveiled on 28 September 1997, the memorial is made of blasted granite and forms a roofless, triangular room with 11-m (36 ft) long sides and a height of 2.5 m (just over 8 ft). The exact position of where the ferry sank is given on a metal ring around a tree in the triangle. With relatives' consent, the names of most of the dead have been carved in the walls.

Vasamuseet ❺

See pp92–4.

Museifartygen ❻

Galärvarvet. **Map** 5 F2.
📞 519 548 91. 🚌 44, 47. 🚊 7
🚢 Djurgårdsfärja. ⏰ 10 Jun–20 Aug: noon–5pm daily; also during various public holidays, ring for details. ♿ 📷 🚻
🌐 www.vasamuseet.se/museifartygen

THE TWO VINTAGE ships moored alongside Vasamuseet are both fine examples of the ships built to handle various tasks in Swedish waters during the early 20th century. The lightship *Finngrundet*, built in 1903, used to be anchored during the ice-free season on the Finngrund banks in the southern Gulf of Bothnia. In the 1960s lightships started to be replaced by permanent automatic lighthouses, so *Finngrundet* was withdrawn from service and became a museum

ship. At 31 m (102 ft) long and 6.85 m (22 ft 6 in) wide, with a draught of 3.1 m (10 ft 3 in), she was designed for a crew of eight. The light had a range of 11 nautical miles.

Built in 1915, *Sankt Erik* was Sweden's first seagoing ice-breaker. This classic Baltic model slides up over the ice and crushes it. She also has a system that enables the ship to be rocked sideways to loosen the ice and widen the channel. One of the two three-cylinder engines is Sweden's largest working marine steam engine. The ice-breaker is 60 m (197 ft) long and 17 m (56 ft) wide and needs a crew of 30.

Biologiska Museet ❼

Lejonslätten. **Map** 6 A3.
📞 442 82 15. 🚌 44, 47. 🚊 7.
⏰ Apr–Sep: 10am–4pm daily, Oct–Mar: 10am–3pm Tue–Sun.
♿ by arrangement. 📷 🚻

THE NATIONAL ROMANTIC influences of the late 19th century inspired the architect Agi Lindegren when he was commissioned to design Biologiska Museet (Museum of Biology) in the 1890s. He based his plans on the simple lines of the medieval Norwegian stave churches.

The man behind the museum was the zoologist, hunter and conservationist Gustaf Kolthoff (1845–1913). In 1892, he persuaded the industrialist

C F Liljevalch – who later financed the nearby art gallery – to form a company whose aim was "to develop and maintain a biological museum to include all the Scandinavian mammals and birds as stuffed specimens in natural surroundings". The result was the world's first museum of its type. Within a few months of opening in autumn 1893, Gustaf Kolthoff had delivered a couple of thousand stuffed animals, as well as birds' nests, young and eggs. Many of the creatures are shown against a diorama background, with about 300 species of Scandinavian birds and land mammals in their respective biotypes. Kolthoff's friend, the artist Bruno Liljefors, was responsible for the paintings.

Since 1970 the Museum of Biology has belonged to the Skansen Foundation. During the 1990s it underwent extensive renovation and was reopened on 13 November 1993 – exactly 100 years after its original inauguration.

Biologiska Museet's wooden façade, inspired by Nordic medieval design

Nordiska Museet ❸

R ESEMBLING AN EXTRAVAGANT Renaissance castle, Nordiska Museet portrays everyday life in Sweden from the 1520s to the present day. It was created by Artur Hazelius (1833–1901), who was also the founder of Skansen *(see pp96–7)*. In 1872, he started to collect objects which would remind future generations of the old Nordic farming culture.

The present museum, designed by Isak Gustaf Clason, was opened in 1907. Today it has more than 1.5 million exhibits, with everything from luxury clothing and priceless jewellery to everyday items, furniture and children's toys, and replicas of period homes.

Dolls' Houses
The dolls' houses show typical homes from the 17th century to modern times. This example illustrates one from 1860.

Level 3

Corridor to staircase

Main Hall

Ground floor

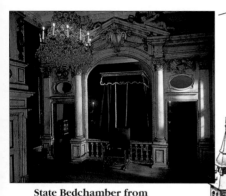

State Bedchamber from Ulvsunda Castle
At the end of the 17th century, the lord of the manor at Ulvsunda accommodated prominent guests in this prestigious bedchamber.

STAR FEATURES

★ **Main Hall**

★ **Strindberg Collection**

★ **Table Settings**

GALLERY GUIDE
The museum has four floors. From the entrance, stairs lead up to the temporary exhibitions in the Main Hall. On the ground level are sections covering Guilds, Folk Costumes and Lapp (Same) *Culture. Floor 3 has the Strindberg Collection, Dolls' Houses, Table Settings, Traditions and the Fashion Gallery. On the fourth floor are sections on Furniture, Swedish Homes, and Small Objects.*

Obelisk with an inscription meaning: "The day may dawn when not even all our gold is enough to form a picture of a bygone era".

Main entrance

★ **Table Settings**
In the mid-17th century, table settings were a feast for the eyes. A swan is the centrepiece at this meal.

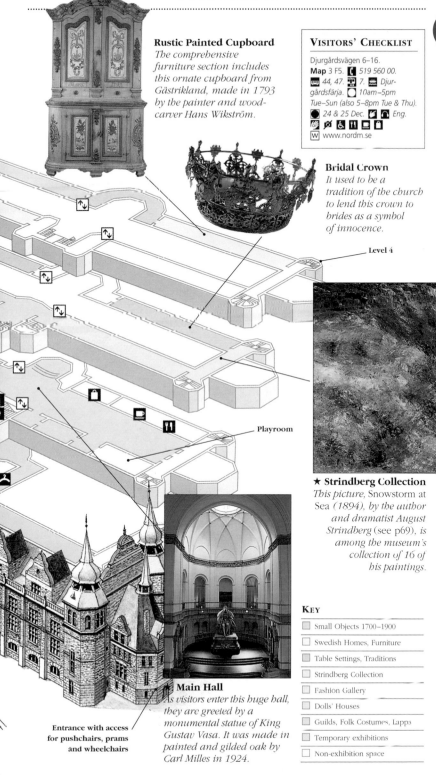

Rustic Painted Cupboard
The comprehensive furniture section includes this ornate cupboard from Gästrikland, made in 1793 by the painter and woodcarver Hans Wikström.

VISITORS' CHECKLIST

Djurgårdsvägen 6–16.
Map 3 F5. 519 560 00.
44, 47. 7. Djurgårdsfärja. 10am–5pm Tue–Sun (also 5–8pm Tue & Thu).
24 & 25 Dec. Eng.
W www.nordm.se

Bridal Crown
It used to be a tradition of the church to lend this crown to brides as a symbol of innocence.

Level 4

Playroom

★ Strindberg Collection
This picture, Snowstorm at Sea *(1894), by the author and dramatist August Strindberg (see p69), is among the museum's collection of 16 of his paintings.*

KEY

	Small Objects 1700–1900
	Swedish Homes, Furniture
	Table Settings, Traditions
	Strindberg Collection
	Fashion Gallery
	Dolls' Houses
	Guilds, Folk Costumes, Lapps
	Temporary exhibitions
	Non-exhibition space

Main Hall
As visitors enter this huge hall, they are greeted by a monumental statue of King Gustav Vasa. It was made in painted and gilded oak by Carl Milles in 1924.

Entrance with access for pushchairs, prams and wheelchairs

Vasamuseet **5**

AFTER A MAIDEN VOYAGE of just 1,300 m (4,265 ft) in calm
weather, the royal warship *Vasa* capsized in Stockholm's harbour on 10 August 1628. About 50 people
went down with what was supposed to be the pride of
the Navy, only 100 m (330 ft) off the southernmost point
of Djurgården. Guns were all that were salvaged from
the vessel in the 17th century and it was not until 1956
that a marine archaeologist's persistent search led to the
rediscovery of *Vasa*. After a complex salvage operation
followed by a 17-year conservation programme, the city's
most popular museum was opened in June 1990, less
than a nautical mile from the scene of the disaster.

Gun-port Lion
*More than 200 carved
ornaments and 500 sculp-
ted figures decorate* Vasa.

★ Lion Figurehead
*King Gustav II Adolf, who com-
missioned* Vasa, *was known as
the Lion of the North. So a
springing lion was the obvious
choice for the figurehead.
It is 4 m (13 ft) long and weighs
450 kg (990 lb).*

To the
restaurant

Museum
shop

Information
desk

Entrance

Emperor Titus
*Carvings of 20
Roman emp-
erors stand on
parade on* Vasa.

Bronze Cannon
More than 50 of Vasa's
*64 original cannons were
salvaged already in the
17th century. Three 11-kg
(24-lb) bronze cannons are
on display in the museum.*

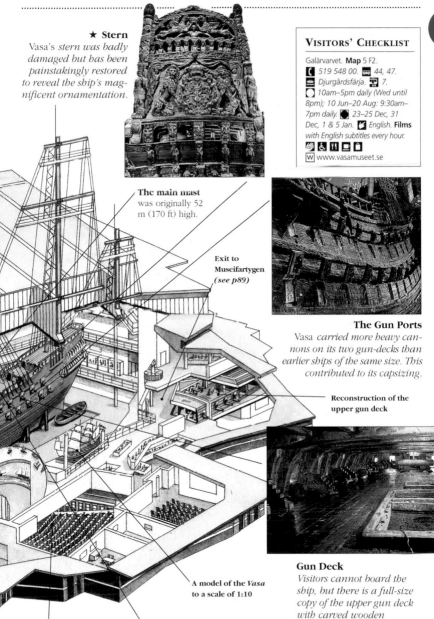

★ Stern
Vasa's *stern was badly damaged but has been painstakingly restored to reveal the ship's magnificent ornamentation.*

VISITORS' CHECKLIST

Galärvarvet. **Map** 5 F2.
519 548 00. 44, 47.
Djurgårdsfärja. 7.
10am–5pm daily (Wed until 8pm); 10 Jun–20 Aug: 9:30am–7pm daily. 23–25 Dec, 31 Dec, 1 & 5 Jan. English. **Films** with English subtitles every hour.
W www.vasamuseet.se

The main mast
was originally 52 m (170 ft) high.

Exit to Museifartygen
(see p89)

The Gun Ports
Vasa *carried more heavy cannons on its two gun-decks than earlier ships of the same size. This contributed to its capsizing.*

Reconstruction of the upper gun deck

A model of the *Vasa*
to a scale of 1:10

Gun Deck
Visitors cannot board the ship, but there is a full-size copy of the upper gun deck with carved wooden dummies of sailors, which gives a good idea of conditions on board.

Main film auditorium

Upper Deck
The entrance to the cabins was towards the stern. This area was the grandest part of the ship, reserved for senior officers. Part of the original mainmast can be seen on the right.

STAR FEATURES

★ **Stern**

★ **Lion Figurehead**

Exploring the Vasa Museum

THE ROYAL WARSHIP *Vasa* has been restored to 95 per cent of its original appearance. The low salt content of the water saved the ship's timber – which came from more than 1,000 oaks – from attacks by ship worms. The hull was all present, but fitting the 13,500 loose pieces together was like doing a jigsaw puzzle without a picture, as there were no detailed designs to follow. The salvage operation produced more than 700 sculpted figures and carved ornaments, as well as many everyday items.

A sailor's simple belongings found on *Vasa*

Carved soldiers on *Vasa*'s stern

THE SHIP

IN 1628 *Vasa* was potentially the world's mightiest ship, able to carry 64 cannons and 300 soldiers (out of a total 450 men on board). *Vasa* was equipped for both traditional close combat and for artillery battles. From its high stern it would have been possible to fire down on smaller ships. The musketeers had shooting galleries for training, and on the upper deck were so-called "storm pieces", erected as protection against musketry fire.

All this may appear very impressive, but it is uncertain exactly what the ship's role would have been if it had survived. The main task of the Swedish navy at that time had been to transport weapons and soldiers as well as to protect shipping or block harbours. It seems doubtful that *Vasa* would have been suitable for these roles.

THE IMAGERY OF POWER

THE WARSHIP'S many figures and carved ornaments formed an important part of that era's language of power and were designed as a type of war propaganda. Most of the sculptors who worked in the shipyard that built *Vasa* came from Germany and Holland, and their work was typical of the late Renaissance and early Baroque eras. The German woodcarver Mårten Redtmer made most of the larger sculptures. Created out of oak, pine and lime wood, the figures were inspired mainly by Greek mythology, as well as the Bible and 17th-century Swedish royal personalities.

Despite the multitude of finds, some mysteries remain. It is, for example, known that the figures were brightly painted but not exactly how.

LIFE ON BOARD

VASA'S DESTINATION on its maiden voyage, with about 150 people on board, was intended to be the Älvsnabben naval base in the southern Stockholm archipelago, where 300 soldiers were to embark. The ship was fully equipped, and the divers were able to recover many everyday items, including food and drink. But when the chief diver, Per Edvin Fälting, tasted the 333-year-old butter from a tub made of wood and tin, sores erupted around his mouth.

The museum has full-scale models of *Vasa*'s upper gun deck and the Admiral's cabin. The sailors and soldiers had to eat and sleep on deck among the cannons. No wonder that in the 17th-century more died from illness than in battle.

In a fascinating exhibition of original artifacts, you can see the medical equipment that was used, an officer's backgammon game, some of the sailors' wooden spoons and plates and the officers' dinner service in pewter and earthenware. The divers also found about 4,000 coins, made mainly from copper, and a chest still neatly packed with hats, clothing and other personal belongings.

Replicas of some of these artifacts are on sale in the museum shop.

THE SALVAGE OPERATION

The marine archaeologist Anders Franzén had been looking for *Vasa* for many years. On 25 August 1956 his patience was rewarded when he brought up a piece of blackened oak on his plumb line. From the autumn of 1957, it took divers two years to clear tunnels under the hull for the lifting cables. The first lift with six cables was a success, after which *Vasa* was lifted in 16 stages into shallower water. Thousands of plugs were then inserted into holes left by rusted iron bolts. The final lift started on 24 April 1961, and on 4 May *Vasa* was finally towed into dry dock.

***Vasa* in dry dock after being salvaged in 1961**

Aquaria ❽

Falkenbergsgatan 2. **Map** 6 A3.
📞 *660 49 40.* 🚌 *44, 47.* 🚢 *Djurgårdsfärja.* 🚆 *7.* 🕐 *10am–4:30pm Tue–Sun; 15 Jun–15 Aug: 10am–6pm daily.* 🎫 *by arrangement.* ♿ 🏪 🛒
🌐 *www.aquaria.se*

FOR MANY YEARS Göran Flodin ran an aquarium shop but always wanted to open his own water museum one day. His dreams were realized towards the end of the 1980s when he took over a waterfront site which had been used to restore the *Vasa* after its salvage. The resulting privately owned water museum was opened in June 1990 and now attracts 250,000 visitors a year.

Aquaria illustrates many habitats, from tropical rainforests to white-water salmon rivers. The South American rainforest is portrayed by thunderstorms and cloudbursts and you can see giant moths, cicadas, stingrays and piranhas. From the rainforest it

Free-swimming sharks in the Aquaria water museum

is only a short step to a scene depicting a northern mountain lake full of Arctic char, alongside a waterfall with trout. Most popular are the free-swimming sharks which you can watch at close quarters from a glass tunnel.

Some 100,000 litres (22,000 gallons) of water are pumped in every hour from nearby Nybroviken. The water runs back into the system via a small lake and a salmon ladder.

Liljevalchs Konsthall ❾

Djurgårdsvägen 60. **Map** 6 A3.
📞 *508 313 30.* 🚌 *44, 47.* 🚆 *7.*
🚢 *Djurgårdsfärja.* 🕐 *11am–8pm Tue & Thu, 11am–5pm Wed & Fri–Sun.* 🎫 *by appt.* ♿ ⓘ 🏪 🛒

ORIGINALLY constructed thanks to a donation from the industrialist Carl Fredrik Liljevalch, this heritage building is regarded as one of northern Europe's most attractive art galleries. It was designed by the architect Carl G Bergsten and built in 1913–16 in a Neo-Classical style which was typical of its era, particularly in Stockholm.

Liljevalch's portrait bust, sculpted in granite by Christian Eriksson, is set in the northern wall of this heritage building. On a high column outside the entrance is Carl Milles' sculpture *The Archer.*

The city of Stockholm owns and administers the gallery, which features Liljevalch's collections of Swedish, Nordic and international art over the 20th century, as well as handicrafts dating from the same period.

Every year four or five major exhibitions are staged, including the Spring Salon which is always a major attraction for Stockholm art-lovers. The exhibitions are complemented by daily guided tours, lectures, debates and concerts.

Children and young people have a special section where they can create their own works of art from various different types of materials.

Gröna Lund funfair seen from Kastellholmen

Gröna Lund ❿

Lilla Allmänna gränd 9. **Map** 6 A4.
📞 *587 502 00.* 🚌 *44, 47.* 🚆 *7.*
🚢 *Djurgårdsfärja.* 🕐 *1 May–11 Sep opening hours vary.* ♿ Ⓖ 🏪 🛒
🌐 *www.gronalund.se*

A TAVERN CALLED Gröna Lund (Green Grove) existed on this site in the 18th century, and it was one of the haunts of the renowned troubadour Carl Michael Bellman *(see p98).* Jakob Schultheis used the tavern's name for the modest-sized funfair which he opened here in 1883 with a two-level horse-drawn round-about as the main attraction. Today Gröna Lund is Sweden's oldest amusement park.

The 130-day season, starting on 1 May, is short but hectic. However, Gröna Lund draws about 10,000 visitors per day to its exciting attractions that include a thrilling roller-coaster, ferris wheel and haunted house. The latest addition is the free-fall "Power Tower", an 80-m (262-ft) high tower from which visitors drop at a frightening speed.

The park also has 13 restaurants and cafés, three stages, a cabaret restaurant with space for 600 guests, and a theatre with 200 seats. The main stage has hosted world stars such as Bob Marley who, in 1980, played to a record audience of 32,000.

Gröna Lund's beautiful gardens include 30,000 pansies and 25,000 summer flowers.

Liljevalchs Konsthall's spacious main exhibition hall

Skansen 12

THE WORLD'S FIRST OPEN-AIR museum, Skansen opened in 1891 to show an increasingly industrialized society how people once lived. About 150 houses and farm buildings were assembled from all over Sweden, portraying the life of both peasants and landed gentry, as well as Lapp (*Same*) culture. The Town Quarter has wooden urban dwellings and crafts like glass-blowing and printing. Nordic flora and fauna feature everywhere, with bears, wolves and elks in natural habitat enclosures and more exotic creatures in the Aquarium. Many festivals are celebrated in Skansen (*see pp26–9*).

★ Älvros Farmhouse
The living room in this 500-year-old wooden cottage from Härjedalen shows the tools for daily tasks.

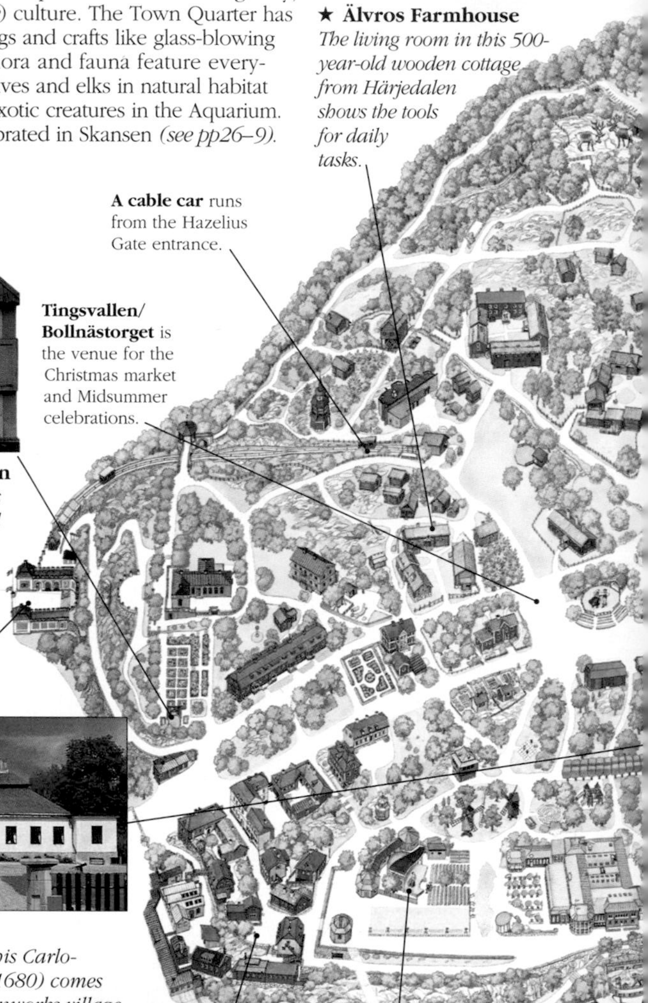

A cable car runs from the Hazelius Gate entrance.

Tingsvallen/ Bollnästorget is the venue for the Christmas market and Midsummer celebrations.

Swedenborg's Pavilion
Set in the rose garden is the pavilion which used to belong to the philosopher and scientist Emanuel Swedenborg (1688–1772).

Hazelius Gate

Skogaholm Manor
The main building in this Carlovingian manor estate (1680) comes from the Skogaholm ironworks village in central Sweden.

★ Town Quarter
Original Stockholm wooden town houses replicate a medium-size 19th-century town. Glass-blowers, shoemakers and other craftsmen demonstrate their traditional skills in restored workshops.

Solliden stage

Main entrance

Skansen Aquarium

Vastveit Loft
This storehouse from eastern Norway was built in the 14th century and is Skansen's oldest building.

VISITOR'S CHECKLIST

Djurgårdsslätten 49. **Map** 6 B3.
442 80 00. 44, 47. 7.
Djurgårdsfärja. daily:
Jan–Apr: 10am–4pm; May:
10am–8pm; Jun–Aug: 10am–
10pm; Sep–Dec: 10am–4pm.
Jun–Aug. 24 Dec.
Seglora Church
11am Sun W www.skansen.se

★ Bear Pit
Skansen's brown bears are firm favourites, not least in April, when the new cubs emerge.

Wolves

Bredablick is a 30-m (98-ft) high viewing tower.

Seglora Church
This shingle-roofed wooden church was built in 1729–30 in western Sweden and has an interesting interior decor with a pulpit which is even older than the church itself. It is popular for weddings.

Skåne farmyard

0 metres 100
0 yards 100

Hornborga Cottage
A timber cottage with a straw and peat roof from western Sweden shows how poorer people lived in the 19th century.

STAR FEATURES

★ **Älvros Farmhouse**

★ **Town Quarter**

★ **Bear Pit**

Djurgårdsstaden & Beckholmen ⓫

Map 6 A4. 🚌 44, 47. 🚃 7.
🚢 Djurgårdsfärja.

BEHIND GRÖNA LUND amusement park lies Djurgårdsstaden, a tranquil oasis of wooden houses, providing flats for about 200 people. The area was originally developed from a town plan drawn up around the Admiralty churchyard in 1736, to house workmen at the nearby Johan Lampas shipyards.

When the Djurgården shipyard took over in 1768 the carpenters were given the opportunity to buy their homes. The company then erected the majestic two-storey stone building at Lilla Allmänna Gränd 15–17 with offices, employees' homes and a chapel. Other buildings on this street also date from the 18th century such as Apotekshuset, the shipyard manager's residence, and Mjölnargården, now belonging to the amusement park. Several two-storey wooden houses were built on the churchyard, which had fallen into disuse, in the 19th century.

At the junction of Östra Varvsgränd and Breda Gatan is the house of the ship's carpenter Sven Månsson. Enlarged in 1749, the building still looks much as it did then, with original tiled stoves and wood fires. It is now used by the Djurgården Local Culture Society and has undergone extensive renovation.

Lying just to the south of Djurgårdsstaden is the island

of Beckholmen which, during the 17th century, was used as a warehouse for commercial goods. It was also used to store tar and pitch. The fire hazard meant that such dangerous items could not be stored any closer to the city centre.

In 1848 the Wholesalers' Society decided to build a shipping repair yard on the island and two docks were blasted out of the solid rock on the southern side. They were later widened to accommodate more wharves. In 1917 another large dock was opened, named after King Gustaf V and they were used by the Navy and the Finnboda shipbuilding firm. The fleet moved to the island of Muskö in 1969 and Finnboda remained until 1982. The docks and houses form an unusual industrial setting. The 18th-century tar inspector's residence, the dockmaster's 19th-century home, and workmen's cottages from the 1890s are well preserved.

Door lintel, Rosendals Slott's Gold Room

Skansen ⓬

See pp96–7.

The Karl Johan-style Rosendals Slott on Djurgården

Rosendals Slott & Trädgårdar ⓭

Rosendalsvägen. **Map** 6 C3. 🚌 47, then 5 min walk. **Palace** [402 61 30. ◯ for guided tours May–Aug: Tue–Sun, Sep: Sat & Sun. 🎫 every hour 11am–3pm. 🖼 ⓰ **Gardens** ◯ all year. 🍴 ⛺ summer.

WHAT WAS CONSIDERED elsewhere as Empire style was named Karl Johan style in Sweden after King Karl XIV Johan (1818–44). One of the best examples is Rosendal Palace, built as a summer retreat for the king. Constructed in the 1820s and designed by Fredrik Blom, a prolific architect of the era, the palace was one of Sweden's first prefabricated homes. In 1913, it was opened to the public as a museum devoted to the life and times of Karl XIV Johan and represents a pioneering work of historic restoration.

The decor is magnificent, with Swedish-made furniture and lavish textiles in wonderful colours. The carpeting and curtains are worth a visit in themselves. The dining room

Well-preserved wooden homes in Djurgårdsstaden

AN IMMORTAL TROUBADOUR

Carl Michael Bellman (1740–95) was a much-loved troubadour. Gustav III gave him a job as secretary of a lottery, but he was best known around Stockholm's many taverns – particularly on Djurgården. His works about the drunken watchmaker Jean Fredman and his contemporaries (*Fredman's Epistles* and *Fredman's Songs*) have never lost their popularity and form part of Sweden's musical heritage. A bust of Bellman was unveiled on Djurgården in 1829 in the presence of Queen Desideria.

Bust of Bellman by J N Byström (1829)

is fitted out in heavily woven fabric to create the impression of being in a tent. Tiled stoves are everywhere, along with some grandiose artifacts and delightful details. In front of the palace is a large bowl made in porphyry from Karl XIV's own workshops at Älvdalen in central Sweden.

Close to the palace is Rosendals Trädgårdar, a biodynamic market garden managed by a foundation since 1984. Its aim is not just to use biodynamic cultivation methods but also to run courses, lectures and exhibitions. Plants are available to buy at the shop and there is a café.

Waldemarsudde ⑭

Prins Eugens Väg 6. **Map** 6 C4.
☎ 545 837 00. 🚌 47. 🚋 7.
⏱ 11am–4pm Tue, Wed & Fri,
11am–8pm Thu, 11am–5pm Sat &
Sun; May–Aug: 11am–5pm Tue–Sun,
11am–8pm Thu. 🎫 📷 ♿ 🚻 🛍
🏠 ⓦ www.waldemarsudde.se

PRINCE EUGEN'S Waldemarsudde, which passed into State ownership after his death in 1947, is one of Sweden's most visited art museums. The prince was trained as a military officer but became a successful artist and was one of the leading landscape painters of his generation. He produced monumental paintings for Kungliga Operan, Kungliga Dramatiska Teatern and Rådhuset. Among his own works hanging in Waldemarsudde, his former home, are three of his most prized paintings: *Spring* (1891), *The Old Castle* (1893) and *The Cloud* (1896).

Based on works by his contemporaries, the collection represents early 20th-century Swedish art with names like Oscar Björck, Carl Fredrik Hill, Richard Bergh, Nils Kreuger, Eugène Jansson, Bruno Liljefors and Anders Zorn. Prince Eugen was a generous patron to the next generation – for example, the group known as "The Young Ones" – so works by younger artists like Isaac Grünewald, Einar Jolin, Sigrid Hjertén and Leander Engström are also in the collection. Sculptors of the same era are well represented, particularly works by Per Hasselberg which can be seen in the gallery and the park.

Along with the architect Ferdinand Boberg, Prince Eugen drew up the sketches for the house, completed in 1905. The same architect was called in later to plan the gallery, which was finished in 1913. This now includes parts of the collection of some 2,000 works, as well as the Prince's own paintings.

The guest apartments remain largely unchanged, and the two upper floors with the Prince's studio at the top are used for temporary exhibitions.

Hornsgatan (1902) by Eugène Jansson, in Thielska Galleriet

Thielska Galleriet ⑮

Sjötullsbacken 6–8. **Map** 7 F4.
☎ 662 58 84. 🚌 69. ⏱ noon–4pm Mon–Sat, 1–4pm Sun.
🎫 by appt. 📷 🛍
ⓦ www.thielska-galleriet.a.se

WHEN THE magnificent apartments of the banker Ernest Thiel (1860–1947) on Strandvägen started to overflow with his excellent collection of contemporary paintings, he commissioned the well-known architect Ferdinand Boberg to design a dignified villa on Djurgården.

However, during World War I Thiel lost most of his fortune. In 1924, the State bought his collection, mostly covering Nordic art from the late 19th and early 20th centuries, and opened Thielska Galleriet in his villa two years later.

Thiel was regarded as something of a rebel in the banking world and he was particularly fond of works by painters in the Artists' Union, which had been formed in 1886 to counter the influence of the traditionalist Konstakademien *(see p66)*.

There are paintings by all the major Swedish artists who formed an artists' colony at Grèz-sur-Loing, south of Paris, such as Carl Larsson, Bruno Liljefors, Karl Nordström and August Strindberg. And there are paintings by Eugène Jansson, Anders Zorn and Prince Eugen, as well as wooden figures by Axel Petersson and sculptures by Christian Eriksson. Thiel also acquired works by foreign artists, not least his good friend Edvard Munch.

Prince Eugen's Waldemarsudde, seen from the water

MALMARNA & FURTHER AFIELD

Window on Vikingagatan

As STOCKHOLM started to grow, the heart of the city, Gamla Stan, became cramped and building spread out to the surrounding areas, known as "Malmarna" (the "ore hills"). Parts of these now make up present-day Stockholm.

Södermalm came into the ownership of the city in 1436. Much of Stockholm's old charm can still be found in the areas around Fjällgatan, Mosebacke and Mariaberget. To the north, the Norrmalm area expanded rapidly and became known as Stockholm's northern suburb in the 17th century. Much of Vasastan is a residential area, but in recent years it has become popular because of its wide choice of restaurants. The once-rural Östermalm was transformed in the late 19th century into an affluent residential area with grand, wide boulevards, contrasting with the 1930s Functionalist style of the adjoining Gärdet district. This is the location of some of Stockholm's most important museums, including Historiska Museet with its impressive Gold Room, and Folkens Museum Etnografiska.

To the west is Kungsholmen, the centre for local government, with distinguished buildings like Stadshuset (the City Hall) and Rådhuset (the Law Court). Ekoparken (the National City Park), the first of its kind in the world, is a green area of ecological and cultural interest surrounding the city and reaching into its central districts.

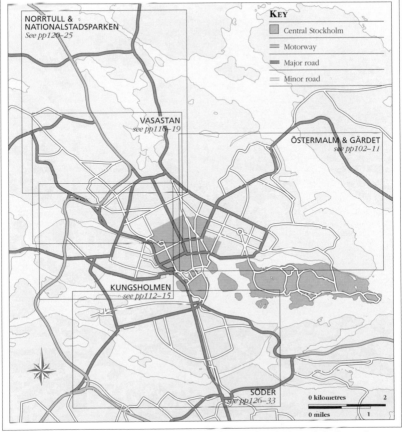

KEY

Central Stockholm

Motorway

Major road

Minor road

NORRTULL & NATIONALSTADSPARKEN
See pp120–25

VASASTAN
see pp116–19

ÖSTERMALM & GÄRDET
see pp102–11

KUNGSHOLMEN
see pp112–15

SÖDER
see pp126–33

0 kilometres 2

0 miles 1

◁ **Stadshuset with Norr Mälarstrand on Kungsholmen and the Västerbron bridge in the background**

Östermalm & Gärdet

T HE FOUR WIDE BOULEVARDS, Strandvägen, Karlavägen, Narvavägen and Valhallavägen, were created around 1870–80 as part of the development of Östermalm into one of the city's most affluent residential districts, adjoining the extensive green area of Ladugårdsgärde. Apart from embassies and the headquarters of Swedish Radio and TV, four leading museums are located in this green oasis, as well as Kaknästornet. The area between Östermalm and the former military exercise grounds was developed in the 1930s with housing in the clean lines of the Functionalist style typical of the period.

Housing at Karlaplan, built in the late 19th century

SIGHTS AT A GLANCE

Berwaldhallen ❺
Diplomatstaden ❻
Engelbrektskyrkan ⓲
Filmhuset ⓭
Folkens Museum Etnografiska ❿
Försvarshögskolan ⓯

Historiska Museet (see pp104–105) ❷
Kaknästornet ⓫
Karlavägen ❸
Ladugårdsgärde ⓬
Sjöhistoriska Museet ❼
Stadion ⓰

Strandvägen ❶
Sveriges Radio och TV ❹
Tekniska Högskolan ⓱
Tekniska Museet ❾
Telemuseum ❽
Tessinparken ⓮

KEY

Central Stockholm

Major street

Other street

Ⓣ Tunnelbana station

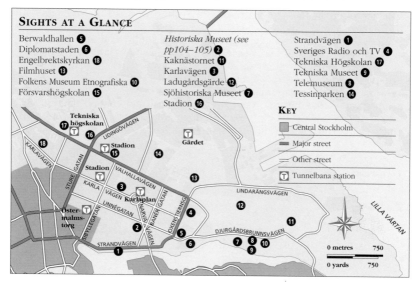

0 metres   750
0 yards   750

Strandvägen ❶

Map 5 E1. 🚌 47, 69, 76.
Ⓣ Östermalmstorg, Karlaplan. 🚊 7.

I N THE EARLY 1900s Stockholm's 10 richest citizens lived in palatial new houses along Strandvägen. Seven of them were wholesale merchants. Up to 1897's major exhibition on Djurgården, the hilly and muddy former Ladugårdslands Strandgata had

been moving towards the goal of becoming "a street, the like of which will not be found anywhere else in Europe". It was a long process. Even after all the stately buildings had been completed the wooden quay erected in the 1860s was something of an eyesore. It was still used up to the 1940s by boats bringing fire wood from the archipelago islands.

All the same, Strandvägen and its three rows of lime

trees soon became the elegant boulevard envisaged and, then as now, it was a popular place for admiring the elegant façades, watching the boats and to see and be seen.

The financiers behind the housing projects of the early 1900s were wealthy and could call on the best architects, including I G Clason (1856–1930). Clason was influenced by Italian and French Renaissance styles for his work on No. 19–21 (Thaveniuska Huset) and No. 29–35 (Bünsowska Huset), where he designed gateways made of ship's timbers. No. 55 (Von Rosenska Palatset) was also created by him.

Historiska Museet ❷

See pp104–105.

Strandvägen with stately houses and boats along the quayside

Karlavägen ❸

Map 3 E3. 🚇 *Karlaplan, Stadion.*
🚌 *1, 42, 44.*

UNTIL 1885 Karlavägen was known as Esplanaden, a 42-m (138-ft) wide avenue planted with lime trees and flower beds. Towards the end of the 19th century several impressive houses were built there, many in Neo-Renaissance style. The street has retained its character as a grand boulevard despite a lot of new building and the arrival of shops and offices.

A major development was undertaken in the 1960s when the central section of the road was gradually converted into an open-air sculpture gallery. At the crossroads with Engelbrektsgatan is *The City* by Lars Erik Husberg; at Villagatan a female figure by the French sculptor Paul Cornet; at Floragatan *Gunnar Nils-son's Mimi*, which can also be seen at other places in the city; at Sturegatan *Living Iron* by Willy Gordon, a gift from the LKAB mining company, whose head office at No. 45 acquired a façade relief by Eric Grate in 1970. Also situated at this crossroads is *Scatola* by the Italian sculptor Arnoldo Pomodoro.

At Nybroplan is *Man –Horse– Carriage* by Asmund Arle; at Sibyllegatan *Woman with Hand Mirror* by Ebba Ahlmark-Hughes; in front of Östra Real a bust of the author August Blanche (1811–68) by Aron Sandberg; the secondary school building designed by Ragnar Östberg with sculptures by Carl Eldh; at Grevgatan *Incoming Sea* by Håkan Bonds; at Karlaplan a marble sculpture by Gert Marcus; at Tysta Gatan *Jeanette* by Curt Thorsjö; and at Banérgatan Urn by Hedy Jolly-Dahlström. Finally at No 100 is the long Garrison administration building with a sculpture group at the entrance, a work in glazed stoneware by Gustav Kraitz.

The fountain and round pond at Karlaplan were added in 1929. *The Aviator* is by Carl Milles and was unveiled two years later.

Fountain on Karlaplan at the end of the tree-lined Karlavägen

Swedish Television's main building at Gärdet, next to Swedish Radio's headquarters

Radio- och TV-husen ❹

Oxenstiernsgatan 20 & 34. **Map** 6 A1.
🚇 *Karlaplan.* 🚌 *4, 56, 76.*
SR 📞 *784 50 00.* 📅 *by appt.* ♿
🌐 *www.sr.se* **SVT** 📞 *784 00 00.*
📅 *by appt.* ♿ 🌐 *www.svt.se*

THE HEADQUARTERS OF Swedish Radio (SR) and Swedish Television (SVT) take up a 12 ha (29.6 acres) site alongside Ladugårdsgärde. The area's long history as a military training depot is reflected by several old buildings once used for stores. Now it is the site not just of the modern radio and TV buildings designed by the architects Erik Ahnborg and Sune Lindström but also of three old buildings with military connections: the gunpowder cellar from 1717, the old stone coach-house from 1750, and the Karl Johan storehouses from 1820. Both architects also designed Berwaldhallen *(see p106)*, the concert hall which is linked to SR and SVT by a tunnel.

Swedish Radio started its transmissions from Malmskillnadsgatan on 1 January 1925. It moved to No. 8 Kungsgatan in 1928 and into its new premises in 1961.

SVT started transmissions from the Svea Artillery Regiment's old premises on 24 October 1954. In 1969 it moved into the new TV building in the former barracks area, where an office block was added four years later. Additions in 1983–7 included a building for news broadcasts. SVT now covers an area of 51,600 sq m (555,220 sq ft) with eight studios, three of which are used for news programmes.

BOATS ALONG STRANDVÄGEN

Until the 1940s sailing vessels used to carry firewood from Roslagen on the Baltic coast to the quayside at Strandvägen. This trade had lost its importance by the 1950s, and boating enthusiasts started buying up these old vessels. Some were

Old wood-carrying boats along the Strandvägen quay

renovated and sailed to the Caribbean, others became illegal drinking or gambling clubs on Strandvägen. New harbour regulations led to the formation of two associations to administer the boats. About 40 have survived and are owned by people who want to preserve a piece of cultural heritage. By every boat there is a sign describing its history.

Historiska Museet ②

Upper floor

Exhibitions showing the mass migrations and the Wendic era.

Sᴡᴇᴅᴇɴ'ꜱ ʜɪꜱᴛᴏʀɪꜱᴋᴀ ᴍᴜꜱᴇᴇᴛ (Museum of National Antiquities) was opened in 1943. It was designed by Bengt Romare and Georg Sherman. Bror Marklund (1907–77) was responsible for the decoration around the entrance and the richly detailed bronze gateways depicting events in early Swedish history. The museum originally made its name with its exhibits from the Viking era, as well as its outstanding collections from the early Middle Ages. Contemporary church textiles are also on show. Many of Historiska Museet's gold treasures have been gathered together to form one of Stockholm's most remarkable sights, Guldrummet (the Gold Room).

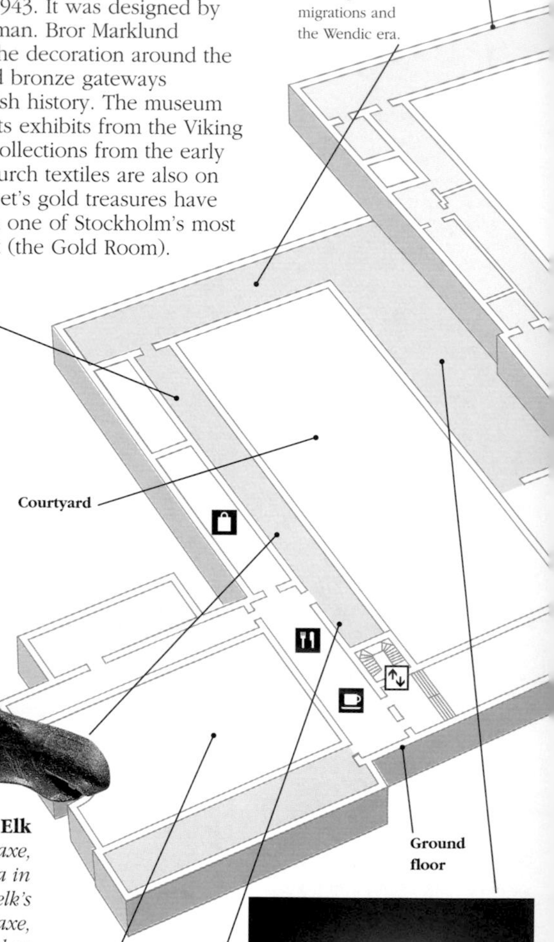

Bronze Age Find
This Bronze Age artifact, thought to be a percussion instrument, was discovered in a bog in southern Sweden in 1847.

Courtyard

★ The Alunda Elk
This 21-cm (8-inch) stone axe, discovered in 1920 at Alunda in central Sweden, resembles an elk's head. It is a ceremonial axe, probably made in Finland or Karelia in around 2000 BC.

Rosen-gården

Ground floor

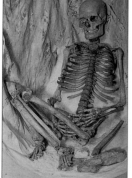

The Bäckaskog Woman
The 155-cm (5-ft) long Bäckaskog woman lived around 5000 BC. She died at the age of 40–50 and was buried sitting in a cramped pit.

The Viking Era
This eventful era is reflected in a new department, whose exhibits include a Viking sword with artistic embellishments, and ornaments in the shape of Nordic animals.

STAR SIGHTS

★ **The Gold Room**

★ **Maria from Viklau**

★ **The Alunda Elk**

The Skog Tapestry
This once hung in the wooden church at Skog in northern Sweden. It is one of the museum's oldest textile treasures.

Baroque Hall

GALLERY GUIDE
The exhibitions are divided chronologically on two floors with the prehistoric section on the ground floor and the Middle Ages on the upper floor, where there is also a Baroque Hall. In the basement, reached by a staircase from the entrance hall, is the Gold Room with priceless exhibits from prehistoric times to the medieval period.

Stairs descending to the Gold Room

Main entrance

★ Maria from Viklau
This Madonna figure without child is the best-preserved example from Sweden's early medieval period. The colourful wooden sculpture is richly gilded.

KEY

☐	Prehistoric Era
☐	Middle Ages and Baroque
☐	Temporary exhibitions
☐	Non-exhibition space

★ THE GOLD ROOM
Since the early 1990s the museum's many priceless gold artifacts have been on show in Guldrummet (the Gold Room), a 700-sq m (7,500-sq ft) underground vault built with 250 tons of reinforced concrete to ensure security. The room is in two circular sections. The inner section houses the main collection, with 50 kg (110 lb) of gold treasures and 250 kg (550 lb) of silver from the Bronze Age to the Middle Ages.

The Elisabeth Reliquary was originally a drinking goblet which was mounted with gold and precious stones in the 11th century. In about 1230 a silver cover was added to enclose the skull of St Elisabeth. In 1631 it was seized as a trophy for Sweden during the Thirty Years War.

The Gold Collars were found between 1827 and 1864; the three-ringed collar in a stone quarry in eastern Sweden, the five-ringed in a ditch on the island of Öland, and the seven-ringed hanging on a spike in a barn.

The underground Gold Room in Historiska Museet

Berwaldhallen, concert hall of the Swedish Radio Symphony Orchestra

Berwaldhallen ❺

Dag Hammarskiölds väg 3. **Map** 6 A2
📞 784 18 00. 🚇 *Karlaplan.* 🚌 *56, 69, 76.* ⭕ *during concerts, call for info on tickets and times.* ⭕ 🖵
🆆 www.sr.se/berwaldhallen

O N 30 NOVEMBER 1979 the
Swedish Radio Symphony
Orchestra and the Radio
Chorus acquired their own
concert hall, Berwaldhallen.
The hall has become a
national showcase for Swedish music. It is named after
Franz Berwald (1796–1868),
one of Sweden's greatest
composers. The architects Erik
Ahnborg and Sune Lindström
won an award for "a
wonderful and sensitively
designed concert hall". Hans
Viksten, Hertha Hillfon and
other artists undertook the
decoration of the foyer.
Nature has made its own
contribution in the form of
untouched areas of rock
which were blasted out to
accommodate two-thirds of
the six-sided building.
The Swedish Radio Sym-
phony Orchestra and Radio
Chorus give 60–70 perform-
ces every season in the hall,
which has become an
internationally renowned
concert stage, attracting
audiences of 120,000 a year.
Visiting ensembles also
perform here and the hall is
often used for other events,
including the annual Polar
Music Prize ceremony in the
presence of the King and
Queen, as well as corporate
functions and conferences.

Diplomatstaden ❻

Map 6 A2. 🚇 *Karlaplan.* 🚌 *56, 69, 76.*

T HE ELEGANT VILLAS which
gave the area of
Diplomatstaden its name
stretch along Nobelgatan and
the eastern part of Strandvägen (from No. 74). The first
house for a foreign diplomat
was built in the 1910s, when
the British ambassador moved
into Nobelgatan 7. Nearby is
Engelska Kyrkan (the English
Church), which was built in
the city centre in the 1860s
but was moved to the
diplomatic quarter in 1913.
In the 1980s the church was
finally completed with the
addition of an octagonal
parish hall. Villa Bonnier at
No. 13 was designed by
Ragnar Östberg and was a gift
to the State by a prominent
publishing family. It is now
used by the Government for
official functions.
The embassies of Hungary,
Turkey, South Korea, Norway,
Germany, the UK and USA are
all located in or near the area.
Nobelparken, the park
adjoining the embassies, is
named after the scientist
Alfred Nobel (1833–96). In the
early 20th century plans for a
Nobel Palace in the park were
drawn up by the architect
Ferdinand Boberg, but the
project never came to fruition.
On the north side of
Strandvägen is the Törner
Villa, a heritage wooden
house built in 1880. The villa
is named after a firemaster at
Nobel's gunpowder factory.

Sjöhistoriska Museet ❼

Djurgårdsbrunnsvägen 24. **Map** 6 C2.
📞 519 549 00. 🚌 69. ⭕ 10am–
5pm daily, spring and autumn; also
10am–11.30pm Tue. 🎫 🎪 ♿ 🖵
📷 🆆 www.sshm.se/sjohistoriska

T HE NATIONAL MARITIME
Museum's architectural
design and location on
Djurgårdsbrunnsviken are
worthy of a country with a
long coastline and numerous
archipelagos and lakes.
Sjöhistoriska Museet focuses
on shipping, shipbuilding and
naval defence, and there are
fascinating exhibits, both
permanent and temporary,
on these themes.
There are some 100,000
exhibits, including more than
1,500 model ships. The oldest
ship was built in the 17th
century and the oldest
Swedish vessel is a
reproduction of the so-called
"Cathedral ship" from the
early 1600s. The collections
include every conceivable
type of ship – from small
coasters and Viking longboats
to oil tankers, coal vessels,

Majestic buildings in the diplomatic quarter at Djurgårdsbrunnsviken

dinghies, full-riggers and submarines. A series of models on a scale of 1:200 show the development of ships in Scandinavia from the Iron Age to the present day.

There are also full-scale settings which give a good idea of life on board the ships. Among them are the beautiful original cabin and elegant stern from the royal schooner *Amphion*. The ship was built at the Djurgården shipyard and designed by the leading shipbuilder F H Chapman. It was Gustav III's flagship in the 1788–90 war with Russia. Contrasting with this is the cramped and damp-preserved forecastle from the schooner *Hoppet*, where four crew members ate, slept and spent their time off watch.

The galley *Lodbrok*, one of many maritime models at Sjöhistoriska Museet

The museum has some notable examples of ship decoration from the late 17th century. They include part of the national coat of arms recovered by divers in the 1920s from the stern of the *Riksäpplet*, which sank at Dalarö in 1676. When *Carolus XI*, an 82-cannon ship, was launched from the shipyard in Stockholm in 1678 the stern had a large relief portrayal of Karl XI on horseback. The relief was possibly removed some years later when the ship was renamed *Sverige*, but it was saved and is now in the museum. There are many fine figureheads in the collection, including one depicting Amphion, the son of Zeus, playing his lyre, which once adorned the schooner of the same name.

Linked to the museum is the Swedish Marine Archaeology Archive, which contains a mass of information, including a complete listing of shipwrecks with 10,000 entries from 1720

Figurehead, about 1850

to the end of the 1920s. The ship-design archive has documents covering most eras of maritime history and is used extensively by researchers. The photographic collection has 300,000 pictures, while the library covers all aspects of seafaring and war at sea. There is a special children's section with a work-shop which is open on Sundays and during school holidays. During the summer a dinghy-sailing school is arranged for children aged 8–14.

The attractive museum building was one of the architect Ragnar Östberg's last works and was opened in 1938. On the gable facing Djurgårdsbrunns-viken is *The Sailor*, a monument to the victims of naval war by Nils Sjögren.

Telemuseum ❽

Museivägen 7. **Map** 6 C2.
☎ 670 81 00. 🚌 69. ⏰ 10am–4pm Mon–Fri, 11am–4pm Sat & Sun.
♿ by appointment. 🎫 ♿ 📷 🚻
ⓦ www.telemuseum.se

FEW SPECIALIST museums can cover such a wide range of interests as Telemuseum (the Telecommunications Museum). The collections go back to the 1850s and cover telegraphy, telephony, radio

and television from the early pioneering days to today. The many milestones in telecommunications depicted include the first electric telegraph line in Sweden opened in 1853 between Stockholm and Uppsala. Other exhibits cover the first test radio transmissions in 1922, and the start of regular broadcasting by Swedish Radio on 1 January 1925. The first trial television broadcasts in 1947 from the Royal Institute of Technology using a camera named Matilda are featured, too. Regular TV transmissions started in 1954.

The museum was opened in 1937 and moved to new premises alongside Tekniska Museet in 1975. It also includes a manned amateur radio station and a news-editing studio for school groups. A room commemorating L M Ericsson (1826–1926), founder of the Swedish telecommunications industry, is among the many other attractions at Telemuseum.

Ericsson telephone made in 1903 for Czar Nicholas II

Tekniska Museet 🄆

Museivägen 7. **Map** 6 C2.
📞 *450 56 00.* 🚌 *69.* 🕐 *10am–4pm Mon–Fri, 11am–4pm Sat & Sun.*
🅿 *by appointment.* 🖼 ♿ 🅿 🍴
📧 🇼 *www.tekmu.se*

A NYONE PLANNING to visit the Museum of Science and Technology should allow plenty of time. Throughout the 20th century it accumulated a wealth of exhibits connected with Sweden's technical and industrial history. It has 12,000 sq m (129,000 sq ft) of well-stocked exhibition space plus a library with 50,000 volumes and a large collection of technical magazines. The archive contains 250,000 maps and designs. It is also the home of Sweden's first Science Centre, Teknorama, with many "hands on" experiments aimed particularly at children and young people, who will also be tempted by the museum shop's selection.

The machinery hall is the largest exhibition area with many powered machines from different eras. Among them is the country's oldest preserved steam engine, built in 1832 and once used in a coal mine in southern Sweden. The locomotive "Lotta" is another favourite. The classic T-Ford is there, too, as well as early Swedish cars from Volvo, Scania and Saab. Swinging above the selection of bicycles and motor bikes is Sweden's first commercial aircraft, built in 1924. There is another rarity – the scientist Emanuel Swedenborg's model of a "flying machine" (1716).

The museum also has sections on electric power and the history of the computer, as well as exhibitions on chemistry, technology in the home, book-printing, building techniques and the Swedish forestry industry. The mining and processing of iron and steel is also highlighted.

Folkens Museum Etnografiska 🄉

Djurgårdsbrunnsvägen 34. **Map** 6 C2.
📞 *519 550 00.* 🚌 *69.* 🕐 *11am–4pm Tue, Thu & Fri, 11am–8pm Wed, noon–5pm Sat & Sun.* 🅿 🖼 ♿ 🍴
📧 🅿 🇼 *www.etnografiska.se*

T HE NATIONAL MUSEUM of Ethnography is a showcase for the collections brought home to Sweden by travellers and scientists from the 18th century to the present day. The imaginative displays are intended to offer visitors a better understanding of the unknown or unfamiliar from around the world. Another aspect of the museum's work is to reflect the multicultural influences on Sweden brought about by the large-scale immigration into the country in the late 20th century.

The explorer Sven Hedin (1865–1952), the last Swede to be ennobled (in 1902), contributed many exhibits, including Buddha figures and Chinese costumes, as well as Mongolian temple tents donated by leaders of the Kalmuck people in western China to King Gustav V. Another section of interest shows masks and totem poles from western Canada.

A Japanese tea house was opened in 1990. It is a work of art in itself where visitors can take part in tea ceremonies during the summer.

The museum runs an extensive educational programme. It has published an international magazine, *Ethnos*, every year since 1936 and maintains a comprehensive reference library.

The "Babajan" restaurant offers a taste of foods from all over the world, and it has an impressive list of beers from far and near.

Religious mask from British Columbia

Kaknästornet 🄊

Ladugårdsgärdet. **Map** 7 D1.
📞 *789 24 35.* 🚌 *69.* 🕐 *May–Aug: 9am–10pm daily, Sep–Apr: 10am–9pm daily.* 🅿 *by appointment.* 🎥
🖼 ♿ 🍴 📧 🅿

A NCHORED BY 72 steel poles, driven 8 m (26 ft) into the rock, the 34-storey Kaknästornet soars to a height of 155 m (508 ft). The tower, designed by the architects Bengt Lindroos and Hans Borgström, was opened in 1967. It was erected as a centre for the country's television and radio broadcasting and also contains technical equipment to conduct conferences by

Tekniska Museet's machinery hall with exhibits from different eras

Kaknästornet with the buildings of Sjöhistoriska Museet, Tekniska Museet and Folkens Museum Etnografiska in the foreground

Filmhuset ⑬

Borgvägen 1–5. **Map** 6 B1.
【 665 11 00. 〔T〕 Karlaplan. ▦ 56, 72, 76. ◯ 8am–6pm Mon–Thu, 8am–4pm Fri, Sat & Sun. **Film club, library & archives** ring for details.
【&】【H】【▯】【W】 www.sfi.se

THE PRODUCTION OF quality Swedish films is supported by the Swedish Film Institute. The institute also acts as guardian of the country's cinematic heritage and promotes Swedish films both at home and abroad. From 1971, all its activities were brought under one roof in Filmhuset, a Modernist structure by P Celsing.

The institute's archives include more than 18,000 films. Also there is a comprehensive library and a film database, accessible on the Internet. The institute publishes the *Film Annual*, and organizes the Film Gala at which the Gold Beetle prizes are presented. The film club shows Swedish and international films daily in their original languages.

Filmhuset, home of the Film Institute and Dramatic Institute

satellite between European cities. Five dishes to the left of the tower – the largest of which has a diameter of 13 m (43 ft) – relay signals to and from satellites. The main hall containing the transmitters and receivers has been blasted out of the rock below the dishes.

The observation points on levels 30 and 31 provide a spectacular view of the city, and the restaurant on the 28th floor has panoramic windows. It is reached by two lifts, travelling at 18 km/h (11 mph). Stockholm Information Service runs a busy tourist information office at the entrance level, selling souvenirs, maps and the Stockholm Card *(see p183)*. Decorative features include a wall relief by Walter Bengtsson, a work inspired by the tower's daunting technology.

Ladugårdsgärde ⑫

Map 6 C1. ▦ 1, 69, 76.

AS EARLY AS THE 15th century there was a royal farm on the site where the Nobel Park now stands. After 250 years it had outlived its usefulness and for a few centuries it was used as a training area for the Stockholm garrison. Between Kungliga Borgen (Royal Fortress) and Hakberget are the remains of Karl XI's fort from 1672, which was largely rebuilt in time for the World Equestrian Championships, held here in 1990. During the 20th century what became

known simply as Gärdet lost its military role. In the early 1900s the area was used for May Day processions, and car races were staged here around 1920.

The fortress of Kungliga Borgen is a relic of the military training era, and it was from here that Karl XIV Johan used to watch his troops manoeuvring. He rode from here to Rosendal Palace on Djurgården *(see p98)* via a pontoon bridge near the present-day National Maritime Museum. The fortress was badly damaged by fire in October 1977, but it has since been rebuilt to its original appearance. A restaurant is open during the summer.

Something is always going on in Gärdet. It is the starting point for major fun runs and the venue for kite-flying festivals, and is used by the city's balloonists. It is also a favourite place to exercise horses and dogs.

INGMAR BERGMAN

The playwright and producer Ingmar Bergman was born at Östermalm in 1918. His long series of masterly films have made him world-famous, but he started his career in the theatre. From 1963–6 he was Director of Dramatiska Teatern, where he is still a guest producer. He has created more than 100 theatrical productions. His international breakthrough as a film producer came with *Smiles of the Summer Night* (1955), and *The Seventh Seal* (1957) was a cinematic milestone. Bergman completed this stage of his career with *Fanny and Alexander* (1982).

Ingmar Bergman at a press conference, 1998

Tessinparken, surrounded by Functionalist-style housing dating from the late 1930s

Tessinparken & Nedre Gärdet ⑭

Map 3 F2. ⊤ *Karlaplan, Gärdet.*
🚃 *1, 4, 72.*

THREE GENERATIONS OF the Tessin family of architects *(see p37)* have given their name to this park opened at Lower Gärdet in 1931. Tessinparken runs from north to south and is attractively designed with lawns, play areas, paths and ponds. The adjoining houses, built between 1932–7, have their own gardens and blend in such a way that they give the impression of being part of the park itself.

The earliest houses, nearest to Valhallavägen, still show signs of 1920s Classicism, although Gärdet's real hallmark is Functionalism *(see p37)*. The lower white houses along Askrikegatan are Functionalist in style and noticeably different from other buildings in Gärdet. They mark the northern boundary of the park. Some 60 different architects were involved in designing the Gärdet development, including Sture Frölén.

A granite statue of a woman with a suitcase, *Housewife's Holiday*, stands in the part of Tessin Park adjoining Valhallavägen. It was made by Olof Thorwald Ohlsson in the 1970s. At the other end of the park is a colourful concrete statue, *The Egg*, by Egon Möller-Nielsen.

Functionalist façade at Tessinparken

Försvarshögskolan ⑮

Valhallavägen 117. **Map** 3 E2.
🚃 *4, 62, 72.* ⊤ *Stadion.*
◐ *to the public.*

TWO DECORATIVE cannons, an aircraft propeller and an 18th-century anchor guard the entrance to Försvarshögskolan (the Military Academy). The building has been sympathetically renovated and appears to be lower than it really is because the adjoining Valhallavägen was built at a higher level.

It was originally the base for the Svea Artillery Regiment and is one of many notable military buildings designed by the architect Ernst Jacobsson. After Nybrogatan was blasted out through the Tyskbagarbergen hill, the regimental building provided a backdrop to the newly extended street.

The regiment moved out in 1949 to make way first for Swedish Radio and later for the Military Academy, in whose present gym Swedish

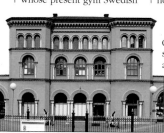

The restored façade of Försvarshögskolan (Military Academy) on Valhallavägen

TV started. A plaque reads: "From this building the first regular television programme was transmitted on 24 October 1954."

Stadion ⑯

Lidingövägen 1–3. **Map** 3 E2.
📞 *508 260 00.* ⊤ *Stadion.* 🚃 *4, 55, 72, 73.* ◐ *15 Apr–15 Oct.*
during events. ♿ ⒒ ▣

A NEW MAIN ARENA was built for the 1912 Olympic Games in Stockholm. The architect of Stadion, Torben Grut (1871–1945), followed the National Romantic influences of the day. His design was based on his own interpretation of the commission to build a stadium "using modern construction methods adapted from traditional medieval brick-building techniques". It is no coincidence that the arena, which is the world's oldest Olympic stadium still in use, is often known as the "Stadium Fortress".

In addition to the 1912 Olympics, the stadium has also been the venue for ice hockey and bandy (a type of hockey) championships, the European Athletics Championships in 1958, and the World Equestrian Championships in 1990. The stadium is renowned for athletics events, and stages an international athletics gala every summer.

Stadion is listed as a heritage building and its twin towers are a familiar landmark. The complex is richly decorated. The clock tower has two figures by Carl Fagerberg, *Ask and Embla*, the counterparts of Adam and Eve in Nordic mythology. There are also busts of Victor Balck, the man behind the 1912 Olympics; P H Ling, the father of Swedish gymnastics; and Edwin Wide, the "flying teacher", who was a leading opponent of the Finnish master-athlete Paavo Nurmi in long-distance races during the 1920s.

Bruno Liljefors's statue *Play* outside Stadion

Four notable sculptures were added in the 1930s. The painter and gymnast Bruno Liljefors created *Play* at the main entrance, Carl Eldh made *The Runners*, and Carl Fagerberg provided *Relay Runners* and *The Shot Putter*.

Tekniska Högskolan ⑰

Valhallavägen 79. **Map** 3 D1.
Ⓣ *Tekniska högskolan.* 🚌 4, 72, 73.

THE RENOWNED higher education establishment, Tekniska Högskolan, accounts for one-third of Sweden's technical research and engineering education at university level. It has 15,000 students, 1,000 active research students and a staff of 2,500. It was founded in 1827, and since 1917 its campus has been housed in heritage buildings on Valhallavägen, as well as in the suburbs of Haninge and Kista, and outside Stockholm in Södertälje, Gävle and Visby.

The main building on Valhallavägen was designed by Erik Lallerstedt and its opening in October 1917 was a milestone in Sweden's technological development.

The architect commissioned several contemporary artists to decorate the austere technical environment, so it has become something of an artistic treasure trove. The sculptors and painters whose works adorn the buildings included Einar Forseth, Olle Hjertzberg, Georg Pauli, Ivar Johnsson, Axel Törneman, Hilding Linnqvist and Carl Milles. Milles was also responsible for the fountain sculpture, *The Industrial Monument*, which rests on a marble base in the courtyard facing Valhallavägen.

Early in the 20th century the main building underwent a painstaking renovation. The surrounding park was also restored to its original state.

Engelbrektskyrkan & Lärkstaden ⑱

Östermalmsgatan 20. **Map** 3 D2.
Ⓣ *Tekniska högskolan.* 🚌 1, 42.
Engelbrektskyrkan 📞 406 98 00.
🕐 11am–3pm Tue–Sun. ✝ 11am Sun, 11:30am Thu. ♿ 🅿

ONE OF SWEDEN'S leading Jugendstil architects, Lars Israel Wahlman, designed the Engelbrekt Church as a result of winning an architectural competition in 1906. The church was opened on 25 January 1914 in the presence of King Gustaf V.

Engelbrektskyrkan gives the appearance of thrusting out from the rocks, and it dominates the surrounding area with its slender brick tower. In the chancel, the monumental paintings are by Olle Hjortzberg (1872–1959). The sculptor Tore Strindberg (1882–1968) was commissioned for the stucco reliefs both in the chancel and above the main entrance. Filip Månsson executed the frescoes in the west portico and elsewhere. The nave is the highest in Scandinavia, and the arches inside the church are supported by eight granite pillars.

Engelbrektskyrkan is located in Lärkstaden, a quarter which was developed around 1910 and is characterized by dark red façades and tiled roofs that blend in well with the church. The area has winding streets and natural differences in level – inspired partly by Austrian patterns.

Engelbrektskyrkan, dominating the surrounding area of Lärkstaden

---

ARENA FOR RECORDS

No other athletics arena can compete with Stockholm's Stadion when it comes to world records. The 1912 Olympics gave the statistics a flying start with 11 world records. The gold medallist Ted Meredith's time of 1 min 51.9 sec in the 800-m event can be compared with Wilson Kipketer's 1997 time of 1 min 41.73 sec over the same distance; the last world record set at Stadion. It has recorded a total of 83 world records. London is second with 68 and Los Angeles is third with 66 records. The top Swedish runner of the 1940s, Gunder Hägg, set seven world records and the Finn, Paavo Nurmi, had six.

Running track at Stadion, 1912

Kungsholmen

ONCE BEST KNOWN for its handicrafts and small industries, Kungsholmen changed in the late 19th century with the emergence of new apartment blocks and institutional buildings. By the early 1900s the area had a different status, exemplified by Ragnar Östberg's Stadshuset (city hall) – Stockholm's most notable architectural project of the 20th century – and Carl Westman's majestic Rådhuset (law court). These were followed by the elegant waterfront houses along Norr Mälarstrand. The area has a high concentration of government buildings, but it also offers many venues for entertainment and nightlife.

Stately buildings on Norr Mälarstrand line the Riddarfjärden waterfront

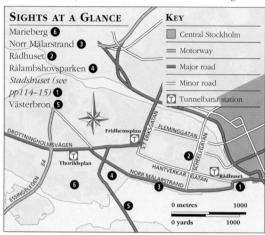

SIGHTS AT A GLANCE	KEY
Marieberg ⑥	▢ Central Stockholm
Norr Mälarstrand ❸	▬ Motorway
Rådhuset ❷	▬ Major road
Rålambshovsparken ❹	▬ Minor road
Stadshuset (see pp114–15) ❶	Ⓣ Tunnelbana station
Västerbron ❺	

Norr Mälarstrand ❸

Map 1 C3. Ⓣ *Rådhuset, Fridhemsplan.* 🚌 *40, 52.*

WHEN INDUSTRIES like textiles and dyeing left Norr Mälarstrand in the early 20th century work began on exploiting Kungsholmen's attractive location along the bay of Riddarfjärden. Gradually an exclusive residential area emerged. During World War II a sculpture park was developed along the waterfront, where the excursion boats and vintage coasters are moored today. Willow, poplar, alder and birch trees thrive along the shoreline. A pavilion with a summer café stands on pillars above the water. It was designed by Erik Glemme, assistant to the city's master gardener Holger Blom (born 1906).

The architect of Stadshuset, Ragnar Östberg, designed Norr Mälarstrand 76. Cyrillus Johansson, Sven Wallander and J Norberg were the architects of Nos. 26, 28 and 30, where the figures on the gables above the steps were created by the metal craftsman Ragnar Myrsmeden. There is much to see in the small side streets, including the façades of No. 5 Jacob Westins Gata (architect Harald Wadsjö) and No. 9 Skillinggränd. The original service-flat building at No. 6 John Erikssongatan was designed by Sven Markelius, who was influenced by the ministerial couple Gunnar and Alva Myrdal. It is the first residential building in the Functionalist style typical of the 1930s to be listed as a heritage site.

Stadshuset ❶

See pp114–15.

Rådhuset ❷

Scheelegatan 7. **Map** 2 A5. Ⓣ *Rådhuset.* 🚌 *40, 52.*

IN THE EARLY 20TH century, the intention was to build a combined city hall and law court, but the plans changed when two separate architectural competitions were launched. The winning entry for Rådhuset (the law court), was a design by Carl Westman (1866–1936), who became a leading exponent of the National Romantic School along with Ragnar Östberg (1866–1945), architect of Stadshuset. Building began in 1911, and

Rådhuset was opened in December 1915. In his design, Westman drew inspiration from the Vasa Renaissance of the 16th century and was probably influenced by Vadstena Castle in southern Sweden. Rådhuset, with its prominent tower, is one of the best examples of the National Romantic style, but its solid scale also shows Jugendstil influences.

The sculptors Christian Eriksson and the brothers Aron and Gustaf Sandberg were responsible for the decoration, which also includes paintings by Olle Hjortzberg and Filip Månsson. Beside the staircase on the fifth floor is a copy of *Kopparmatte*, the pillory which once stood on Stortorget in Gamla Stan. The original pillory is at Stockholms Stadsmuseum *(see p127).*

Rådhuset, exterior detail

Rålambshovsparken ❹

Map 1 B3. 🅣 *Fridhemsplan.*
🚌 *1, 4, 40, 56, 57, 62, 74.* 🚊

RÅLAMBSHOVPARKEN was created in 1935, when the Västerbron bridge was built. It adjoins other green areas, including Smedsudden and Marieberg and Fredhäll parks. These open spaces attract joggers and sun-bathers. In summer it is possible to swim from the beach at Smedsudden or the cliffs at Fredhäll.

When the city celebrated its 700th anniversary in 1953 an amphitheatre was opened in Rålambshovsparken, and a paddling pool and playgrounds were added. The park has been enhanced with Elli Hemberg's sculpture *The Butterfly*, Eric Grate's *Monument to an Axeman*, *Judgement* by Egon Möller-Nielsen and Lars Erik Falk's *Colour Tower*.

Rålambshovsparken on the north side of Västerbron bridge

Västerbron ❺

Map 1 B4. 🚌 *4, 40, 74.*

AS STOCKHOLM expanded and car use increased in the 1920s, it became necessary to build an additional bridge between the northern and southern shores of Lake Mälaren. German experts dominated the architectural competition launched in 1930, but their plans were implemented by Swedish architects and engineers and the bridge was completed in 1935.

The attractive design blends well with the landscape. The bridge is built in two spans of 168 m (551 ft) and 204 m (669 ft) with a vertical clearance of 26 m (85 ft). It is used by an average of 12,000 vehicles daily. A walk to the centre of Västerbron is rewarded with a magnificent view of central Stockholm.

Marieberg ❻

Map 1 A3. 🅣 *Thorildsplan.* 🚌 *1, 49, 56, 62.* **Riksarkivet** 🎧 *737 63 50.*

THE AREA at the northern end of the Västerbron bridge, Marieberg, was once known for its porcelain factory and military installations. But since the early 1960s it has become the city's main newspaper district and the home of three of the four Stockholm dailies.

The architect Paul Hedqvist's 98.6-m (323-ft) high building for *Dagens Nyheter* and *Expressen* is one of the city's landmarks. The neon sign which tops the building at Gjörwellsgatan 30 was designed by P O Ultvedt, who also created the relief at the entrance. Works of art include Lennart Rodhe's walls made from glazed stoneware, *Day and Night*, and Arne Jones' sculpture *Nova*. Some older works of art were brought from the papers' original building in the central Klara district, including Stig Blomberg's copper sculpture,

***The Orb* by Elli Hemberg (1970) in front of Riksarkivet**

Freedom our Watchword, made in 1951.

The offices of *Svenska Dagbladet* are not as richly decorated as their neighbours', but they are no less interesting architecturally. The building was inspired by Pirelli's high-rise offices in Milan and designed by Tengbom Architects in 1960–2.

The third interesting building in Marieberg in Riksarkivet, the state archive. It was built in 1968 by architects Åke Ahlström and Kjell Åström. Riksarkivet is one of Sweden's oldest public bodies, dating from the Middle Ages. At the entrance is Elli Hemberg's iron sculpture, *The Orb*. The main hall, which has 56 seats for researchers and 18 individual study rooms, is dominated by Lennart Rodhe's tapestry, *Symbol in the Archive*, which was created by the Friends of Handicrafts. In a smaller adjoining room the public has access to archive documents, microfilm and microfiche.

Among the archives is one of the world's largest books – the accounts for the province of Östergötland dating from 1813. It has 12,390 pages, weighs 42 kg (92 lb) and is 1.13 m (3.7 ft) wide.

Guided tours of Riksarkivet can be arranged.

Västerbron bridge, opened in 1935, linking Kungsholmen with Södermalm across Lake Mälaren

Stadshuset ❸

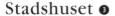

Probably sweden's biggest architectural project of the 20th century, the City Hall was completed in 1923 and has become a symbol of Stockholm. It was designed by Ragnar Östberg (1866–1945), the leading architect of the Swedish National Romantic style, and displays influences of both the Nordic Gothic and Northern Italian schools. Several leading Swedish artists contributed to the rich interior design. The building contains the Council Chamber and 250 offices for city administrative staff. The annual Nobel Prize festivities take place in the Blue Hall.

Engel-brekt

★ The Golden Room
The Byzantine-inspired wall mosaics by Einar Forseth (1892–1988) have 19 million fragments of gold leaf. The theme of the northern wall is Queen of Lake Mälaren.

Norra Trapptornet, crowned by a sun.

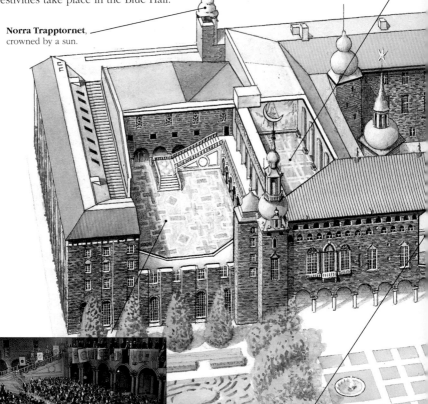

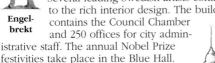

★ The Blue Hall
The banqueting room is made from hand-shaped dark bricks. The name comes from the original plan to use polished blue-painted bricks.

★ The Prince's Gallery
A fresco, The City on the Water, *in the Prince's Gallery, was painted by Prince Eugen (see p99), who donated it to the City Hall.*

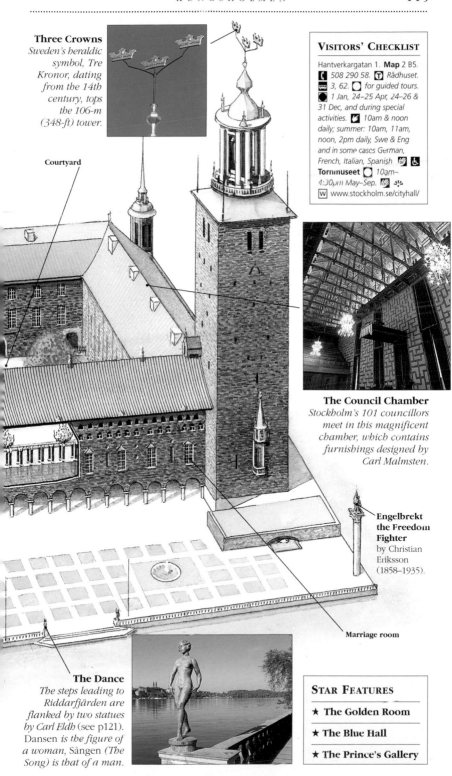

Three Crowns
Sweden's heraldic symbol, Tre Kronor, dating from the 14th century, tops the 106-m (348-ft) tower.

Courtyard

VISITORS' CHECKLIST

Hantverkargatan 1. **Map** 2 B5.
508 290 58. Rådhuset.
3, 62. for guided tours.
1 Jan, 24–25 Apr, 24–26 & 31 Dec, and during special activities. 10am & noon daily; summer: 10am, 11am, noon, 2pm daily, Swe & Eng and in some cases German, French, Italian, Spanish
Tornmuseet 10am–4:30pm May–Sep.
www.stockholm.se/cityhall/

The Council Chamber
Stockholm's 101 councillors meet in this magnificent chamber, which contains furnishings designed by Carl Malmsten.

Engelbrekt the Freedom Fighter
by Christian Eriksson (1858–1935).

Marriage room

The Dance
The steps leading to Riddarfjärden are flanked by two statues by Carl Eldh (see p121). Dansen is the figure of a woman, Sången (The Song) is that of a man.

STAR FEATURES

★ The Golden Room

★ The Blue Hall

★ The Prince's Gallery

Vasastan

BUILDING STARTED in Vasastan, the most northerly part of Norrmalm, in the 18th century. Today it is both a residential area, with houses built around 1900 for manual workers and craftsmen, and a lively part of the city with a wide choice of bars and restaurants. The area also includes some of Stockholm's most agreeable green open spaces, including Vasaparken and Vanadislunden. Stadsbiblioteket, the city library *(see p117)*, is one of Stockholm's most distinctive buildings, and there are several architecturally outstanding churches.

The old observatory (1748–53) at the top of the Observatory hill

SIGHTS AT A GLANCE	KEY
Gustav Vasa Kyrka **⑤**	▢ Central Stockholm
Handelshögskolan **③**	▬ Motorway
Judiska Museet **⑥**	▬ Major road
Karlbergs Slott **⑨**	▬ Minor road
Observatoriemuseet **②**	▬ Minor road
Röda Bergen **⑩**	🅣 Tunnelbana station
Rörstrandsgatan **⑧**	
Spökslottet **①**	
Stadsbiblioteket **④**	
Vanadislunden **⑪**	
Vasaparken **⑦**	

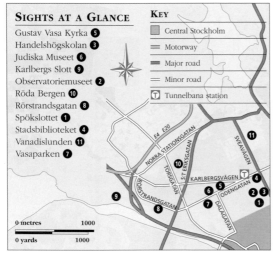

0 metres 1000
0 yards 1000

Spökslottet **①**

Drottninggatan 116. **Map** 2 B3.
🛈 *16 41 07.* 🅣 *Rådmansgatan.*
🚌 *52.* ⃝ *only during prearranged
tours.* 🏛 *groups only, by appt.* 🅿 🚻
limited access. 🚫

UNTIL ABOUT 1900 the most northerly section of Drottninggatan formed the main road into the city from the north. Here is Spökslottet (the "haunted palace"), built in the grand style popular during Sweden's time as a great power, thus dating it to around 1700. It has been suggested that it was designed by Tessin the Elder, but it is more likely that it was by his stepson, Abraham Winantz, who was ennobled in 1693 for his

**Orrefors bowl
by Simon Gate, 1925**

services as an architect. On show in the palace is Stockholm University's collection of 360 paintings from the 16th to the 19th century, and the Hellner collection of 700 pieces made at the Orrefors glassworks. Pehr Hilleström's painting *With the Fortune Teller* is included in the collection, but the emphasis is on foreign works such as *The Assault*, attributed to Pieter Bruegel the Elder (1567), and *Danae Banquet* and *Cleopatra's Banquet* by Tiepolo. The property was acquired in 1925 by the College of Higher Education, later Stockholm University, which handed it over to the State. Legend has it that the house has a ghost.

Observatoriemuseet **②**

Map 2 B2. 🛈 *31 58 10.* 🅣 *Odenplan.* 🚌 *52.* ⃝ *during guided tours.*
🏛 *guided tours in English by
appointment.* 🚻 🅿

A NUMBER OF institutions connected with science and education can be found on and around the hill of Brunkeberg. The oldest is the former observatory designed by Carl Hårleman for the Royal Scientific Academy and opened in 1753. In 1931 its astronomical research was moved to Saltsjöbaden in the Stockholm archipelago. The building has since become Observatoriemuseet (the Observatory Museum), where visitors can see the observation room with its instruments, the two median rooms, the weather room and the instrument workshop. In good weather one can view the stars. There is a splendid view of Stockholm from the museum's dome.

The grove which surrounds the old observatory began to take shape in the 18th century. It is an idyllic enclosed area which was first opened to the public in the 20th century.

On top of Brunkeberg is Sigrid Fridman's statue *The Centaur*. A park stretches down to Sveavägen, where a large pond is fed by water from a stream running down the hillside. The statue *Dancing Youth* is by Ivar Johnsson. At the southern entrance of the park is Nils Möllerberg's sculpture *Youth*.

Handels-högskolan ❸

Sveavägen 65. **Map** 2 C2. Ⓣ Råd-mansgatan. 🚌 52.

Wᴴᴇɴ ᴛʜᴇ ᴀʀᴄʜɪᴛᴇᴄᴛ Ivar Tengbom (1878–1968) designed Handelshögskolan, Stockholm's School of Economics, in the early 1920s he was inspired mainly by the Renaissance and Neo-Classical styles. Tengbom himself took charge of the construction and the building was officially opened in 1926 in the presence of King Gustav V. The façade has stone reliefs and a gilded Mercury – the god of commerce – all by Ansgar Almquist, who also contributed a stucco relief with a lion gate based on the one in ancient Mycenae in Greece.

The school was founded in 1909 and was previously based in premises at Brunkebergs-torg before moving to the newly built Handelshögskolan.

Entrance of Handelshögskolan, the School of Economics

Vasastaden with Stadsbiblioteket (top left) and Gustav Vasa Kyrka

Stadsbiblioteket ❹

Sveavägen 73. **Map** 2 B2. 📞 508 311 00. Ⓣ Rådmansgatan. 🚌 4, 42, 46, 52, 53, 72. 🕐 10am–8.30pm Mon–Thu, 10am–6pm Fri, noon–4pm Sat & Sun. 25 May–22 Aug: 11am–7pm Mon–Thu, 11am–5pm Fri. ♿ 🖥

Gᴜɴɴᴀʀ Aꜱᴘʟᴜɴᴅ's master work, Stadsbiblioteket (City Library), is one of the capital's most architecturally important buildings (see p36). Asplund, the champion of the Functionalist style prevalent in the 1930s, designed a library which was dominated by Classic ideals. It was opened in 1928.

Internally, the furnishings and many of the lightfittings were designed by Asplund himself. In the entrance hall are Ivar Johnsson's stucco reliefs with themes from Homer's *Iliad*. The sparkling mural painting in the children's section, *John Blund*, is by Nils Dardel, and the depiction of the stars in the heavens by Ulf Munthe. The door lintels, fine door handles and drinking fountains are by Nils Sjögren. Hilding Linnquist was responsible for the giant-sized tapestry, and also for four mural paintings using ancient fresco techniques.

The library lends more than a million books every year.

Gustav Vasa Kyrka ❺

Odenplan. **Map** 2 B2. 📞 31 66 97. Ⓣ Odenplan. 🚌 4, 40, 42, 46, 53, 69, 72. 🕐 11am–6pm Mon–Thu, 11am–3pm Fri–Sun. ✝ noon Mon & Fri, 8am Wed, 6pm Thu, 11am Sun, in Swedish. ♿

Sᴡᴇᴅᴇɴ's ʟᴀʀɢᴇꜱᴛ Baroque sculpture forms the altar in Gustav Vasa Kyrka, which was opened in 1906. The piece, by the court sculptor Burchardt Precht (1651–1738), was made for Uppsala Cathedral, from where it was removed in the late 19th century. It was bought by the Gustav Vasa parish congregation, whose church immediately gained a notable attraction.

The architect Agi Lindegren designed the central part of the church in Italian Neo-Baroque style with a 60-m (197-ft) high dome. Lindegren himself designed the marble pulpit and the font was created by Sigrid Blomberg. In the baptismal chapel there is a 15th-century painting by an unknown Dutch artist. The paintings on the dome are by Vicke Andrén, who also portrayed the four evangelists in the transepts. The organ was built with the help of the composer Olle Olsson, the church organist for 50 years.

GᴜNNAR AꜱPLUND

Gunnar Asplund (1885–1940) was the dominant figure among Swedish and internationally renowned architects between the two world wars. His first major commission was the chapel at the Skogskyrkogården Cemetery, designed in National Romantic style. His last work was Heliga Korsets Kapell, the cemetery's crematorium (1935–40). Regarded as a masterpiece in the Functionalist style, it has earned a place on the UNESCO World Heritage list (see p133). Asplund also designed Stadsbiblioteket (City Library, 1920–28). He pioneered the Functionalist style as chief architect for the Stockholm Exhibition in 1930.

Stockholm Exhibition, by Gunnar Asplund, 1930

An eight-stemmed *chanuki* (candlestick) in the collection of Judiska Museet

Judiska Museet ⑥

Hälsingegatan 2 **Map** 2 A2.
【 31 01 43. ⊤ Odenplan. 🚌 4,
47, 72. ○ noon–4pm Mon–Fri &
Sun. 🎫 in English by appointment.
🖼️ 🔥 🏠 🛒

IN 1774 AARON ISAAC became the first Jewish immigrant to settle in Stockholm and practise his religion. Half of Sweden's Jewish population of around 18,000 live in the Stockholm area. Judiska Museet depicts the history of the Swedish Jews from Isaac's time up to the present day. It focuses on Judaism as a religion, its integration into Swedish society and, naturally, the Holocaust. A comprehensive collection of pictures and other items provide an insight into Jewish life in Sweden with its important traditions and customs. The beautiful *Torah* (the five books of Moses), the bridal canopy, and the collection of eight-stemmed *chanukis* (candlesticks) are just some of the museum's remarkable spiritual artifacts.

Vasaparken ⑦

Map 2 A3. ⊤ S:t Eriksplan.
🚌 3, 4, 47, 72.

VASAPARKEN DATES from the early 20th century. It was typical of parks of its time with its emphasis on sport exemplified by the inclusion of a spacious grass sports field. During World War I the field was used for growing potatoes. A playground area was added in 1911.
    It is a leafy and pleasant park. With few exceptions the trees were planted when the

park was opened, but a lime tree in the shape of a candelabra is believed to be more than 200 years old.
    During a major facelift in the 1940s, the appearance of the section along Torsgatan was changed. Three terraced gardens were added with granite and concrete walls and reliefs. Gottfrid Larsson's bronze statue *The Workman* has stood in this part of the park since 1917. On the opposite side of the park is *Romeo and Juliet*, a small granite sculpture by Olof Th Ohlsson.

Vasaparken, a green lung in the built-up area of Vasastan

Rörstrandsgatan ⑧

Map 1 C1. ⊤ S:t Eriksplan. 🚌 3, 4, 42, 57, 72.

THIS STREET TAKES its name from the no longer existing Rörstrand palace, built in the early 1630s. In the summer of 1726 the manufacture of Delft-style porcelain started in the building. Two hundred years later the now-famous

Rörstrand porcelain factory was moved to the Gothenburg area and then to its current home at Lidköping in south-west Sweden.
    Rörstrandsgatan has become a popular street for restaurants and pubs, and it was the site of one of the city's first Chinese restaurants. Today a wide range of restaurants offer cuisine from all over the world. The many outdoor cafés give the street a colourful atmosphere during summer.

Karlbergs Slott ⑨

Map 1 B1. 【 562 813 05. 🚌 42, 72 to the station of Karlberg, then 15 min walk. 🎫 groups only, by appointment.

ADMIRAL KARL Karlsson Gyllenhielm started to build Karlbergs Slott in the 1630s, during the Thirty Years War. From 1670 the palace was extended and rebuilt by Magnus Gabriel de la Gardie, with Jean de la Vallée as his architect. When Karlberg became royal property in 1688, it was one of Sweden's most majestic palaces. It was where the "hero King" Karl XII (1682–1718) grew up, and it was here that he lay in state after his death at the Battle of Fredrikshald *(see p19)*.
    In 1792 the architect C C Gjörwell converted the property into the Royal War Academy, which later became the Karlberg Military School, and since 1999 it has been one of the country's military academies.
    Cadet balls at Karlberg are unforgettable experiences, not

Rörstrandsgatan, a popular area for restaurants and pubs

Karlbergs Slott, a palace dating from the 1630s – now one of Sweden's military academies

least because of the magnificent setting. The interior decorations include Carl Carove's magnificent stuccowork which can be seen in the grand hall. The palace church has been renovated, but the 17th-century lamps are original. De la Gardie's "rarities room" is now the sacristy but once housed his collection of valuables.

Röda Bergen ⓿

Map 2 A2. Ⓣ S:t Eriksplan.
🚌 3, 42, 47, 57, 69.

TURNING OFF from Sveavägen into Vanadisvägen one soon reaches Matteus Kyrka which dates from 1902–3. This church was designed by Erik Lallerstedt, who 20 years later undertook its renovation. The figure of St Matthew at the entrance, as well as the reredos figures, are the work of Ivar Johnsson. The mural paintings are by the artist Olle Hjortzberg.

The Röda Bergen ("Red Mountains") district starts at Vanadisplan with a sculpture made from reinforced plastic, *Transformation*, by Chris Gibson (1984). The area is a typical 1920s garden city where, as in Lärkstaden *(see p111)*, the architects abandoned the normal rigid road layout and allowed the

street plan to follow the terrain. After the rose gardens of Rödabergsbrinken, flanked by the parkland oases of Hedemora and Sätertäppan, comes Rödabergsgatan, an avenue of horse chestnut trees typical of the area. A Modernist sculpture in steel has sneaked in here – Björn Selder's *1 1/2 Spheres* (1979). In the background is a playground with Bo Englund's sculpture *Genesis* (1984).

Vanadislunden ⓫

Map 2 B1. 🚌 40, 46, 52. **Vanadisbadet** Ⓒ 30 12 11. ⏰ 22 May–22 Aug: 10am–6pm daily. 🈂 ♿ 🍴 ▯

MANY PLACES in Vasastan are named Vanadis, which derives from Norse mythology. It was not until the late 19th century that the area around the northern end of Sveavägen started to be developed. In the 1880s a park was laid out on the nearby hillside in which

the cultivated areas were created from a landfill site. A chapel, Stefanskapellet, at the southern end of the park, was opened in 1904. It was designed by Carl Möller, who was the architect responsible for Johannes Kyrka. During renovation in 1925–6 the chapel acquired its painted altar by Einar Forseth depicting the Passion.

It took almost a half-century to complete Vanadislunden The Vanadisbadet outdoor swimming pool was opened in 1938. Above the pool the sculpture *Girl in the Evening Sun* by Anders Jönsson looks out over Vasastaden. This is the highest part of Vanadislunden, and the streets around here have attractive black and white paving stones.

At one time there were numerous suburban mansions in the area. One of them, Cederdals Malmgård, can still be seen towards the northern end of the park.

Houses in Röda Bergen with their typical façades in warm colours

Norrtull & Nationalstadsparken

LARGE PARTS OF EKOPARKEN, the world's first National City Park, are spread around the Brunnsviken inlet, only a few kilometres north of the city centre. The English-style park, Hagaparken, with its many 18th-century buildings, extolled by the poet Carl Bellman *(see p98)*, is located in this oasis. To the north lies the majestic Baroque Ulriksdals Slott. In stark contrast, to the south visitors come abruptly to the inner city's built-up area at the old Norrtull gateway. The area has several museums, including Naturhistoriska Museet, Sweden's largest.

The Wenner-Gren Center's main building, Pylonen

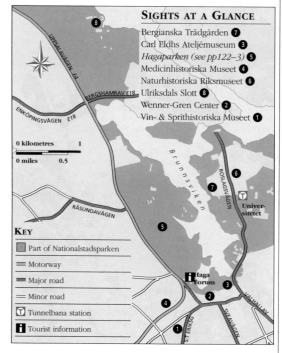

SIGHTS AT A GLANCE

Bergianska Trädgården **7**
Carl Eldhs Ateljémuseum **3**
Hagaparken (see pp122–3) **5**
Medicinhistoriska Museet **4**
Naturhistoriska Riksmuseet **6**
Ulriksdals Slott **8**
Wenner-Gren Center **2**
Vin- & Sprithistoriska Museet **1**

KEY

▪ Part of Nationalstadsparken
═ Motorway
▬ Major road
═ Minor road
🅃 Tunnelbana station
🅸 Tourist information

Vin- & Sprithistoriska Museet **1**

Dalagatan 100. **Map** 2 A1.
📞 744 70 70. 🅃 S:t Eriksplan.
🚌 69. 🕐 10am–7pm Tue, 10am–4pm Wed–Fri, noon–4pm Sat & Sun.
♿ 🎧 ♿ 🎁 🛍
🅆 www.vinosprithistoriska.a.se

SWEDISH PUNSCH and schnapps are the themes of Vin- & Sprithistoriska (Wine and Spirits Historical Museum), located in an old wine warehouse. It was designed by Cyrillus Johansson and built in 1923. As the wine trade decreased over the years, the building was used for other purposes until 1967, when the first exhibition was staged. Today's museum dates from 1989 and covers 1,700 sq m (18,300 sq ft). It shows how a wine shop would have looked around 1900. From the same era is a typical southern Swedish distillery in which potatoes were used to make the best schnapps. There is also a collection of spices used for schnapps and liqueurs, and over 50,000 labels are on show.

Visitors can listen to some 200 "schnapps songs" via a computer which also has the texts of 2,000 drinking songs.

Schnapps label, Vin- & Sprithistoriska Museet

Wenner-Gren Center **2**

Sveavägen 166. **Map** 2 B1. 🚌 40, 46, 52, 69.

THE INDUSTRIALIST Axel Wenner-Gren (1881–1961) had an almost religious faith in the potential of science. "Let us use science to solve mankind's problems" is an expression attributed to him. During the 1920s he launched products like vacuum cleaners and refrigerators through his company, Electrolux, which he founded in 1919. His name is preserved in three foundations and in the Wenner-Gren Center, whose 24-storey headquarters, Pylonen, stands like an exclamation mark at the northern end of Sveavägen.

It was opened in 1962, but Wenner-Gren lived only long enough to see the topping-out ceremony in 1961. In the semi-circular Helicon are 155 apartments for the use, at subsidized rents, of foreign scientists undertaking long-term research in Sweden.

The Wenner-Gren Foundation was set up to encourage scientific exchanges between Sweden and other countries. About 250 scientists take part in these every year, and international symposiums are arranged.

Carl Eldhs Ateljémuseum ❸

Lögbodavägen 10, Bellevueparken.
📞 612 65 60. 🚌 40, 46, 52, 53.
🕐 Apr: noon–4pm Sun; May: noon–
4pm Sat & Sun; Jun–Aug: noon–4pm
Tue–Sun; Sep: noon–4pm Sat & Sun;
Oct: noon–4pm Sun. 🛒 📷 ♿
🚫 📁 🖥

Carl Eldh's Ateljémuseum containing gypsum originals of his works

IT IS NOT EASY to find Löge-bodavägen, but those who do are richly rewarded. It has a viewpoint looking out over the Brunnsviken inlet and is close to the monument *The Young Strindberg in the Archipelago* by Carl Eldh (1873–1954). The sculptor's studio, now Carl Eldh's Ateljémuseum, is only a few metres from the viewpoint.

In his time Carl Eldh was one of Sweden's most prolific sculptors. Like his colleague Carl Milles, he lived in Paris for several years and was influenced by Rodin's Impressionist style. Later his works were characterized by a more robust Realism. Eldh's sculptures can be seen at 16 public sites in Stockholm. The gypsum forms of these works are on show in the studio. Examples include the *Branting Monument* at Norra Bantorget, the statue of Strindberg in Tegnérparken, and *The Runners* at Stadion *(see pp110–11)*. The original studio, built in 1918–19, was designed by the City Hall's architect, Ragnar Östberg.

Medicinhistoriska Museet Eugenia ❹

Karolinska Sjukhuset. **Map** 2 A1.
📞 34 86 20. 🚌 3, 52.
🕐 11am–4pm Tue, Thu, Fri; 11am–7pm Wed; noon–4pm Sun.
📷 by appointment. ♿ 🖥

PRINCESS EUGENIE (1830–89), the daughter of Oscar I, founded the Eugenia Home in 1879, where handicapped children could be taught and cared for. It closed in 1971. The building, in the Karolinska Hospital area, became the home of Medicinhistoriska Museet Eugenia (Museum of Medical History) in 1995. Its exhibits highlight the development of medical and dental skills, as well as pharmacy and medical care.

The accent of the museum's collection is on the 19th and 20th centuries, but medieval medicine is also covered.

A 19th-century dentist's reception in Medicinhistoriska Museet

---

EKOPARKEN – NATIONALSTADSPARKEN

Ekoparken – the world's first National City Park – was established by the Swedish Parliament in 1995. This has enabled the capital to safeguard the ecology of its "green lung", a 27-sq km (10.5-sq miles) area for recreation and outdoor activities in an urban setting. In fact, the park covers an area that is as large as Stockholm's inner-city. Ekoparken includes central districts like Skeppsholmen and the southern part of Djurgården, and continues north-west to northern Djurgården, Hagaparken, Brunnsviken and Ulriksdal. Much of the park was a royal hunting ground as early as the 16th century, scattered with beautiful palaces and other sights. The archipelago is represented with the Fjäderholmarna islands in the south.

Information on the park is available at Haga Forum *(see map p120)*, which is a natural entry point. From here there are guided boat tours around Brunnsviken, with stops at some of the more important sights. For more information on Ekoparken and bookings inquiries, telephone 587 140 40.

Isbladskärret in Ekoparken with its rich bird-life, including breeding herons

Hagaparken ⑤

IN THE MID-18TH CENTURY King Gustav III decided to
create a royal park in the popular Haga area.
The king's vision was realized by the fashionable
architect Fredrik Magnus Piper (1746–1824) with the
help of leading architects and decorators, and the
result was an English-style park with some unusual
buildings. A royal palace inspired by Versailles in
France was also planned, but construction halted
after the king's death and it remained unfinished.
Today Hagaparken is part of Ekoparken (see p121),
the world's first national city park – an oasis of
nature and culture in the city centre.

*Gustav III's Pavilion painted in
1811 by A F Cederholm*

Fjärils- & Fågelhuset
*Hundreds of exotic butterflies
and birds fly freely around the
greenhouses containing
humid tropical rainforest with
waterfalls and luxuriant
growth at a temperature of
25°C (78°F).*

**Haga Park-
museum**

These ruins are
all that remain
of Gustav III's
unfinished
royal palace.

★ **Koppartälten**
*These "Roman battle tents" designed
by Louis Jean Desprez were completed in 1790. They were originally
used as stables and accommodation, but now house a restaurant,
café and the Haga Parkmuseum.*

Stora Pelousen
*The lawns stretching down from
Koppartälten to Brunnsviken
are popular with Stockholmers for
sun-bathing and picnics in the
summer, and skiing or sledging
in the winter. At the rear is
Gustav III's Paviljong.*

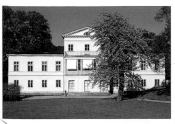

Haga Slott
Built in 1802–4 for Gustav IV Adolf, the palace was the childhood home of the present monarch, Carl XVI Gustaf, and his sisters. Now it is used for government receptions.

VISITORS' CHECKLIST

4 km (2.5 miles) N of Stockholm. *515.* **Haga Parkmuseum** *402 61 30.* *May–Aug: 11am–4pm Tue–Sun.* **Gustav III's Paviljong** *402 61 30.* *every hour May–Aug: 11am–3pm Tue–Sun; Sep: 11am–3pm Sat & Sun.* **Fjärils- & Fågelhuset** *730 39 81.* *May–Sep: 10am–4pm Tue–Fri, 11am–5.30pm Sat & Sun; Oct–Apr: 10am–3pm Tue–Fri, 11am–4pm Sat & Sun.* *24, 25 & 31 Dec.* *in Koppartälten and Fjärils- & Fågelhuset.*

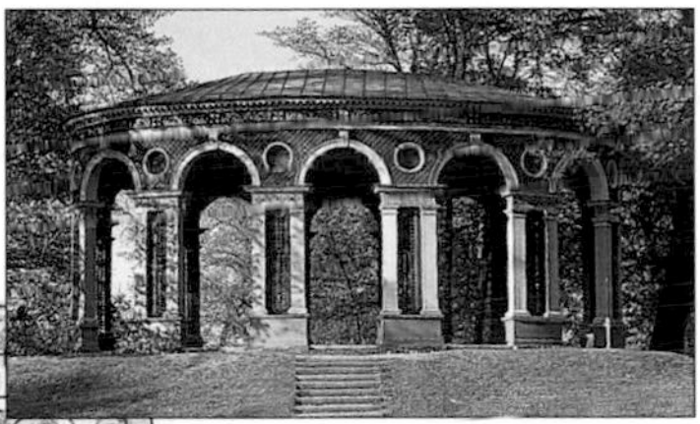

Ekotemplet
This building designed by Louis Jean Desprez in the 1790s was a royal summer dining room. The acoustics made it possible to eavesdrop on secret conversations.

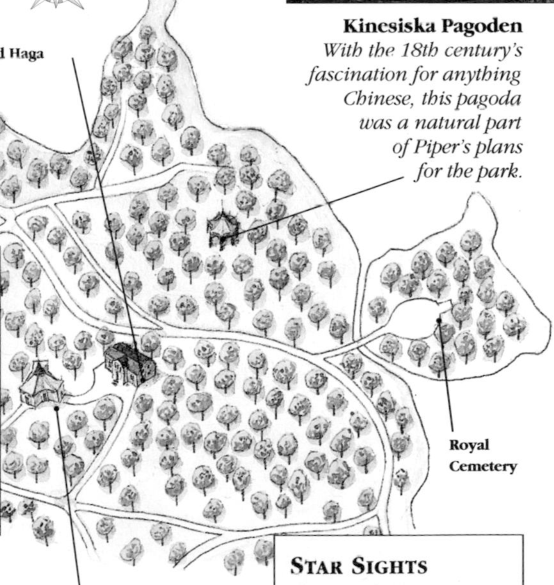

Old Haga
Royal Cemetery
Turkish Pavilion
0 kilometres 2
0 miles 1

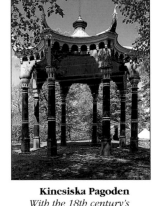

Kinesiska Pagoden
With the 18th century's fascination for anything Chinese, this pagoda was a natural part of Piper's plans for the park.

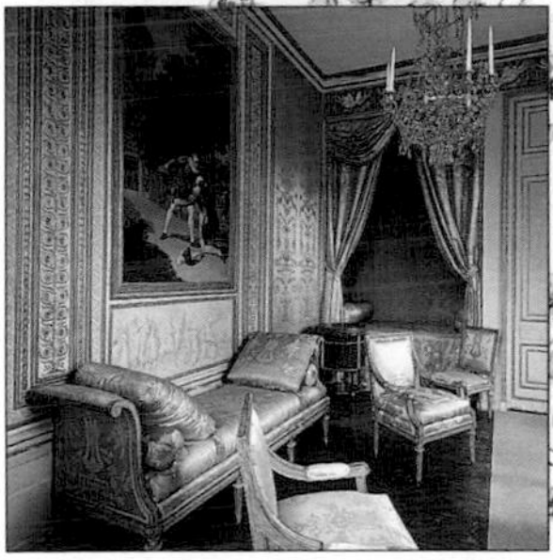

★ Gustav III's Paviljong
Olof Tempelman designed this Gustavian masterpiece and Louis Masreliéz undertook the interior decoration. The magnificent hall of mirrors is particularly worth seeing.

STAR SIGHTS

★ Gustav III's Paviljong

★ Koppartälten

Polar bear in a natural setting at Naturhistoriska Riksmuseet

Naturhistoriska Riksmuseet ❻

5 km (3 miles) N of Stockholm. 519 540 00. Ⓣ Universitetet. 40, 540. 🅾 10am–6pm Tue & Wed, 10am–8pm Thu, 10am–6pm Fri–Sun, (Jun–Jul: also 10am–6pm Mon). ☑ by appointment. 📷 ♿ 🅿 🅱 ⓦ www.nrm.se

COMPLETED IN 1916, the vast Naturhistoriska Riksmuseet (Natural History Museum) was designed by Axel Anderberg and decorated by Carl Fagerberg. The museum is a venerable institution, founded in 1739 by Carl von Linné (1707–78) as part of Vetenskapsakademien (the Academy of Science). It is one of the 10 largest museums of its kind in the world. Over the centuries, the number of exhibits has risen to about 17 million.

During the 1990s it was modernized with the aim of providing "experience-based knowledge". Three permanent collections are sited here along with temporary exhibitions. In "1.45 Billion Years" visitors can get acquainted with the dinosaurs and the earliest human beings. "Life and Water" presents both

the smallest creatures and the giants of the sea, while penguins, sea lions and polar bears await visitors in "The Polar Regions".

During the 1980s the restaurant and museum courtyard were given an artistic facelift by Nils Stenqvist, Gunnar Larsson and Pål Svensson, and a major extension was added in the early 1990s. This also saw the opening of Cosmonova, which is both a planetarium and an IMAX cinema. The architects were Uhlin & Malm. The dome-shaped cinema screen is 25 times the size of a normal screen. It is largely due to Cosmonova that the museum is now a major visitor attraction.

The *Vega Monument* was erected in front of the museum in 1930 to mark the 50th anniversary of explorer Adolf Erik Nordenskiöld's return from the first voyage through the North-East Passage in his ship *Vega*. Designed by Ivar Johnsson, it is an obelisk in dark granite topped with a copper ship.

Lumpfish, Naturhistoriska Riksmuseet

Bergianska Trädgården ❼

5 km (3 miles) N of Stockholm. 15 65 45. Ⓣ Universitetet. 40, 540. **Edvard Andersons Växthus** 🅾 11am–5pm daily. **Victoriahuset** 🅾 May–Sep: 11am–5pm daily; Oct: 11am–5pm Sat & Sun. 📷 ♿ 🅱 🔲 ⓦ www.bergianska.se

BERGIANSKA TRÄDGÅRDEN features more than 9,000 types of plants in beautiful natural settings, and provides an attractive display throughout the year. The most important parts of the gardens are the herb area with its botannical planting scheme, the park with its flower borders, Victoriahuset and the conservatories of Edvard Anderson Växthus, and the fruit and berry beds. There is a kitchen garden in the shade of 100-year-old spruce hedges, and an area for spices and medicinal plants.

There are also trees and shrubs from northern Europe, Asia and America, as well as flowerbeds with both Nordic and Mediterranean plants, and rhododendrons. The spring spectacle of seas of flowering bulbs is the result of 100 years of dedicated care. The Japanese pool was added in 1991 to mark the 200th anniversary of the Bergius foundation which made these gardens possible.

The Victoriahuset conservatory (1900) houses tropical water plants, utility plants and epiphytes. Edvard Andersons Växthus (1995) has large sections for Mediterranean and tropical plants.

An environmental trail offers information on subjects linked with the garden.

Edvard Andersons Växthus in Bergianska Trädgården featuring Mediterranean and tropical plants

Ulriksdals Slott with its magnificent 18th-century Baroque exterior, seen from the palace park

Ulriksdals Slott ❽

7 km (4.3 miles) N of Stockholm.
☎ 402 61 30. 🚌 503. **Palace**
🕐 May–Aug: 10am–4pm daily; Sep:
10am–4pm Sat & Sun. **Orangery**
🕐 May–Aug: 10am–4pm daily; Sep:
10am–4pm Sat & Sun; Oct–Apr:
noon–4pm Sun. **Coronation
Carriage** 📷 May–Aug: 1.40pm &
3.40pm daily. ⊘ 🈺 ♿ 🚻 🍴 🛒

ULRIKSDALS SLOTT is situated
between the two main
roads in the northern outskirts
of Stockholm – the E4 and
Norrtäljevägen. The palace
sits on a headland in the bay
of Edsviken. Its attractive
buildings and lush and leafy
surroundings are well worth a
visit. At the entrance to the
grounds is one of Stockholm's
best-known restaurants,
Ulriksdals Wärdshus *(see p163)*.

The original palace was
built in the 1640s and designed by Hans Jakob Kristler in
German/Dutch Renaissance
style. The owner, Marshal of
the Realm Jakob de la Gardie,
named the palace Jakobsdal.
It was bought in 1669 by the
Dowager Queen Hedvig
Eleonora. When she had a
grandson, Ulrik, 15 years later
she donated the palace to
him as a christening gift, and
it was renamed Ulriksdal.

Around this time the architect Tessin the Elder *(see p37)*
suggested some rebuilding
work, but only a few of his
proposals saw the light of
day. However, the stucco
work by Carlo Carove in the
southern wing can still be
seen. In the 18th century the
palace acquired its Baroque

exterior. After being a popular
place for festivities in the time
of Gustav III (1746–92), it
began to lose its glamour and
at one time was used as a
home for war invalids.

Interest in the palace was
revived under Karl XV
(1826–72), and furnishings
and handicrafts many
hundreds of years old are on
show in his rooms. The living
room of Gustav VI Adolf
(1882–1973) in the rebuilt
Knights' Hall, contains furnishings by the great architect
and designer Carl Malmsten.
The suite was a gift from the
Swedish people in 1923 to the
then Crown Prince when he
married Louise Mountbatten.
A new staircase was built at
the same time to designs
which Tessin the Elder had
suggested 250 years earlier.

The park was laid out in the
mid-17th century. It has 300-
year-old lime trees, as well as
one of Europe's most
northerly beechwoods. Carl
Milles's two sculptures of wild
boars stand by the pool in

front of the palace. A stream
is crossed by a footbridge,
which is supported by Per
Lundgren's *Moors Dragging
the Nets*. More art can be seen
in the orangery, designed by
Tessin the Elder in the 1660s
and rebuilt in 1705. It now
houses a sculpture museum.

The palace chapel, a popular
place for weddings, was designed by F W Scholander and
built in 1865 in Dutch Neo-
Renaissance style. It has some
notable medieval stained-
glass windows.

It was from Ulriksdal that
Queen Kristina's Coronation
procession departed in 1650.
Legend has it that by the time
the queen reached the city,
some of her retinue had still
not left Ulriksdal. In one of
the stables there is a replica
of Kristina's carriage. A riding
school, built in 1671, was
converted into a theatre by
Carl Hårleman and C F
Adelcrantz in the 1750s. Performances are staged in the
theatre, named Confidencen,
every summer *(see p168)*.

Sculpture on display in the 17th-century orangery at Ulriksdals Slott

Södermalm & South of Söder

THE SÖDERMALM AREA, generally known as "Söder", rises steeply from the water and is something of a city in itself with its own character, charm and dialect. The slopes are lined with old wooden cottages with an unrivalled view of Stockholm. The dramatic topography has provided some hilly parks, and allotments are scattered among the built-up areas. The area has plenty of shops, bars and restaurants and a lively nightlife, as well as the latest in modern architecture. South of Söder is Globen, a spectacular indoor arena, and Skogskyrkogården Cemetery which is on the UNESCO World Heritage list.

The towers of Mariaberget on a steep hillside close to Slussen

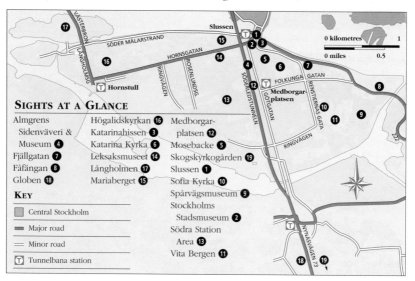

SIGHTS AT A GLANCE

Almgrens Sidenväveri & Museum **4**
Fjällgatan **7**
Fåfängan **8**
Globen **18**
Högalidskyrkan **16**
Katarinahissen **3**
Katarina Kyrka **6**
Leksaksmuseet **14**
Långholmen **17**
Mariaberget **15**
Medborgarplatsen **12**
Mosebacke **5**
Skogskyrkogården **19**
Slussen **1**
Sofia Kyrka **10**
Spårvägsmuseum **9**
Stockholms Stadsmuseum **2**
Södra Station Area **13**
Vita Bergen **11**

KEY

- Central Stockholm
- Major road
- Minor road
- T Tunnelbana station

Slussen **1**

Map 4 C4. T Slussen. 3, 43, 46, 53, 55, 59 76. Djurgårdsfärja.

STEADILY INCREASING traffic in the early 1900s turned the narrow road between Södermalm and Gamla Stan into a bottleneck. All the boats sailing between Lake Mälaren and the Baltic had to pass through the locks here, and land traffic was confined to a narrow bridge. The congestion was eased in 1928, when some of the boat traffic was transferred to a new canal, but the problem needed a more radical solution. This took the form of a clover-leaf system of roundabouts devised by Tage William-Olsson and Gösta Lundborg. It was opened in 1935 and was so well designed that it was able to cope with the change to right-hand driving in 1967.

At Slussplan, facing Södermalm and the lock that bears his name, is a bronze statue of Karl XIV on horseback by Bengt Fogelberg, unveiled in 1854 by Oscar I on the 40th anniversary of the union between Sweden and Norway (1814–1905). Around the same time, the locks were rebuilt. New machinery devised by the inventor Nils Ericsson was installed. Today the locks are used mostly by pleasure boats, whose erratic manoeuvres provide entertainment for onlookers.

Although the construction of Västerbron bridge and Söderleden road have eased the traffic burden, Slussen is still a busy junction and is in need of a thorough facelift.

The intricate traffic system at Slussen, opened in 1935

Stockholms Stadsmuseum ❷

Ryssgården. **Map** 4 B5.
📞 508 316 00. Ⓣ Slussen. 🚌 3, 43, 46, 53, 55, 59, 76. 🕐 11am–5pm Tue–Sun (Sep–May: also 5pm–9pm Thu; Jun–Aug: also 5pm–7pm Thu).
🚻 🚫 📷 ♿ 🎁 🏪

HEMMED IN between the traffic roundabouts of Slussen and the steep hill up to Mosebacke Torg is Stockholms Stadsmuseum (City Museum). It is housed in a late 17th-century building originally designed by Tessin the Elder as Södra Stadshuset (Southern City Hall). After a fire, it was completed by Tessin the Younger in 1685. It has been used for various purposes over the centuries, including law courts and dungeons, schools and city-hall cellars, theatres and churches. It became the city museum in the 1930s.

The museum documents the history of Stockholm and its people. The city's main stages of development are described in a slideshow and a series of four permanent exhibitions. The first starts with the Stockholm Bloodbath of 1520 (see p54) and continues through the 17th century. The eventful 18th century is illustrated with exhibits that include the Lohe treasure – 20 kg (44 lb) of silver discovered in Gamla Stan in 1937. The other sections depict the industrialization in

Almgrens Sidenväveri (*silk mill*), now a museum with working 19th-century looms

the 19th century and the tremendous growth in the 20th century with the emergence of a new city centre and many new suburbs.

The library has a large archive of pictures and a reference room where visitors can find out virtually anything they want to know about Stockholm. There are also children's activities, concerts and lectures

Katarinahissen ❸

Stadsgården. **Map** 4 C5.
Ⓣ Slussen. 🚌 3, 43, 46, 53, 55, 59, 76. 🕐 7.30am–10pm Mon–Sat, 10am–10pm Sun. ♿ 🍴 ✶

KATARINAHISSEN IS THE oldest of Stockholm's "high-rise" attractions. The 38-m (125-ft) high lift was opened to the public in March 1883 and is still a prominent silhouette on the Söder skyline. The first Swedish neon sign was erected here in 1909 – a legendary advertisement for Stomatol toothpaste. Since the 1930s, the sign has been placed on a nearby rooftop.

The Stomatol sign

The original lift was driven by steam, but it switched to electricity in 1915. In the 1930s it was replaced by a new lift when the Cooperative Association (KF) built its large new office complex at Slussen. In its first year the lift was used by more than a million passengers, but its

record year was 1945, when it carried 1.8 million people between Slussen and Mosebacke Torg.

The lift is still used every year by about 500,000 passengers who can enjoy a spectacular view of the city from the top.

Almgrens Sidenvaveri & Museum ❹

Repslagargatan 15 a. **Map** 9 D2.
📞 642 56 16. Ⓣ Slussen. 🚌 59. 🕐 8 Aug–24 Jun: during guided tours and 2pm–5pm Mon–Thu, 9am–4pm Fri; 25 Jun–7 Aug: only during guided tours. 📷 during and off opening hours, call for details. 🎁 🏪 W www.kasiden.se

KARL AUGUST ALMGREN was the founder of Almgren's silk-weaving mill, now a museum, in 1833. While on a study tour to Lyon and Tours in France in 1825, Almgren learned about the punch-card system, which was one of the secrets of France's dominance of the silk business. Armed with this information, he returned to Sweden with designs for modern looms and opened his own mill. It soon became a leader in the market, which in the 1700s had seen more than 30 silk-weaving mills in Stockholm.

The Almgren family continued the business until 1974, when the mill closed. Everything was left intact, and the mill took on a new role in 1991 as a living museum. In the weaving room there is a museum shop selling textiles. The area where the old steam-driven machinery stood is now a banqueting room with well-preserved 19th-century decorations.

Katarinahissen with Stockholms Stadsmuseum in the background

Mosebacke ❺

Map 9 D2. 🇹 *Slussen, then a short walk or take the lift at Katarinahissen.* 🚌 *59, then a short walk.* ♿

BY TAKING the lift at Katarinahissen *(see p127)* from Slussen, the district of Mosebacke with its distinctive atmosphere can be reached. The area got its name from a miller and landowner, Moses Israelsson, the son-in-law of Johan Hansson Hök who managed two mills on the hilltop plateau in the 17th century.

In the mid-19th century Mosebacke became increasingly attractive to Stockholmers as a centre for entertainment. A theatre was built in 1852. However, it was destroyed by fire soon after and replaced in 1859 by a new building, Södra Teatern, designed by Johan Fredrik Åbom. The gateway leading to Mosebacke Terrass and its spectacular panoramic views of the city was added at the same time.

Södra Teatern is a classic among Stockholm's stages. Around 1900 the new auditorium was enhanced with a ceiling painting by Vicke Andrén. In the 1930s murals were added, some by Isaac Grünewald. Carl Eldh's bronze bust, *The Young Strindberg*, placed on the theatre's terrace in 1975, shows the author looking across to the city from this very terrace, recalling the character of Arvid Falk in the beginning of Strindberg's novel *The Red Room* (1879).

Nils Sjögren's *The Sisters* stands behind railings on Mosebacke Torg. Attractive

Katarina Kyrka (1695) after its extensive restoration due to a devastating fire in 1990

steps lead up to Fiskargatan. At No. 12 is an experimental fireproof-gable design, *Morning Light*, an *al secco* painting on limestone plaster.

Katarina Kyrka ❻

Högbergsgatan 13. **Map** 9 D2. 🇹 743 68 40. 🇹 *Medborgarplatsen, then 3 min walk.* 🚌 *3, 46, 53, 76.* ⏰ *Apr–Sep: 11am–5pm Mon–Fri, 10am–5pm Sat & Sun; Oct–Mar: 11am–4pm Mon–Fri, 10am–4pm Sat & Sun.* 🎫 *by appointment.* ✝ *11am Wed, 11am Sat, 11am Sun.* ♿ 🚻

THE BUILDINGS ON Katarinaberget date partly from the 18th century and surround a hilltop where various churches have been sited since the late 14th century. The earlier chapels were replaced in the 17th century by a more impressive and appropriate building, Katarina Kyrka, designed by one of the era's greatest architects, Jean de la Vallée (1620–96). King Karl X Gustaf was also deeply involved in the project, and he insisted that the church should have a central nave with the altar and pulpit right in the middle. The church was founded in 1656, although it was not completed until 1695. In 1723 it was badly damaged by fire, along with large parts of the surrounding built-up area, but it was restored over the next couple of decades. Major restoration was also carried out in the 20th century, and a new copper roof was added in 1988. Two years later, on the night of 16 May 1990, there was another fire and, apart from the outer walls, the church and virtually all its fittings were destroyed.

The architectural practice of Ove Hidemark was commissioned to design a new church which, as far as possible, would be a faithful reconstruction of the original. It was not just the outer shell of the building that had to undergo detailed restoration. In order to make the best use of the surviving walls it was necessary to adopt 17th-century building techniques. Experts and craftsmen managed to join heavy timbering on to the central dome in the traditional way, and the collapsed central arch was rebuilt with specially made bricks in 17th-century style.

In 1995, the church was reconsecrated, more beautiful than ever in the view of many people, with the altar sited exactly where it was originally planned.

The reconstruction cost 270 million kronor, of which 145 million kronor was covered by insurance. The remainder was raised through public donations.

Mosebacke Torg with Södra Teatern in the background

Fjällgatan ❼

PER ANDERS FOGELSTRÖM (1917–98), probably Söder's best-known author, wrote: "Fjällgatan must be the city's most beautiful street. It's an old-fashioned narrow street which runs along the hilltop with well-maintained cobble-stones ... and with street lights jutting out from the houses. Then the street opens up and gives a fantastic view of the city and the water..." This area offers an experience of the authentic Söder and its unique atmosphere.

Street light, Fjällgatan

The Heights of Söder
With its 300-year-old houses and terraced gardens, the Söder hilltop stands like a giant stage-set behind Stadsgården harbour.

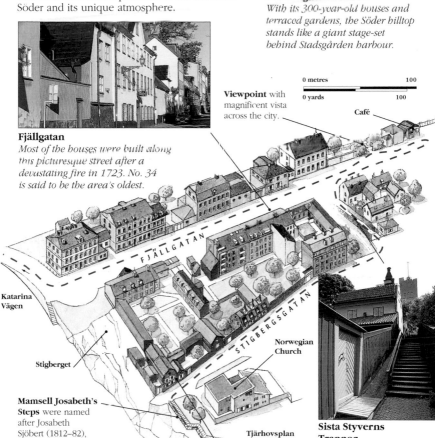

Fjällgatan
Most of the houses were built along this picturesque street after a devastating fire in 1723. No. 34 is said to be the area's oldest.

Viewpoint with magnificent vista across the city.

| 0 metres | 100 |
| 0 yards | 100 |

Café

Katarina Vägen

Stigberget

Norwegian Church

Mamsell Josabeth's Steps were named after Josabeth Sjöbert (1812–82), a local painter.

Tjärhovsplan

Sista Styverns Trappor
This alley of steps was once known as Mikaelsgränd after a 17th-century executioner. Later it was named after the inn on the harbour, Sista Styvern ("The Last Penny").

Söder Cottages
Typical well-preserved cottages can be found along Stigbergsgatan. One of them is No. 17, the house of the blockmaker Olof Krok during the 1730s.

KEY

‒ ‒ ‒ Suggested route

Fåfängan ❽

Map 6 A5. 🚃 *53.* 🚇 ⚓

FÅFÄNGAN, at Södermalm's
most easterly point, pro-
vides a grandstand view of
the boats sailing in and out
of Stockholm's harbour. In the
1650s, Field Marshal Erik
Dahlberg made full use of its
strategic location on a hilltop
to build a defensive fortress.
Some relics of this period
can still be seen.

The hill and its park were
given the name Fåfängan in
the 1770s. The wholesale
merchant Fredrik Lundin
owned the area at that time,
and he built a pavilion which
still stands on the hilltop in a
square garden filled with
flowerbeds. The word
"Fåfängan" ("Vanity") originally denoted an area of land
which was not worth using.
But in Stockholm it has a
special meaning: "The
pavilion on the hilltop with a
marvellous view." It is a
delightful place for a coffee
break while exploring Söder.

Spårvägsmuseet ❾

Tegelviksgatan 22. **Map** 9 F3.
📞 *559 031 80.* 🚃 *46, 55, 66.*
🕐 *10am–5pm Mon–Fri, 11am–4pm
Sat & Sun.* 📷 *by appt.* 🏛 ♿ ⬛ 🚇
📶 *www.sparvagsmuseet.sl.se*

THE TRAM MUSEUM, Spårvägsmuseet, covers the
development of the
Stockholm public transport
system, SL, from the horse-
drawn buses of the 19th
century to the high-tech
underground trains of today.
Visitors can try out old and
new trams and buses for

**Horse-drawn tram from the 1890s on
display in Spårvägsmuseet**

Sofia Kyrka and Vita Bergen park with its 18th-century cottages

comfort and can experience a
driver's-eye view of the city
traffic on film.

The museum has three per-
manent exhibitions covering
5,000 sq m (53,800 sq ft). One
shows the history of public
transport with the help of
some 50 vehicles. Another
section traces technical developments from different eras.
The third section focuses on
the artistically decorated
underground stations *(see
p195)*. There is also a library
and archive. On Saturdays
and Sundays for most of the
year visitors can take two free
round trips on a vintage bus.

Sofia Kyrka ❿

Vitabergsparken. **Map** 9 F3.
📞 *641 83 01.* 🚃 *3, 46, 76.*
🕐 *9.30am–4pm Mon–Fri, noon–4pm
Sat & Sun.* ⛪ *6.30pm Thu, 11am
Sun.* 📷 *by appt.* ♿ ⬛
Concerts *3pm Sat.*

HIGH UP ON Vita Bergen,
surrounded by a leafy
green park, is Sofia Kyrka,
named after Oscar II's consort
and built in 1902–06.

The 35-year-old architect
Gustaf Hermansson, who had
already designed
several churches,
including Oscars-
kyrkan at Östermalm,
created a monumental
design with both
National Romantic and
Gothic influences and
tall spires, the highest
reaching 78 m (256 ft).

Three windows by
Olle Hjortzberg are all
that remain of the
original decorations.
The early 1950s saw

the addition of the large altar
fresco by Hilding Linnqvist
with themes from the Old and
New Testaments. The interior
acquired its present appearance as part of a major
renovation in the early 1980s
when the layout of the church
was radically altered.

Vita Bergen ⓫

Map 9 F3. 🚃 *3, 46, 55, 66, 76.*

VITA BERGEN (White Moun-
tains) is best known as a
park, largely because of
Swedish TV broadcasts from
its open-air theatre. But it is
more than just a park. Houses
for workers at Söder's
harbours and factories were
built on and around the hilltop in the 18th century. They
were simple homes, often
with a small garden and
surrounded by a fence. In
1736 the building of new
wooden houses was forbid-
den because of the fire risk,
but the slum districts were
exempted. As a result, areas
like Bergsprängargränd still
have houses which have
retained their original
character and give a good
idea of life in bygone days.

Around 1900, when Sofia
Kyrka was built, the area was
turned into a leafy hillside
park. This was complemented
to the east by an area of
allotment-garden cottages.
Towards Malmgårdsvägen is
the 300-year-old Werner
Groen Malmgård (suburban
mansion). The park has a
bronze statue, *Elsa Borg*, by
Astri Bergman Taube (1972),
wife of the great troubadour
Evert Taube *(see p57)*.

Medborgar-platsen **⑫**

Map 9 D3. **T** *Medborgarplatsen.* 59, 66.

SÖDERMALM'S NATURAL centre is Medborgarplatsen. The square had been called Södra Bantorget for more than 100 years, but in 1939 it was renamed Medborgarplatsen (Citizen's Square) on completion of Medborgarhuset. The building, designed by Martin Westerberg in Functionalist and Neo-Classical styles, contains an auditorium, gym, swimming pool and library.

On the west side of the square is Söderhallarna, a complex of restaurants, delicatessens and a cinema. In 1984 the Göta Ark offices, designed by Claes Mellin and Willy Hermansson, were added on the north-west side. Alongside the stairway to Södra Station is the Södertorn apartment block designed by the Danish architect Henning Larssen. At the entrance is *Nana's Fountain* by Niki de Saint-Phalle, who also created a large sculpture group at the Moderna Museet *(see pp80–81)*. The western corner of Medborgarhuset features a 17th-century gateway. Closer to Götgatan is Gustaf Nordahl's *The Source of Life* (1983).

Göran Strååt's sculpture *Kasper* can be seen at the 17th-century Lillienhoffska Palatset. Stefan Thorén's sculpture *Dawn* in welded iron is a dominant feature on the square outside.

Södertorn tower and Ricardo Bofill's curved building near Södra Station

Södra Station Area **⑬**

Map 8 C3. **T** *Medborgarplatsen or Mariatorget, then a short walk.* 43, 55, 66.

IN THE MID-19TH century Fatburen lake existed to the west of Medborgarplatsen. It was filled in and in the 1860s a train station called Södra Station was opened nearby. In the 1980s the track site was transformed into a new residential area with about 3,000 apartments.

The district became a test-bed for the design concepts of the 1980s shaped by architects' efforts towards Stockholm's urban renewal. The most interesting developments were the work of the Spanish architect Ricardo Bofill. He designed the tower blocks near to the station building as well as the curved residential building – the area's most impressive Neo-Classical feature – which adjoins the new Fatbur Park.

The park has an open section close to Bofill's curved building with a wooded area further away. It is crossed by a path which links Medborgarplatsen with Södermalmsallén and the rail-shuttle station. A 200-m (660-ft) long avenue with 16 sculptures cuts diagonally across the park with a fountain and pool in the middle. In the northern part of the park a flower garden has been named after the Swedish composer Johan Helmich Roman (1694–1758). The arches of Bofill's curved building shelter some interesting works of art.

Leksaksmuseet **⑭**

Mariatorget 1 C. **Map** 8 C2
C 641 61 00. **T** *Mariatorget.* 43, 55. ◯ *10am–4pm Tue–Fri. noon–4pm Sat & Sun.* 🖊 *by appt.*
🖼 🅰 🗋 🖳

TOYS WHICH have delighted children and adults alike over the past century are on show at Leksaksmuseet (the Toy Museum). The museum was opened in 1980, and the main exhibition changes continuously as new toys are added to the collection.

One floor features musical instruments, including musical boxes, barrel organs and accordions. Another floor is devoted to mechanical toys, models and dioramas. A third section has dolls, dolls' houses, wooden toys, steam engines, and several working model railways. Private collections are also on show. There is a playroom and children's theatre.

Medborgarplatsen, central Södermalm, with Lillienhoffska Palatset, once a poorhouse

Bastugatan, one of Mariaberget's well-preserved 18th-century streets

Mariaberget ⓯

Map 8 C2. Ⓣ *Mariatorget.*
🚌 *43, 55.*

A FIRE IN 1759 destroyed the old buildings of Mariaberget. The area was rebuilt according to a 1736 law forbidding the construction of wooden houses in this part of Söder. The result of this purposeful 18th-century town planning remains intact. Mariaberget's stone buildings on the slopes down towards Riddarfjärden are among Stockholm's most distinctive, and the character of the steep winding streets and alleys has been well preserved.

Towards the end of the 20th century a conservation programme was implemented to safeguard the area's cultural heritage, including the view over Riddarfjärden. Near Bastugatan an attractive promenade, Monteliusvägen, has been built along the rock's edge. A new flight of steps leads down to the Söder Mälarstrand quayside.

The author Ivar Lo-Johansson (1901–90) lived in this area for more than half a century. A small park with a bust of the artist bears his name. The 18th-century poet C M Bellman *(see p98)* was born at Mariaberget, although he is more usually associated with Haga and Djurgården.

Mariaberget presents a pleasant contrast to the busy traffic artery of Hornsgatan. When the street was widened and levelled in 1901 a number of 18th-century buildings came into view. The area now features galleries and antique shops. On the opposite side of Hornsgatan is Maria

Magdalena Kyrka on a site where there have been religious buildings since the 14th century. The predecessor of the present building was constructed in 1634. It burnt down in 1759 and was rebuilt four years later.

Högalidskyrkan ⓰

Högalids Kyrkväg. **Map** 1 C5.
📞 *616 88 00.* Ⓣ *Hornstull.*
🚌 *4, 66, 74.* ⏱ *11am–6pm Mon–Fri, 11am–2pm Sat, 10am–4pm Sun.* ⏱ *noon Wed, 11am Sun.* ♿ ⬛

T HE OCTAGONAL twin towers of Högalidskyrkan make the church easy to identify from many parts of the city. The impressive brick building in National Romantic style was completed in 1923. It was designed by Ivar Tengbom. He also put his mark on the interior decoration, which involved a number of leading artists and craftsmen.

Tengbom was enlisted to design the columbarium which was added in 1939. The most prolific artist was Gunnar Torhamn, who provided the Crucifix – the

The distinctive twin towers of Högalidskyrkan, built in 1923

largest in Scandinavia – as well as the frescoes in the baptismal chapel and the decoration of the pulpit and organ loft. Erik Jerke created the reredos in Byzantine style. In the cemetery chapel below the chancel, Einar Forseth designed an apse mosaic using the same techniques that he employed for Gyllene Salen (the Golden Room) in Stadshuset *(see p114)*.

By no means everything in the church is new. The font is from the 16th century, and the seven-stemmed candlestick on the altar dates from the 18th century.

Exercise yard in the former royal prison on Långholmen

Långholmen ⓱

Map 1 B5. Ⓣ *Hornstull, then 3 min walk.* 🚌 *66.* 🚢

B ELOW THE MAJESTIC Västerbron bridge *(see p113)* is the island of Långholmen, which is linked to Södermalm by two bridges. Långholmen is best known for the various prisons which have been located here since 1724. During the 20th century the prison here was the largest in Sweden, housing 620 inmates. When it closed in 1975, the island became a popular recreational area.

The prison buildings were demolished in 1982, but the old royal jail dating from 1835 remains. The one-time cells now form part of a hotel, as well as a prison museum. There is also a youth hostel and an excellent restaurant, as well as a small museum to the poet C M Bellman with a café in the gardens which run down towards Riddarfjärden.

Långholmen's park has an open-air theatre, and offers excellent swimming both from the beaches and the rocks.

Globen ⓲

3 km (1.9 miles) S of Stockholm.
Ⓣ *Globen.* Ⓒ *725 10 00.* ◯ *during events.* Ⓖ Ⓔ Ⓦ *www.globen.se*

IN 1989 STOCKHOLM acquired a new symbol in the shape of the indoor arena Globen. It is the world's largest spherical building and has given the southern part of the city a completely new silhouette.

Globen offers a wide programme, including 125 annual events. The ice hockey world championship in 1989 was the first major competition to be staged here. It has been followed by other world championships, including handball, boules, wrestling and indoor bandy (a type of hockey). Globen has also hosted European championships in gymnastics, athletics and volleyball and key equestrian events.

Concerts at Globen have featured international stars like Pavarotti, Sinatra, Roxette and the Rolling Stones, as well as Bruce Springsteen, who attracted a record audience of 16,357. World figures who have appeared here have included Pope John Paul II and Nelson Mandela.

Globen, designed by Berg Architects, has a circumference of 690 m (2,260 ft) and a roof height of 85 m (279 ft). The viewing screens each cover 13 sq m (140 sq ft). Globen City has sprung up around the arena with more than 150 shops, hotels and other services.

Chapel of the Holy Cross by Gunnar Asplund at Skogskyrkogården

Skogskyrko-gården ⓳

6 km (3.7 miles) S of Stockholm.
Ⓒ *508 301 00.* Ⓣ *Skogskyrko-gården.* ⓖ *5pm Mon.* Ⓖ Ⓔ

NATURE AND the splendid buildings have combined to provide a harmonious setting which has placed Skogskyrkogården Cemetery on the UNESCO World Heritage list. It is sited amid pine-woods which provide a justly sombre frame-work for the chapels and crematorium.

The winners of a competition to de-sign the cemetery in 1914 were Gunnar Asplund *(see p117)* and Sigurd Lewerentz, whose proposals were considered the most likely to safeguard the area's special character. Asplund's first significant work, Skogs-kapellet (Woodland Chapel), with its steep shingled roof,

Epitaph to Gunnar Asplund

was opened at the same time as the cemetery in 1920. This was followed five years later by Uppståndelsekapellet (Resurrection Chapel), designed by Lewerentz.

In 1940 Asplund's last great work, Skogskrematoriet (Woodland Crematorium), was opened, along with its three chapels representing Faith, Hope and the Holy Cross. They are sited along Korsets Väg. John Lundqvist's *The Resurrection* stands in the pillared hall of Heliga Korsets Kapell – the largest of the three. Adjoining the chapel is Asplund's black granite cross.

A memorial park was added in 1961 on the wooded slopes to the north-west of the chapel. The Hill of Meditation lies to the west. The chapel has been decorated by artists like Carl Milles, Sven Erixson and Gunnar Torhamn.

Skogskyrkogården is the last resting place of both the unknown and the celebrated, among whom is Greta Garbo.

The silhouette of Globen arena dominating the surrounding area

---

GRETA GARBO

The legendary Greta Garbo, one of the 20th century's out-standing film stars, was born in 1905 in a humble part of Södermalm. At the age of 17 she joined the theatre academy of Dramaten and made her film debut in *Peter the Tramp.* Her breakthrough came in 1924 in Mauritz Stiller's film of Selma Lagerlöf's book *The Atonement of Gösta Berling.* The following year she moved to Hollywood, where she soon became the reigning star. Garbo appeared in 24 films, including *Anna Karenina* (1935) and *Camille* (1936). She never married and lived a solitary life until her death in 1990. Her ashes were interred at the Skogskyrkogården Cemetery in 1999.

Garbo in *As You Desire Me* (1932)

EXCURSIONS FROM STOCKHOLM

TOCKHOLM'S STRATEGIC LOCATION *between the Baltic Sea and Lake Mälaren provides the backdrop for a range of excursions which offer an insight into Swedish life and history. To the east lies the beautiful archipelago with its 24,000 islands and skerries. To the west are the more sheltered beaches and islands of Mälaren with a cultural heritage stretching back to the time of the Vikings and before.*

The wide stretches of water to the east and west of the capital are markedly different, in terms of both their natural environment and history. The Vikings and their ancestors headed west towards the present-day Lake Mälaren for defensive reasons before the gradual rising of the land transformed what was once a Baltic inlet into a freshwater lake.

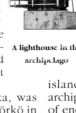

A lighthouse in the archipelago

Sweden's first town, Birka, was founded on the island of Björkö in the 8th century, but archaeological finds indicate that the area was used for trading with other countries as long as 1,500 years ago. Evidence of these early residents can be found on Björkö to this day. Along with the royal palace of Drottningholm, on nearby Lovön, Birka is included on the UNESCO World Heritage list.

Around Lake Mälaren's sheltered shores are many other majestic palaces, elegant manor houses and several small towns like Mariefred, which has retained its old-time character.

To the east of the city, the rising of the land since the Ice Age has provided a fantastic and largely untouched archipelago with over 24,000 islands, rocks and skerries. The archipelago has often been the scene of enemy attacks from the sea, so it lacks the wealth of cultural treasures that characterize Mälaren. Instead, visitors are attracted by the natural scenery. The boat trip to the leafy Fjäderholmarna islands takes less than half an hour, but a full day should be allowed for an excursion to the outer archipelago with its smooth rocks and wide bays.

Archipelago boats ready for departure from Strömkajen, outside Stockholm's Nationalmuseum

◁ **Gripsholms Slott, King Gustav Vasa's Renaissance fortress at Mariefred, founded around 1540**

Excursions around Stockholm

Stockholm is surrounded by a remarkable
natural landscape which provides an
attractive setting for excursions. Idyllic towns,
majestic castles and prehistoric settlements dot
the shores of Mälaren to the west. On the
eastern side are the islands of the archipelago
with their traditional wooden houses, and cosy
hotels and youth hostels. Annual sailing regattas
attract yachting enthusiasts from all over the
world. Everything is easily accessible by
scheduled boat services, making the journey
itself a memorable experience.

KEY

════ Motorway

████ Major road

──── Minor road

──── Railway

Drottningholms Slott on Lovön in Lake Mälaren

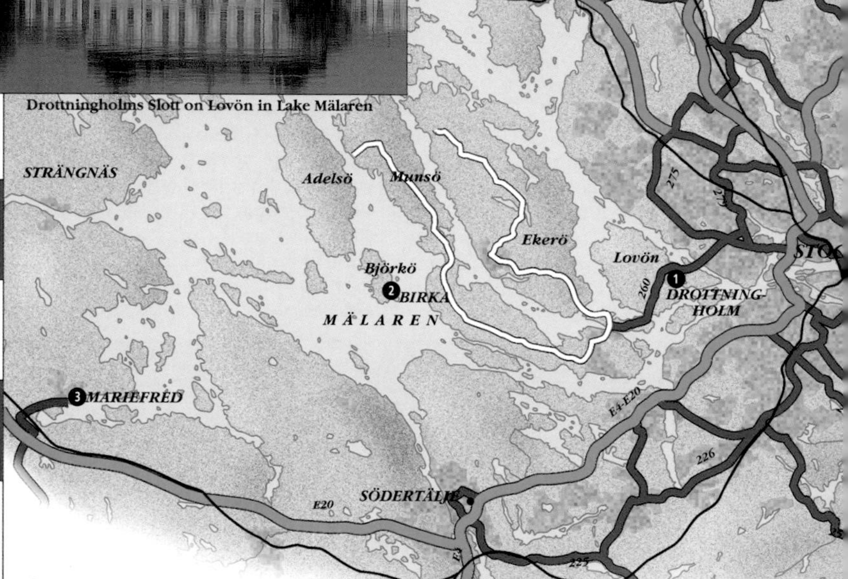

GETTING THERE

All the excursion destinations on this map
can be reached in the summer by
scheduled boat services from Stockholm's
city centre. Those on Lake Mälaren are
operated by Strömma Kanalbolaget or
Gripsholms-Mariefreds Ångf. AB. Most of
those in the archipelago are operated by
Waxholmsbolaget (see p197). Other destinations on the mainland can be reached
by car or bus, and by train to Mariefred.
See also the checklist for individual sights.

SIGHTS AT A GLANCE

Birka ❷

Drottningholm pp140–43 ❶

Finnhamn ❾

Fjäderholmarna ❻

Grinda ❽

Mariefred ❸

Millesgården ❺

Sandhamn ❿

Steninge Slott ❹

Utö ⓫

Vaxholm ❼

EXCURSIONS BY STEAMBOAT

SS *Blidösund*, one of the oldest in Stockholm's fleet of renovated steamboats still in regular service

Traditional steamboats are a picturesque feature on the waters around Stockholm. Both in the archipelago and on Lake Mälaren visitors can still enjoy the quiet, calm atmosphere of a steamboat voyage. One of the real veterans, *SS Blidösund* (1911), is operated by voluntary organizations and serves mostly the northern archipelago. Some routes, for example Stockholm–Mariefred, are operated partly or completely by steamers. Most of the other passenger boats from the early 20th century have been fitted with oil-fired engines but still provide a nostalgic journey back in time.

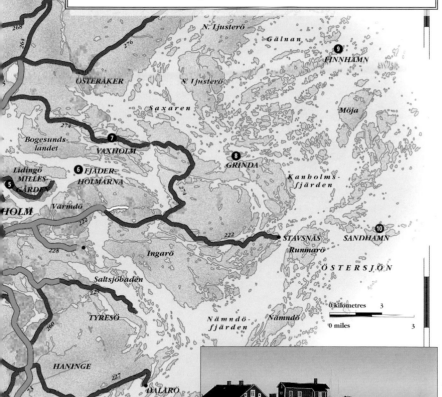

Huvudskär in Stockholm's outer archipelago

Drottningholm ❶

See pp140–43.

Birka ❷

30 km (19 miles) W of Stockholm.
🚢 May–Sep from Stadshusbron.
Birkamuseet 📞 560 514 45.
⭕ 1 May–26 Sep: 10am–5pm daily.
(15 Jun–15 Aug: 10am–7pm daily).
📷 of exhibitions and excavations.

The 16th-century Gripsholms Slott just outside Mariefred

THE FIRST TOWN in Scandinavia was called Birka, on the island of Björkö in Lake Mälaren. It was founded in the 8th century by the king of Svea who then reigned over the central parts of present-day Sweden. His royal residence was on the nearby island of Adelsö. About 100 years later a contemporary writer gave the town this description: "In Birka there are many rich merchants and an abundance of all types of goods, money and valuable items." It was not a large town. There were only about 700 inhabitants, but they included a variety of craftsmen, whose products attracted merchants from distant countries.

The town was planned on simple lines. People lived in modest houses which stood in rows overlooking the jetties where ships were moored. These vessels were used by the king's warriors, the Vikings, for their marauding expeditions. In 830 a monk named Ansgar came to

Birka crucifix

Birka, bringing the Christian faith to Sweden. In the 10th century Birka was abandoned in favour of Sigtuna, 15 km (9 miles) to the north, which is now Sweden's oldest town.

Today Björkö is a flourishing island with gardens and juniper-covered slopes. But, most importantly, it is a popular excursion destination with a fascinating museum and continuing archaeological digs. During the early 1990s these extensive excavations provided a lot of new information about Birka and the Viking era. More recently, work has continued around the old fortifications, revealing much about the town's defences and the life and work of its inhabitants. The museum shows how Birka would have looked in its heyday, along with some of the archaeological finds. Visitors can also see freshly dug artifacts while excavations are in progress.

Mariefred ❸

50 km (31 miles) W of Stockholm.
ℹ️ 0159–297 90. 🚢 summer from Stadshusbron. 🚆 from Central-stationen to Läggesta, then bus.
Gripsholms Slott ⭕ May–Aug: 10am–4pm daily; Sep: 10am–3pm Tue–Sun; Oct–Apr: noon–3pm Sat & Sun. **Grafikens Hus** ⭕ May–Aug: 11am–5pm daily; Sep–Apr: 11am–5pm Sat & Sun.

MARIEFRED should ideally be approached from the water to get the best view of the magnificent Gripsholms Slott in all its splendour. The first fortress on this site was built in the 1380s by the Lord High Chancellor, Bo Jonsson Grip, who gave the castle its name. Work on the present building, initiated by King Gustav Vasa, started in 1537 but parts have been rebuilt or added – most notably during the time of Gustav III in the late 18th century. It was during this period that the National Portrait Gallery was established. It now contains more than 4,000 portraits and covers some 500 years, from the time of Gustav Vasa to the present day. It also has a collection of notable foreign portraits which are shown in a separate section.

Gripsholms Slott's well-preserved interiors feature a wide collection of furniture, art and handicrafts. There are about 60 rooms. Highlights include Gustav III's late 18th-century theatre and the White Salon from the same era.

The town of Mariefred, in the shadow of the castle, derives its name from a late 15th-century monastery,

Iron Age burial ground at Birka on the island of Björkö in Lake Mälaren

Monasterium Pacis Mariae. It received its charter as a town in 1605, and an inn has stood on the site of the monastery since the early 17th century. The elegantly restored and rebuilt restaurant is an attraction in itself.

Visitors to Mariefred can stroll through the town and admire the 17th-century church and the

Duke Karl's bedchamber, Gripsholms Slott

18th-century Rådhus (law courts' building) with the Tourist Information Office. There is a number of specialist shops, galleries and an excellent antiques shop.

Children between 2 and 10 will enjoy old-fashioned go-carting at Lådbilslandet, while the vintage railway attracts visitors of all ages. Those interested in art should head for Grafikens Hus (House of Graphics) on a hill leading up to the former royal farm, where stables and haylofts have been converted into an exhibition area.

The excursion can be made into a varied round trip. From Stockholm to Mariefred one can travel on Sweden's oldest steamboat service, dating from 1832. The steamboat *Mariefred*, which has operated on the route since 1903, travels at 6–7 knots and the journey takes about three and a half hours. Beautiful scenery and

a lunch of classic "steamboat beef" is on offer along the way. For the return, a vintage steam railway runs from Mariefred to Läggesta (a 20-minute journey) from where there is an express train to Stockholm (30 minutes).

Steninge Slott ❹

40 km (25 miles) N of Stockholm.
📞 592 595 00. 🚌 *summer from Stadshusbron to Rosersberg and connecting bus.* **Cultural Centre** ⬜
10am–5pm Mon–Sat, 11am–5pm Sun.
Palace ⬜ *11am–2pm Sat,*
11am–3pm Sun; 10 Jun–20 Aug:
11am–4pm Mon–Fri & Sun,
11am–2pm Sat. 🎫 🏠 🍽

SOUTH-EAST OF Sigtuna, Sweden's oldest town, and only 10 minutes from Arlanda Airport is Steninge Slott, one of the gems of Lake Mälaren. The palace ranks among the finest works of Tessin the

Younger *(see p37)* and was designed a decade before he started on Stockholm's Royal Palace. The roof is that of a traditional Swedish manor house of the time, but otherwise the design is influenced by Tessin's studies, mainly in Italy and France. The result is an Italianate palace in a rural Swedish setting which Carl Gyllenstierna gave to his wife Anna Soop as a wedding gift in 1706. Since then Steninge has had several owners, the best known of whom was Count Axel von Fersen, reputed to have been the lover of the French Queen Marie Antoinette (1755–93). The park, planned by the landscape architect Johan Hårleman, has a monument of Count von Fersen.

In 1999 the estate was transformed into a cultural centre. The biggest attraction is the elegant Baroque palace. The staircase has similarities to its counterpart at the Royal Palace *(see p50)*, and elsewhere there are details which can also be seen in Tessinska Palatset *(see p48)*. The oval hall is a masterpiece of Swedish Baroque, decorated by the Italian stucco artist Giuseppe Marchi. It regained its original splendour as part of restoration work in the early 20th century, planned by the architect G Clason. At the same time Julius Kronberg contributed paintings on the door lintels and ceilings.

A 19th-century stone barn houses a gallery, glassworks, pottery, candle-making workshop, shop and restaurant.

Steninge Palace, one of the most perfect examples of late 17th-century manor house design

Drottningholm ❶

WITH ITS PALACE, THEATRE, PARK and Chinese Pavilion, the whole of Drottningholm has been included in UNESCO's World Heritage list. The royal palace on the island of Lovön emerged in its present form towards the end of the 17th century, and was one of the most lavish buildings of its era. Contemporary Italian and French architecture inspired Tessin the Elder (1615–81) in his design, which was also intended to glorify royal power. The project was completed by Tessin the Younger, while 18th-century architects like Carl Hårleman and Jean Eric Rehn put the finishing touches to the interiors. The Royal Family uses part of the palace as its private residence.

Baroque Garden
The bronze statue of Hercules *(1680s) by the Dutch Renaissance sculptor Adrian de Vries adorns the parterre in the palace's Baroque Gardens.*

The Upper South Bodyguard Room
This ante-room to the State Room, used for ceremonial occasions, was decorated with stucco works by Giovanni and Carlo Carove, and ceiling paintings by Johan Sylvius.

Apartments of the Royal Family

STAR FEATURES

★ **The Staircase**

★ **Queen Lovisa Ulrika's Library**

★ **Queen Hedvig Eleonora's State Bedroom**

Writing Table by Georg Haupt
Standing in the Queen's Room is this masterpiece (1770) commissioned by King Adolf Fredrik as a gift to Queen Lovisa Ulrika. Textiles for the walls and furnishings date from the 1970s.

★ Queen Lovisa Ulrika's Library

The Queen commissioned Jean Eric Rehn (1717–93) to decorate this splendid library which emphasizes her influence on art and science in Sweden in the 18th-century.

VISITORS' CHECKLIST

10 km (6 miles) W of Stockholm.
🚇 Brommaplan, then bus 177,
300–323. 🚢 May–Sep fr Stadshusbron. **Palace** 📞 402 62 80.
🕐 May–Aug: 10am–4:30pm
daily; Sep: noon–3:30pm daily;
Oct–Apr: noon–3:30pm Sat & Sun.
⬤ public hols. 🎫 📷 🚫 🕐
Chinese Pavilion 🕐 Apr–Oct.
🎫 📷 🚫 **Theatre Museum**
📞 759 04 06. 🕐 May–Sep.
🎫 📷 🌐 www.royalcourt.se

The Palace Church
in the northern
cupola was com-
pleted by Hårleman
in the 1720s.

Entrance

★ Queen Hedvig Eleonora's State Bedroom

Morning receptions ("levées") were held in this lavish Baroque room designed by Tessin the Elder. It took about 15 years for Sweden's foremost artists and craftsmen to decorate the room, which was completed in 1683.

★ The Staircase

Trompe l'oeil paintings by Johan Sylvius adorn the walls, giving the impression that the already spacious interior stretches further into the palace.

Exploring Drottningholm

T HE PALACE OF DROTTNINGHOLM IS complemented by the Court Theatre (Slottsteatern), the world's oldest theatre still in active use, the Theatre Museum (Teatermuseum) and the elegant Chinese Pavilion (Kina Slott). The complex is situated on the shores of Lake Mälaren, surrounded by Baroque and Rococo gardens, and lush English-style parkland. In summer there are jousting tournaments; the theatre stages opera and ballet; and the church is used for High Mass and concerts.

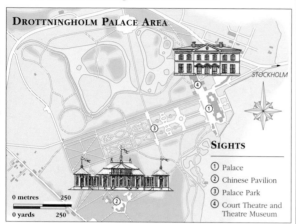

DROTTNINGHOLM PALACE AREA

STOCKHOLM

0 metres 250
0 yards 250

SIGHTS

① Palace
② Chinese Pavilion
③ Palace Park
④ Court Theatre and Theatre Museum

Karl XI's gallery at Drottningholm, featuring the victory at Lund, 1667

THE PALACE APARTMENTS

T HE FIRST THING that meets the eye on entering the apartments is a Baroque corridor with a view that frames part of the gardens in all their splendour. The central part of the palace is dominated by the staircase, crowned by a lantern with ceiling paintings by Ehrenstrahl. There are examples of Baroque stucco work by Giovanni and Carlo Carove. Marble statues of the nine muses and their protector, Apollo, are placed at the corners of the balustrades.

The Green Salon is reached from the lower vestibule via the Lower Northern Bodyguard Room. This is the beginning of the main ceremonial suite, which continues with Karl X's Gallery where paintings illustrate his major military exploit, the crossing of the ice in the Store Bælt (Great Belt) by the Swedish army in 1658.

Medallion showing life and death

Queen Hedvig Eleonora (1636–1715) held audiences in the Ehrenstrahl Salon, named after the artist whose paintings dominate the walls. More prominent guests were received in the State Bedroom which later in Queen Lovisa Ulrika's time was in fact used for sleeping. Her Meissen porcelain can be seen in the Blue Cabinet; the Library has her collection of more than 2,000 books. Behind the Upper Northern Bodyguard Room with a ceiling by Johan Sylvius is a Gustavian drawing room with a bureau by Johan Niklas Eckstein. In 1777, following Gustav III's assumption of power, the Blue Salon was decorated in the Neo-Classical style.

The Chinese Salon was used as a private bedroom by King Adolf Fredrik. It is directly above the Queen's State Bedroom and there is a hidden staircase linking the two floors. The "bureau"

opposite the tiled stove is also a sofa bed. The Oscar Room was refurbished by Oscar I (1799–1859) and is adorned by a tapestry dating from the 1630s. After the General's Room, Karl XI's Gallery commemorating the victory at Lund (1667), and the Golden Salon comes the Queen's Salon. Just as the adjoining State Room had portraits of all the European monarchs, the portraits in the Queen's Salon were of European queens. This floor finishes with the Upper South Bodyguard Room, an ante-room to the State Room and lavishly decorated by the Carove stucco artists and the ceiling painter Johan Sylvius.

THE CHINESE PAVILION

O N HER 33RD birthday in 1753 Queen Lovisa Ulrika was given a Chinese pavilion by her husband, King Adolf Fredrik. It had been manufactured in Stockholm and the previous night it was shipped to Drottningholm and assembled a few hundred metres from the palace. It had to be taken down after 10 years because rot had set in, and was

The Chinese Pavilion, an extravaganza in blue and gold

replaced by the Chinese Pavilion (Kina Slott) which is still one of the major attractions at Drottningholm. The polished-tile building was designed by D F Adelcrantz (1716–96).

At this time there was great European interest in all things Chinese. In 1733 the newly formed East India Company made its first journey to China. After Lovisa Ulrika's death in 1782 this interest waned, but it was rekindled in the 1840s. The Chinese Pavilion is a mixture of what was considered 250 years ago to be typical Chinese style along with artifacts from China and Japan. Efforts have been made to restore the interior to its original state with the help of a 1777 inventory.

Four smaller pavilions belong to the building. In the north-eastern pavilion the king had his lathe and a carpenter's bench. Alongside is the Confidencen pavilion, where meals were taken if he wished to be left undisturbed. The food was prepared in the basement, the floor opened and the dining table hauled up. The adjoining Turkish-style "watch tent" was built as a barracks for Gustav III's dragoons. It now houses a museum about the estate.

THE PALACE PARK

THE PALACE'S three gardens are each of a completely different character but still combine to provide a unified whole. The symmetrical formal garden started to take shape in 1640. The garden was designed to stimulate all senses with sights, sounds and smells. It starts by the palace terrace with its "embroidery" parterre and continues as far as the Hercules statue. The water parterre is situated on slightly higher ground and is broken up with waterfalls and topiaries. The sculptures, mainly carved by the Flemish

sculptor Adrian de Vries (1560–1626) were war trophies from Prague in 1648 and from Fredriks-borg Castle in Denmark in 1659.

The avenues of chestnut trees were laid out when the Chinese Pavilion was completed, as well as the Rococo-inspired garden area – a cross between the formal main garden and the freer composition of the English park. The English park has natural paths and a stream with small islands, along with trees and bushes at "natural" irregular intervals. Gustav III is reputed to have been responsible for its design and also planned several buildings. Not all his plans were realized, but he added four statues which he had bought during his travels in Italy.

The first 300 of a total of 846 lime trees were planted in the avenues flanking the Baroque garden as early as 1684.

Tiled stove in a cabinet in the Chinese Pavilion

THE COURT THEATRE AND THEATRE MUSEUM

THE DESIGNER of the Chinese Pavilion, Carl Fredrik Adelcrantz, was also responsible for the Drottningholm Court Theatre (Slottsteatern), which dates from 1766. The theatre was commissioned by Queen

Court Theatre stage machinery: the world's oldest still in use

The magnificent 18th-century stage in the Drottningholm Court Theatre

Lovisa Ulrika, but Adelcrantz did not have the same resources as the architects of the palace itself. This simple wooden building with a plaster façade is now the world's oldest theatre still preserved in its original condition. The interior and fittings are masterpieces of simple functionality. The pilasters, for example, are made from gypsum and the supports from papier maché. The scenery, with its wooden hand-driven machinery, is still in working order.

After Gustav III's death in 1792 the theatre fell into disuse until the 1920s, when the machinery ropes were replaced, electric lighting was installed, and the original wings were refurbished.

The scenery is adapted to 18th-century plays. It can be changed in just a few seconds with the help of up to 30 scene-shifters. The sound effects are simple but authentic: a wooden box filled with stones creates realistic thunder, a wooden cylinder covered in tent cloth produces a howling wind. Every summer there are about 30 performances, mainly opera and ballet from the 18th century. The theatre is open daily for visitors to the palace.

A Theatre Museum and shop are housed in Duke Carl's pavilion, built in the 1780s. The museum focuses on 18th-century theatre, with decoration sketches, paintings, scenery models and costumes. A *Commedia dell'arte* room contains paintings by Pehr Hilleström and sketches for Gustav III's dramatic productions by Louis Jean Desprez.

Millesgården, home of the sculptor Carl Milles in the early 20th century

Millesgården ❺

Herserudsvägen 30, Lidingö. **T** *Ropsten, then bus 203 or train to Torsvik.* **C** *446 75 90.* ○ *May–Sep: 10am–5pm daily; Oct–Apr: noon–4pm Tue–Fri, 11am–5pm Sat & Sun.* 🎨 *by appointment.* ♿ 🍴 ⬛ **W** *www.millesgarden.a.se*

CARL MILLES (1875–1955) was one of the 20th century's greatest Swedish sculptors and the best known internationally. From 1931 he lived for 20 years in the USA, where he became a prolific monumental sculptor with works like the *Meeting of the Waters* fountain in St Louis and the *Resurrection* fountain in the National Memorial Park outside Washington DC. In Stockholm visitors can see 15 of his public works, including the *Orpheus* fountain in front of Konserthuset *(see p68)*.

In 1906 Milles bought land on the island of Lidingö on which he built a house, completed in 1908. He lived here with his wife until 1931, and also after his return from the USA. In 1936 he and his wife donated the property to the Swedish people.

Millesgården covers 18,000 sq m (194,000 sq ft) in a series of terraces and includes Milles' studios with originals and replicas of his work. It has a magnificent garden – a work of art in itself – and a fine view over the water.

Fjäderholmarna ❻

6 km (4 miles) E of Stockholm. 🚌 *53.* ⛴ *May–Sep from Nybrokajen and Slussen.* **Baltic Aquarium** **C** *718 40 55.* ○ *1 May–25 Sep.* 📷 *ring to book: 715 80 65.* ⬛ 🍴

WITH THE INCLUSION of the Fjäderholmarna islands in The National City Park *(see p121)* the city's "green lung" has acquired a small part of the archipelago. The main island, Stora Fjäderholmen, is only a 25-minute boat journey from Nybrokajen or Slussen.

The island already boasted an inn in the 17th century, conveniently sited for the archipelago islanders on their way to and from the city to sell their wares. The inn was closed during World War II when the area was taken over by the military and landing was forbidden.

Access to the public was restored in the mid-1980s and the main island now has an attractive harbour, three restaurants and an ice-cream parlour. There are also three museums, two of which are devoted to traditional and recreational boating. The third covers angling in conjunction

with the Baltic Aquarium, which has some interesting displays showing where different types of fish can be found in the archipelago.

Various handicrafts are practised on the island, including metalwork, weaving, textile printing, wood-carving, pottery and glassmaking. There is also an art gallery. During the summer there are popular theatre weeks for children.

The other three islands have a rich bird-life and one of them, Libertas, has Sweden's last remaining gas-powered lighthouse.

Vaxholm Fortress, strategically sited on the approach to Vaxholm

Vaxholm ❼

25 km (16 miles) NE of Stockholm. 🎫 *541 314 80.* 🚌 *670.* ⛴ *from Strömkajen and Nybrokajen.* **Vaxholm Fortress** ○ *May–Aug: 11:45am–3:45pm daily or by booking on telephone: 541 721 57.*

THE ARCHIPELAGO'S main community, Vaxholm, has been a strategic point for shipping since the 19th century. It is easily reached by boat from Stockholm on a delightful one-hour journey through the inner archipelago.

Vaxholm has been inhabited since the 16th century. In 1548 Gustav Vasa ordered that the nearby island of Vaxholmen should be fortified. Some 300 years later a new fortress was built here, but it soon lost its military importance and was used as a civil prison. Today the imposing citadel houses an interesting military museum.

Two of Stockholm's best-known architects have left their mark on Vaxholm town. The 100-year-old law-courts' building was given its present appearance in 1925 by Cyrillus Johansson. On the headland nearest to the

The Fjäderholmarna islands, a popular summer excursion just 25 minutes by boat from the city

harbour is a rather stately hotel designed in 1899 by Erik Lallerstedt, and traces of its Jugendstil ornamentation can still be seen.

The wooden buildings around the square and along Hamngatan with their souvenir shops provide a pleasant stroll, and the harbour is always busy.

Grinda ❽

30 km (19 miles) E of Stockholm.
📞 542 490 72. 🚌 670 from Östra station to Vaxholm, then boat.
🚢 from Strömkajen and Nybrokajen.
🍴 (summer only).

Grinda is a leafy island, typical of the inner archipelago. It has some excellent beaches and rocks for swimming, as well as good fishing. Boats and bicycles can be hired, making it an ideal place to visit while exploring the archipelago. It takes about one and a half hours by boat from the city.

The architect Ernst Stenhammar, who designed the Grand Hôtel *(see p79)*, built a large Jugendstil villa here, which is now a restaurant and pub and has guest rooms. There are chalets for rental, a campsite and a youth hostel in a former military barracks.

Finnhamn ❾

40 km (25 miles) NE of Stockholm.
📞 542 462 12. 🚢 from Strömkajen and Nybrokajen. 🅿 🍴

Finnish ships used to moor at Finnhamn on their way to and from Stockholm. This attractive group of islands lies two and a half hours by boat from the city at the point where the softer scenery of the inner archipelago gives way to the harsher landscape of the outer islands. As on Grinda, the main island has a wooden villa designed by Ernst Stenhammar (1912). Today it is the largest youth hostel in the archipelago. There is a restaurant, chalets for rental and a campsite. Smaller islands nearby are accessible by rowing boat.

Sandhamn, the yachting centre in Stockholm's outer archipelago

Sandhamn ❿

50 km (31 miles) E of Stockholm.
📞 571 530 00. 🚌 433, 434 from Slussen to Stavsnäs, then boat. 🚢 from Strömkajen and Nybrokajen. 🅿 🍴

Over the past 200 years Sandhamn, on Sandön, has been a meeting point for sailors, particularly yachting enthusiasts. The Royal Swedish Yacht Club has been based at Seglarrestaurangen (Sailors' Restaurant) for more than 100 years. Every year the world's yachting elite flock to Sandhamn to take part in the Round Gotland Race.

Once a pilot station, Sandhamn is a charming village with narrow alleys and houses adorned with decorative carvings. There are now about 100 permanent residents. The Customs House, built in 1752, is a listed heritage building. A

Smooth rock formations at Utö in the southern archipelago

customs inspector who worked here, Elias Sehlstedt (1808–74), made his name as a poet and artist.

Sandhamn has shops, handicraft centres, and a swimming pool. Guided tours can be arranged. Camping is not permitted, but hotel, bed-and-breakfast and chalet accommodation is available.

Utö ⓫

50 km (31 miles) SE of Stockholm.
📞 501 574 10. 🚢 in summer, from Strömkajen. 🅿 🍴

No other island in the archipelago has as rich a history as Utö, which was inhabited before the Viking era. In the 12th century the islanders started to mine iron ore, and this activity continued until 1879. Their story is told in the Mining Museum adjoining the hotel. Today's holiday homes along Lurgatan were built as miners' cottages in the 18th century. A windmill, built in 1791, provides an unrivalled view of the island.

Utö is now one of the best seaside resorts in the Stockholm area, and is ideal for a weekend or full-day excursion. It has all the usual facilities, including a variety of restaurants. The hotel's restaurant is sited in the old mine offices.

Hotel, youth hostel, camping, chalet and bed-and-breakfast accommodation are all available. Bicycles, rowing boats and canoes can be hired, and there are also regular fishing trips and archipelago safaris.

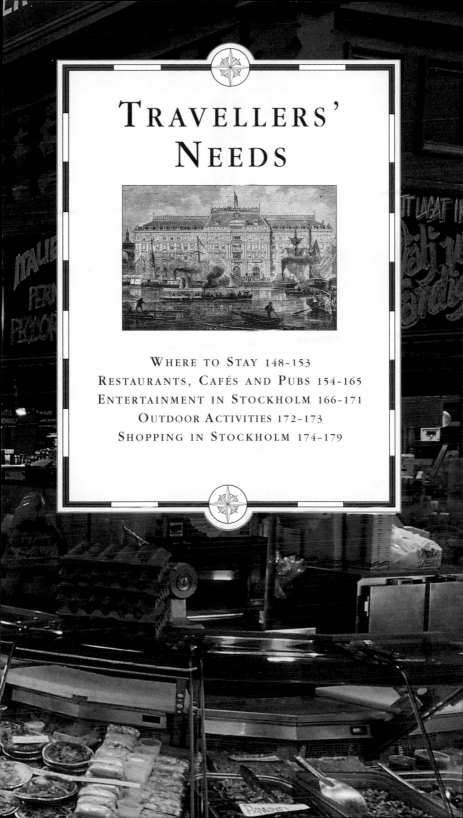

TRAVELLERS' NEEDS

WHERE TO STAY 148-153
RESTAURANTS, CAFÉS AND PUBS 154-165
ENTERTAINMENT IN STOCKHOLM 166-171
OUTDOOR ACTIVITIES 172-173
SHOPPING IN STOCKHOLM 174-179

WHERE TO STAY

Doorman

STOCKHOLM'S HOTEL SCENE could be said to revolve around Blasieholmen, where the Grand Hôtel offers accommodation which is just as princely as the Royal Palace on the opposite side of Norrström. Only a short distance away is *af Chapman*, a ship which is probably one of the world's most beautiful youth hostels. Stockholm's hotels are not usually built in the same grandiose style as their counterparts in southern Europe, but they offer a high level of comfort and service and often have magnificent views or locations.

The listings on pages 150–53 cover about 50 hotels in Stockholm and the immediate area, from budget accommodation and youth hostels to luxury hotels, with the large medium-price chain hotels in between.

Exterior of the elegant Hotell Diplomat *(see p152)*

CHOOSING A HOTEL

WHEN YOU STAY at a beautifully located classic hotel, you pay for the quality. But although most of Stockholm's hotels fall into the rather expensive category, it also has perfectly acceptable budget accommodation, maybe with a shower and toilet along the corridor.

The cheapest accommodation is offered by the dozen or so youth hostels, most of which have high standards. Other value-for-money options include the many Bed & Breakfast establishments.

Stockholm has become one of the world's most important cities for conferences, so occupancy at the city's hotels is high – around 80 per cent between May and November but much lower in July. Visitors are strongly advised to book hotel accommodation well in advance.

You should also try to avoid the peak seasons for trade fairs, or events like the Stockholm Marathon in June. The **Stockholm Information Service** (SIS) events calendar posted on the Internet (www.stockholmtown.com) is useful for finding out when the busiest periods are.

HOW TO BOOK

IF YOU DO NOT book a hotel through your travel agent, you can easily make your own reservation through SIS's **Hotellcentralen** agency, either over the counter or on the SIS/Hotellcentralen website. This user-friendly site includes a simple booking form (in English) which you complete and send back to Hotellcentralen by e-mail. The agency makes bookings for hotels in the whole of Greater Stockholm, including the archipelago and the Mälardalen area. Advance booking on the Internet and by telephone or fax is free of charge, but a small fee is charged for bookings over the counter.

Of course, reservations can also be made directly with the hotel by telephone or fax, and in most cases also on the

The lobby at the Victory Hotel in Gamla Stan *(see p150)*

Internet. Web addresses for the larger hotel chains' reservation centres are listed opposite.

HOTEL CHAINS

SEVERAL INTERNATIONAL and national hotel chains are represented in Stockholm. **Scandic Hotels**, with more than 100 hotels, is the leading Scandinavian chain and it puts emphasis on its environmentally friendly policies. It has eight hotels in the city and six outside, including two on the way to Arlanda Airport.

Radisson SAS, a chain partly owned by Scandinavian Airlines, has three large hotels in Stockholm and two at Arlanda Airport.

Choice Hotels Scandinavia has two hotels in Stockholm under the "Comfort" banner, indicating a high-standard room-and-breakfast hotel. It also has a hotel near Arlanda and three conference hotels in the "Quality" category.

The environmentally conscious Scandinavian chain **First Hotels** has three categories – First Hotel, First Express and First Resort. There are three First Hotels in the city centre and three First Express properties outside the city.

Rica City Hotels, a partner chain of Braathens and Supranational Hotels, has three centrally located hotels in Stockholm, two near Hötorget and one in Gamla Stan.

Tre Hotell i Gamla Stan is a group of three small and exclusive hotels located in the Old Town – Victory, Lord Nelson and Lady Hamilton – which all have artistic and maritime features.

◁ **Östermalmshallen houses an abundance of delicacies in a well-preserved 1880s setting**

Grand Hôtel's Bernadotte Suite *(see p151)*

PRICES AND PAYMENT

PRICES IN THE hotel listing are for the cheapest double room, including breakfast, service and VAT. All hotels offer rooms at much reduced rates at weekends year-round and daily in the summer. For the cheaper hotels this involves a price reduction of 100–300 kr per night; for the medium-priced hotels about 500 kr; and for de luxe hotels up to 1,000 kr.

Nearly all hotels accept the main credit cards. The larger hotels will also change foreign currency, but the best and cheapest way of changing money is to use one of the bureaux de change *(see p186)*.

YOUTH HOSTELS

THERE ARE 13 youth hostels in Stockholm, the four largest of which are affiliated to the **Swedish Touring Club** (STF/IYHF). Apart from the city's flagship, *af Chapman*, three more floating hostels are moored right in the city centre: *Gustav af Klint* at the Stadsgården quay, and *MS Rygerfjord* and *Den röda båten Mälaren* at Söder Mälarstrand. The ships each

Cabin at the floating youth hostel *af Chapman (see p151)*

have about 100 beds, as well as fully licensed restaurants and superb views.

The standard of Stockholm's youth hostels is generally high, especially the four affiliated to STF. Some hostels are open only in the summer.

Prices are around 200 kr per night in a double room, with a discount of about 40 kr for STF members, but come down to about 100 kr in a larger room or dormitory. Prices usually exclude breakfast and bed linen hire.

The **Hotellcentralen** agency can book youth hostel accommodation, but only over the counter and for a stay the same night. Beds can be booked directly with the hostel. A complete list of hostels is available from Hotellcentralen or on the Internet.

BED & BREAKFAST

BED & BREAKFAST accommodation is widely available in central Stockholm and the suburbs, as well as the archipelago. There is usually a choice between a single room, double room or a whole apartment. Breakfast is normally included in the price – apart from apartments, where self-catering is the rule – and bed linen and hand towels always are. B&B prices range from 300–500 kr per person per night. A double room costs 500–700 kr while an apartment, which often has to be rented for four or five days, costs from 600 kr per night.

B&B can be booked in advance through **Bed & Breakfast Service Stockholm** directly or via the Internet. A small booking fee is charged.

DIRECTORY

CENTRAL BOOKING

Hotellcentralen
(Central booking agency for hotels and youth hostels)
Centralstationen, Vasagatan.
111 20 Stockholm. **Map** 2 C5.
☎ 08-789 24 25.
FAX 08 791 86 66.
W www.stockholmtown.com
@ hotels@stoinfo.se

HOTEL CHAINS

Choice Hotels Scandinavia
☎ 020-666 000
(freephone.)
W www.choicehotels.se

First Hotels
☎ 08-458 78 60.
FAX 00 458 95 20.
W www.firsthotels.com

Radisson SAS
☎ 020-79 75 92.
FAX see individual hotel.
W www.radisson.com

Rica City Hotels
☎ 08-723 72 72.
FAX see individual hotel.
W www.rica.cityhotels.se

Scandic Hotels
☎ 08-517 517 00.
FAX 08-517 517 11.
W www.scandic-hotels.com

Tre Hotell i Gamla Stan
☎ 08-506 400 00.
FAX 08-506 400 10.
W www.victory-hotel.se

YOUTH HOSTELS

Swedish Touring Club (STF)
☎ 08-463 22 70.
FAX 08-463 21 06.
W www.meravsverige.nu
@ info@stfturist.se

BED & BREAKFAST

Bed & Breakfast Service Stockholm
Sidenvägen 17,
178 37 Ekerö.
☎ 08-660 55 65.
FAX 08-663 38 22
W www.bedbreakfast.a.se
@ info@bedbreakfast.a.se

Choosing a Hotel

THE HOTELS LISTED HERE have been selected on the basis of their price category, value for money, comfort and location. The listings start with the central areas and continue with hotels outside the city centre. Many hotels have a recommended restaurant – for a separate listing of restaurants, see pages 158–63. For map references, see pages 198–207.

	CREDIT CARDS	CHILDREN'S FACILITIES	PARKING FACILITIES	RESTAURANT	PUBLIC BAR

GAMLA STAN

FIRST HOTEL REISEN ①①①
Skeppsbron 12, 111 30 Stockholm. **Map** 4 C3. (22 32 60. FAX 20 15 59.
Old building in lovely location, with one of Stockholm's most popular piano bars. Primo Ciao Ciao restaurant serves the city's best pizzas.
▦ TV ⏲ ⚡ ⛟ ♿ **Rooms:** 144

	AE DC MC V		■	●	■

LADY HAMILTON HOTEL ①①①
Storkyrkobrinken 5, 111 28 Stockholm. **Map** 4 B3. (506 401 00. FAX 506 401 10.
Exquisite folk art and maritime antiques adorn the rooms and corridors of this delightful hotel. ▦ TV ⏲ ⚡ ⛟ **Rooms:** 34

	AE DC MC V		■	●	■

LORD NELSON HOTEL ①①①
Västerlånggatan 22, 111 29 Stockholm. **Map** 4 B3. (506 401 20. FAX 506 401 30.
Nautical antiques make this beautiful hotel a fascinating maritime museum where guests can imagine themselves as a ship's captain. ▦ TV ⚡ ⛟ **Rooms:** 31

	AE DC MC V		■		■

MÄLARDROTTNINGEN HOTEL & RESTAURANT ①①
Riddarholmen, 111 28 Stockholm. **Map** 4 A3. (24 36 00. FAX 24 36 76.
Barbara Hutton's former luxury yacht, moored at Riddarholmen, has elegant decor, well-equipped cabins and excellent restaurants. ▦ TV ⚡ ⛟ **Rooms:** 60

	AE DC MC V		■	●	■

RICA CITY HOTEL GAMLA STAN ①①①
Lilla Nygatan 25, 111 28 Stockholm. **Map** 4 B4. (723 72 50. FAX 723 72 59.
Newly renovated rooms in Gustavian style in a building dating from the 1650s. Conference facilities in the historic cellars. ▦ TV ⏲ ⚡ ⛟ **Rooms:** 51

	AE DC MC V		■		

VICTORY HOTEL ①①①①
Lilla Nygatan 5, 111 28 Stockholm. **Map** 4 B3. (506 400 00. FAX 506 400 10.
Flagship of the Tre Hotell i Gamla Stan chain with a Lord Nelson theme. An original letter written by him to Lady Hamilton is one of the many unique treasures. Includes Leijontornet Restaurant. ▦ TV ⏲ ⚡ ⛟ ▦ **Rooms:** 48

	AE DC MC V		■	●	■

CITY

BERNS' HOTEL ①①①①
Näckströmsgatan 8, 111 47 Stockholm. **Map** 3 D4. (566 322 00. FAX 566 322 01.
Exclusive small hotel in the heart of the entertainment area. Adjoins Berns Salonger, where breakfast is served. Free entry to the Grand Hôtel fitness centre. ▦ TV ⏲ ⚡ ♿ **Rooms:** 65

	AE DC MC V		■	●	■

CASTLE HOTEL ①①①
Riddargatan 14, 114 35 Stockholm. **Map** 3 E4. (679 57 00. FAX 611 20 22.
Visiting world-famous jazz musicians stay and sometimes perform here. Decorated in 1930s' Art Deco style. ▦ TV ⚡ **Rooms:** 50

	AE DC MC V				

COMFORT HOTEL PRIZE ①①
Kungsbron 1, 111 22 Stockholm. **Map** 2 B4. (566 222 00. FAX 566 224 36.
Modern business hotel in the World Trade Centre. Breakfast not served but extra bed costs only 100 kr. ▦ TV ⚡ ⛟ ♿ **Rooms:** 162

	AE DC MC V		■		■

FIRST HOTEL CRYSTAL PLAZA ①①①
Birger Jarlsgatan 35, 111 45 Stockholm. **Map** 3 D3. (406 88 00. FAX 24 15 11.
Newly renovated rooms in an 1895 building close to Stureplan (see pp70–71). Restaurant Glas serves Swedish/French/Italian cuisine.
▦ TV ⏲ ⚡ ⛟ ▦ **Rooms:** 99

	AE DC MC V	●	■	●	■

LYDMAR HOTEL ①①①
Sturegatan 10, 114 36 Stockholm. **Map** 3 D3. (566 113 00. FAX 566 113 01.
New hotel with the accent on quality, both in the rooms adorned with antiques and modern art and in the two restaurants. Regular jazz evenings and art exhibitions are staged. ▦ TV ⏲ ⚡ ⛟ ♿ **Rooms:** 56

	AE DC MC V			●	■

Price categories apply to a double room per night including breakfast unless otherwise stated and VAT.

🛏 Youth hostel *(see pp148–9)*
Ⓚ under 700 kr
⒦Ⓚ 700–1,400 kr
⒦ⓀⓀ 1,400–2,100 kr
ⓀⓀⓀⓀ over 2,100 kr

CHILDREN'S FACILITIES
Cots and highchairs are available and some hotels will also provide a baby-sitting service.

PARKING FACILITIES
Parking provided by the hotel in either a private car park or a private garage nearby.

RESTAURANT
The hotel has a restaurant for residents which also welcome non-residents – usually only open for evening meals

PUBLIC BAR
The hotel has a bar that is open to non-residents as well as those staying in the hotel.

	CREDIT CARDS	CHILDREN'S FACILITIES	PARKING FACILITIES	RESTAURANT	PUBLIC BAR
PROVOBIS SERGEL PLAZA HOTEL ⓀⓀⓀⓀ Brunkebergstorg 9, 103 27 Stockholm. **Map** 4 A1. 📞 22 66 00. FAX 21 50 70. "Hotel of the Year" four times since its opening in 1984. Full range of services for both tourists and business travellers 🛏 📺 🍸 ⤢ 🔒 📶 ♨ ♿ *Rooms:* 405	AE DC MC V		■	●	■
RADISSON SAS ROYAL VIKING HOTEL ⓀⓀⓀⓀ Vasagatan 1, 101 24 Stockholm. **Map** 2 C5. 📞 14 10 00. FAX 411 86 92. One of Stockholm's top hotels with the excellent Stockholm Fisk Restaurant and the exciting Sky Bar. 🛏 📺 🍸 ⤢ 🔒 📶 ♨ ♿ *Rooms:* 351	AE DC MC V	●	■	●	■
RICA CITY HOTEL KUNGSGATAN ⓀⓀ Kungsgatan 47, 111 56 Stockholm. **Map** 2 C4. 📞 723 72 20. FAX 723 72 99. Views of Hötorget *(see p68)* and modern, well-equipped rooms. Located on the upper storeys of the PUB store. 🛏 📺 🍸 ⤢ 🔒 ♿ *Rooms:* 270	AE DC MC V	■		●	
RICA CITY HOTEL STOCKHOLM ⓀⓀ Slöjdgatan 7, 111 81 Stockholm. **Map** 2 C4. 📞 723 72 72. FAX 723 72 09. Large hotel with buffet breakfast in beautiful winter garden, lunch restaurant with traditional Swedish food. Good conference facilities. 🛏 📺 ⤢ 🔒 ♿ *Rooms:* 292	AE DC MC V		■	●	
SCANDIC HOTEL ANGLAIS ⓀⓀⓀ Humlegårdsgatan 23, 102 44 Stockholm. **Map** 3 D3. 📞 517 340 00. FAX 517 340 11. Offers a relaxing stay right in the heart of the city with Sturetorget lunch restaurant. Discount for guests in nearby Sturebadet *(see p71)*. Piano bar with an international atmosphere. 🛏 📺 🍸 ⤢ 🔒 *Rooms:* 212	AE DC MC V	●		●	■
SCANDIC HOTEL CONTINENTAL ⓀⓀⓀ Klara Vattugränd 4, 101 22 Stockholm. **Map** 2 C4. 📞 517 342 00. FAX 517 342 11. Modern and well-equipped hotel with popular Niki Restaurant and bar in pleasant bistro style. Extensive conference facilities. 🛏 📺 🍸 ⤢ 🔒 ♿ *Rooms:* 268	AE DC MC V	●		●	■
SHERATON STOCKHOLM HOTEL & TOWERS ⓀⓀⓀⓀ Tegelbacken 6, 101 23 Stockholm. **Map** 4 A1. 📞 412 34 00. FAX 412 34 09. Newly renovated large international de-luxe hotel with central location. Piano bar and two restaurants – the American-style Liberty Kitchen and the pleasant Bavarian-style Die Ecke. 🛏 📺 🍸 ⤢ 🔒 📶 ♿ *Rooms:* 459	AE DC MC V		■	●	■

BLASIEHOLMEN & SKEPPSHOLMEN

	CREDIT CARDS	CHILDREN'S FACILITIES	PARKING FACILITIES	RESTAURANT	PUBLIC BAR
AF CHAPMAN & SKEPPSHOLMEN (STF/IYHF) 🛏 Västra Brobänken, 111 49 Stockholm. **Map** 5 D3. 📞 463 22 66. FAX 611 71 55. The world's most beautiful youth hostel, with beds on board the classic ship *(see p79)* or in Hantverkshuset. 210 kr/person in 2-bedded room. ⤢ *Beds:* 290	AE MC V		■	●	
GRAND HÔTEL STOCKHOLM ⓀⓀⓀⓀ Södra Blasieholmshamnen, 103 27 Stockholm. **Map** 4 C1. 📞 679 35 00. FAX 611 86 86. The Grand *(see p79)* is one of the world's great hotels, with a magnificent location. The Cadier Bar and Franska Matsalen Restaurant are unrivalled in Sweden. 🛏 📺 🍸 ⤢ 🔒 📶 *Rooms:* 307	AE DC MC V	●	■	●	■
RADISSON SAS STRAND HOTEL ⓀⓀⓀⓀ Nybrokajen 9, 103 27 Stockholm. **Map** 5 D1. 📞 506 64 000. FAX 506 64 001. First-class hotel with view over Nybroviken from the Piazza Restaurant and Meeting Point bar. Sauna and fitness club in the tower. 🛏 📺 🍸 ⤢ 🔒 📶 ♿ *Rooms:* 148	AE DC MC V		■	●	

DJURGÅRDEN

	CREDIT CARDS	CHILDREN'S FACILITIES	PARKING FACILITIES	RESTAURANT	PUBLIC BAR
SCANDIC HOTEL HASSELBACKEN ⓀⓀⓀ Hazeliusbacken 20, 100 55 Stockholm. **Map** D3. 📞 517 343 00. FAX 663 84 10. Beautifully restored hotel adjoining Skansen, dating from 1765. Excellent restaurant, terrace grill and summerhouse bar. Extensive conference and banqueting facilities. 🛏 📺 🍸 ⤢ 🔒 ♿ *Rooms:* 112	AE DC MC V	●	■	●	■

For key to symbols see back flap

Price categories apply to a double room per night including breakfast unless otherwise stated and VAT.

🛏 Youth hostel *(see pp148–9)*
Ⓚ under 700 kr
⒦Ⓚ 700–1,400 kr
⒦ⓀⓀ 1,400–2,100 kr
Ⓚ⒦ⓀⓀ over 2,100 kr

CHILDREN'S FACILITIES
Cots and highchairs are available and some hotels will also provide a baby-sitting service.

PARKING FACILITIES
Parking provided by the hotel in either a private car park or a private garage nearby.

RESTAURANT
The hotel has a restaurant for residents which also welcome non-residents – usually only open for evening meals.

PUBLIC BAR
The hotel has a bar that is open to non-residents as well as those staying in the hotel.

ÖSTERMALM & GÄRDET

	Credit Cards	Children's Facilities	Parking Facilities	Restaurant	Public Bar
COMFORT HOME HOTEL TAPTO ⒦Ⓚ Jungfrugatan 57, 115 31 Stockholm. **Map** 3 F2. 📞 664 50 00. ⒻⒶⓍ 664 07 00. Homely hotel with name inspired by nearby military academy – "tattoo", the signal for rest at the end of the day. 🛏 📺 📶 ♨ 🅿 ♿ *Rooms: 86*	AE DC MC V	●	■	●	■
DIPLOMAT, HOTELL ⒦ⓀⓀ Strandvägen 7C, 104 40 Stockholm. **Map** 3 E4. 📞 459 68 00. ⒻⒶⓍ 459 68 20. Offers Stockholm's only "tea house". Typical Swedish decor with elegant bathrooms in well-preserved Jugendstil building from 1911. 🛏 📺 📶 ♨ 🅿 *Rooms: 136*	AE DC MC V		●	■	
ESPLANADE, HOTEL ⒦ⓀⓀ Strandvägen 7A, 114 56, Stockholm. **Map** 3 E4. 📞 663 07 40. ⒻⒶⓍ 662 59 92. Majestic patrician house on fashionable Strandvägen with individually and tastefully decorated rooms in Jugendstil style. 🛏 📺 📶 ♨ *Rooms: 34*	AE DC MC V				
MORNINGTON HOTEL ⒦ⓀⓀ Nybrogatan 53, 102 44 Stockholm. **Map** 3 E3. 📞 663 12 40. ⒻⒶⓍ 662 21 79. Tartan-clad staff and decor from the theatre world in this pleasant hotel with British atmosphere. Near Östermalmshallen *(see p71)*. 🛏 📺 ♨ ♿ *Rooms: 141*	AE DC MC V		●	■	
PÄRLAN HOTELL ⒦Ⓚ Skeppargatan 27, 114 52 Stockholm. **Map** 3 E4. 📞 663 50 70. ⒻⒶⓍ 667 71 45. Very popular hotel in a large patrician building with high ceilings, tiled stoves and oriel windows. 🛏 📺 ♨ *Rooms: 9*	AE DC MC V				
SCANDIC HOTEL PARK ⒦ⓀⓀ Karlavägen 43, 102 46 Stockholm. **Map** 3 E3. 📞 517 348 00. ⒻⒶⓍ 517 348 11. Just by Humlegården with high service standards and Jacuzzis in all eight suites. Piano bar and outdoor café in summer. 🛏 📺 📶 ♨ 🅿 ♿ *Rooms: 198*	AE DC MC V	●	■	●	■
VILLA KÄLLHAGEN ⒦ⓀⓀ Djurgårdsbrunnsvägen 10, 115 27 Stockholm. **Map** 6 B2. 📞 665 03 00. ⒻⒶⓍ 665 03 99. Elegant establishment with outstanding location on Djurgårdsbrunnsviken Bay. Top-class restaurant and garden café. 🛏 📺 📶 ♨ 🅿 *Rooms: 20*	AE DC MC V	●	■	●	■

KUNGSHOLMEN & VASASTAN

	Credit Cards	Children's Facilities	Parking Facilities	Restaurant	Public Bar
AUGUST STRINDBERG, HOTEL ⒦Ⓚ Tegnérgatan 38, 113 59 Stockholm. **Map** 2 C3. 📞 32 50 06. ⒻⒶⓍ 20 90 85. Newly renovated small hotel with own inner courtyard in a quiet location. Shower and toilet along corridor for cheaper rooms. 📺 *Rooms: 21*	MC V				
BIRGER JARL, HOTEL ⒦ⓀⓀ Tulegatan 8, 104 32 Stockholm. **Map** 2 C3. 📞 674 10 00. ⒻⒶⓍ 673 73 66. Swedish designers and artists have given the hotel a new nature-inspired look, but room No. 247 has been preserved in 1970s' style. 🛏 📺 📶 ♨ 🅿 🍴 *Rooms: 230*	AE DC MC V		●	■	
CLAS PÅ HÖRNET, VÄRDSHUSET ⒦Ⓚ Surbrunnsgatan 20, 113 48 Stockholm. **Map** 2 C2. 📞 16 51 30. ⒻⒶⓍ 612 53 15. Authentic 18th-century atmosphere in rooms dedicated to various Swedish celebrities. Excellent Swedish food in the restaurant. 🛏 📺 📶 ♨ 🅿 ♿ *Rooms: 10*	AE DC MC V	■		●	■
FIRST HOTEL AMARANTEN ⒦ⓀⓀ Kungsholmsgatan 31, 104 20 Stockholm. **Map** 2 A4. 📞 654 10 60. ⒻⒶⓍ 652 62 48. Excellent hotel with several bars and restaurants; claims to serve Sweden's best hotel breakfast. 🛏 📺 📶 ♨ 🅿 🍴 ♿ *Rooms: 423*	AE DC MC V	●	■	●	■
PALACE HOTEL, BEST WESTERN ⒦ⓀⓀ S:t Eriksgatan 115, 100 31 Stockholm. **Map** 2 A1. 📞 566 217 00. ⒻⒶⓍ 566 217 01. Comfortable hotel, particularly for families with children. Bishop's Arms pub at street level serves beer and whisky. 🛏 📺 📶 🅿 🍴 *Rooms: 216*	AE DC MC V	●	■	●	■

SANDSTRÖM, HOTEL　　⑯　　MC V
S:t Eriksgatan 75, 113 32 Stockholm. **Map** 1 C1. ☎ 30 83 32. FAX 30 74 76.
Small and friendly hotel with inexpensive accommodation in a good location
near Odenplan. 🚇 TV **Rooms:** 8

TEGNÉRLUNDEN, HOTEL　　⑯⑯　　AE DC MC V
Tegnérlunden 8, 113 59 Stockholm. **Map** 2 B3. ☎ 54 54 55 50. FAX 54 54 55 51.
Hotel with a family atmosphere in a quiet location near August Strindberg's
residence and museum on Drottninggatan (*see p69*). 🚇 TV 🍽 **Rooms:** 103

SÖDERMALM

COLUMBUS HOTELL　　⑯⑯　⌇　　AE MC V
Tjärhovsgatan 11, 116 21 Stockholm. **Map** 9 E3. ☎ 644 17 17. FAX 702 07 64.
Located in listed former barracks on the heights of Söder, with buffet breakfast in
the courtyard in the summer; bar open in the evening. 🚇 TV 🍽 **Rooms:** 38
Also youth hostel open daily all year (price: about 200 kr/night). **Beds:** 100

ERSTA KONFERENS & HOTELL　　⑯⑯　　AE DC MC V
Erstagatan 1 K, 116 91 Stockholm. **Map** 9 F2. ☎ 714 63 41. FAX 714 63 51.
Large and busy complex in an historic setting with hotel, conference facilities,
café, restaurant, bookshop, museum and church, all with a fantastic view of Stockholm. Also dormitory accommodation with 18 beds. 🚇 TV 🍽 🛁 ⓰ **Rooms:** 16

LÅNGHOLMEN HOTELL & VANDRARHEM (STF/IYHF)　　⑯⑯　⌇　　AE DC MC V
Kronohäktet, Långholmen, 102 72 Stockholm. **Map** 1 B5. ☎ 668 05 00. FAX 720 85 75.
This former prison offers accommodation in modernized cells on a leafy island in
the city centre. Excellent restaurant and wine cellars. 🚇 TV 🍽 🛁 ⓰ **Rooms:** 101
From 19 June to 9 August also youth hostel for about 195 kr/night. **Beds:** 125

SCANDIC HOTEL SLUSSEN　　⑯⑯⑯⑯　　AF DC MC V
Guldgränd 8, 104 65 Stockholm. **Map** 9 D2. ☎ 517 353 00. FAX 517 353 11.
Well-equipped modern hotel with several restaurants and bars, extensive
conference facilities and fitness and beauty centres. Magnificent view across
Riddarfjärden and Gamla Stan. 🚇 TV 🍸 🍽 🛁 ⓰ 🛎 **Rooms:** 292

TRE SMÅ RUM HOTEL　　⑯　　AE MC V
Högbergsgatan 81, 118 54 Stockholm. **Map** 8 C3. ☎ 641 23 71. FAX 642 88 08.
Prepare your own breakfast in this inexpensive but personal and modern
small hotel. 🚇 TV 🍽 🛁 **Rooms:** 7

ZINKENSDAMM VANDRARHEM (STF/IYHF).　　⌇　　AE DC MC V
Zinkens Väg 20, 117 41 Stockholm. **Map** 8 A3. ☎ 616 81 00. FAX 616 81 20.
Stockholm's largest youth hostel with an international clientele and a quiet
location in the Tantolunden park area. Bistro/pub. TV 🛁 ⓰ **Beds:** 466

FURTHER AFIELD

FIRST HOTEL ROYAL STAR　　⑯⑯　　AE DC MC V
Mässvägen, 125 30 Älvsjö. ☎ 99 02 20. FAX 99 39 09.
Personal business and conference hotel, close to the Stockholm International Fairs
exhibition centre; 10 min from City by shuttle train. 🚇 TV 🍸 🍽 🛁 ⓰ **Rooms:** 103

GOOD MORNING HOTELS STOCKHOLM-SYD.　　⑯　　AE DC MC V
Västertorpsvägen 131, 129 53 Hägersten. ☎ 55 63 23 30. FAX 97 64 27.
Located on the southern approach to Stockholm near IKEA. High standards
and reasonable prices. 🚇 TV 🍽 🛁 🍴 ⓰ **Rooms:** 190

HOTEL FLICKORNA TROBERG　　⑯⑯　　AE DC MC V
Stockholmsvägen 70, 181 42 Lidingö. ☎ 767 91 20. FAX 636 99 80.
Three sisters run this pleasant hotel in a quiet area, about 15 min by car from
the city centre. Squash court in the hotel and other sporting facilities nearby.
🚇 TV 🍸 🍽 🛁 🍴 ⓰ **Rooms:** 29

QUALITY HOTEL GLOBE　　⑯⑯　　AE DC MC V
Arenaslingan 7, 121 26 Stockholm-Globen. ☎ 686. FAX 686 63 01.
Well-equipped large hotel near the Globe Arena, with ladies-only rooms and
facilities for conferences and special events. 🚇 TV 🍽 🛁 🍴 ⓰ **Rooms:** 287

QUALITY HOTEL PRINCE PHILIP　　⑯⑯　　AE DC MC V
Oxholmsgränd 2, 127 24 Skärholmen. ☎ 680 25 00. FAX 680 25 25.
Well-equipped modern hotel, 10-min walk from IKEA, 15 min by car from the
city or 20 min by Tunnelbana. Floodlit jogging track, free golf course and
lavish buffet breakfast. 🚇 TV 🍸 🍽 🛁 🍴 ⓰ **Rooms:** 201

For key to symbols see back flap

RESTAURANTS, CAFÉS AND PUBS

STOCKHOLM HAS BECOME one of Europe's liveliest and most varied cities for eating out. Swedish cuisine has won many international awards in recent years, and seven of the country's restaurants have been awarded Michelin stars. Many of the best restaurants are relatively small and informal as a number of top chefs have opened their own establishments. Various ethnic styles of cooking are often combined to

Swedish hot dog

create innovative and delicious dishes in what is called "cross-over" cuisine. Traditional Swedish dishes are frequently served at lunchtime and are excellent value for money. If you want to eat inexpensively in the evening there are plenty of fast-food outlets, pubs, Chinese restaurants, pizzerias and kebab houses. Hot-dog kiosks, providing filling snacks, can be found dotted all over the city.

WHERE TO EAT

THERE IS A WIDE choice of restaurants all over the capital, not just in the city centre or the busiest shopping streets. Restaurants and cafés can also be found in the larger department stores and shopping malls, as well as at most museums. Hot meals can be had on many of the archipelago ferries, and several of the boats offering sightseeing tours also include dinner *(see p197)*.

The market halls at Östermalmstorg, Hötorget and Medborgarplatsen have some excellent restaurants and cafés but they are not open in the evening for dinner.

Sandwiches with a variety of fillings can be bought at cafés and cake shops, which often serve inexpensive hot dishes at lunchtime as well.

Outdoor cafés spring up in the summer on many streets and squares, and also in green areas like Djurgården and Hagaparken *(see p122)*.

TYPES OF RESTAURANT

FASHIONABLE restaurants usually attract a young clientele, and the most trendy places sometimes have a rather stark decor and extremely high noise levels. If you are looking for somewhere quieter which also has good service, it is often best to choose an established restaurant. There are many specialist restaurants serving cuisine from abroad, or "cross-over" cooking, which is a combination of styles.

Inn sign, Gamla Stan

Most restaurants charge roughly the same prices, regardless of quality. If you are looking for somewhere cheaper to eat, there are plenty of pizzerias, pubs, kebab houses, hamburger joints or cafés to choose from.

Those with a sweet tooth will be well-catered for in

Stockholm's many modern cafés or traditional cake shops which offer delicious Danish pastries, cinnamon buns, cakes and gateaux.

Stockholm has few bars as such and the best can be found at the most popular restaurants *(see pp158–63 and pp170–71)*.

Dress is usually informal, even at the more elegant restaurants, although shorts are not acceptable. Men are not normally required to wear a tie.

Larger restaurants often have a no-smoking section, although only a very few have a complete ban on smoking.

OPENING TIMES

MOST RESTAURANTS open for lunch at 11.30am and close at around 10pm. Dinner is served from 6pm or even earlier. A number of restaurants are closed on Sundays or Mondays. Smaller restaurants may close for their annual holiday during July.

Prices for lunch are often extremely reasonable, even at the more elegant establishments, so lunchtime can be spent enjoying an inexpensive meal at a pleasant restaurant. *Dagens lunch* (Lunch of the Day) is generally not served after 2pm, even if the restaurant is open in the afternoon.

A number of restaurants and pubs serve food right up to midnight or even later, particularly those which have

Magnificent interior of Café Opera, next to Operakällaren *(see p160)*

Outdoor café in Riddarhustorget in Gamla Stan

entertainment, music or a disco. Anyone still hungry during the night can find 24-hour hot-dog kiosks.

VEGETARIAN FOOD

INTEREST IN vegetarian food is increasing in Sweden, and this is reflected by the fact that excellent vegetarian cuisine now is served at most Stockholm restaurants. There are also several completely vegetarian restaurants.

BOOKING A TABLE

RESERVATIONS should be made for evening meals, but many restaurants do not accept bookings for lunch. If you want to be sure of a table at midday, it is best to arrive at the restaurant before 11.30am or after 1pm, by which time most of the lunchtime clientele will have left.

CHILDREN

ALL CHILDREN ARE welcome in restaurants without exception. They will usually be offered a special children's menu, or half portions from the normal menu. Highchairs are generally available.

PRICES

PRICES OF MEALS at Stockholm restaurants are very similar. At most places hot dishes cost from about 100 kr, or 200 kr at the more expensive restaurants. Lunch prices are around 70 kr, and that often includes bread, salad, a soft drink and coffee. However, the price of beer, wine and other alcoholic drinks can vary considerably. It generally follows that the more expensive the restaurant, the higher the price of the wine. The house wine is usually the cheapest, with a bottle normally costing from 150 kr. Beer is cheaper in pubs than in restaurants. Tap water is free of charge, and Stockholm's drinking water is of excellent quality.

Tips are always included in the price, but if you want to reward good service you can round up the bill. If the restaurant has a manned cloakroom, the normal price is 10 kr per person. A number of restaurants do not allow guests to take their outdoor clothing into the dining room. Credit cards are accepted in virtually every restaurant.

READING THE MENU

DINNER AT A Stockholm restaurant usually includes a starter, hot main course and dessert. Most offer one or more fixed-price meals with a choice of two or three dishes at a lower price than the à la carte menu. It is perfectly acceptable to have just a starter or main course. At lunchtime most people order only one course. The meal is nearly always served on the plate, but the more elegant restaurants often have dessert or cheese trolleys. Many restaurants have menus in English. But if they don't, the serving staff are usually familiar with English and will be pleased to explain the menu. A number of menus have a section labelled *Husmanskost*, which features traditional dishes of Swedish "home-cooking".

Some restaurants serve a typical Swedish *smörgåsbord*, usually on Sundays. During December a *Julbord* is usually available. This is similar to the normal *smörgåsbord*, but with a lavish buffet selection of traditional seasonal dishes. You can eat as much as you like at a fixed price, but drinks are not included.

WHAT TO DRINK

WINE AND BEER are the normal accompaniments to a meal, as well as mineral water. The wine list often features wine from countries outside Europe, along with a house wine. Vintage wines are usually not available at medium-price restaurants.

Beer is graded into three classes, with class I the weakest. Many pubs and restaurants offer a wide selection, often with one or more on draught. A few smaller Swedish breweries make an excellent non-filtered beer.

Herring or "home-cooking" is usually washed down with beer, sometimes accompanied by one of the many varieties of schnapps as well.

Spirits and wines are more expensive in Swedish restaurants than in most other countries because of the high duty on alcohol and the State retail alcohol monopoly.

Café Tranan in Vasastan, one of Stockholm's many popular small restaurants (*see p163*)

What to Eat in Stockholm

Crisp-bread

Sweden can offer some unique gastronomic ingredients such as elk, reindeer, bleak roe, shellfish and local fish. Thanks to strict regulations, Sweden's food is among the purest in Europe. Salmon can be caught in the heart of the city, zander and Baltic herring are fished in the archipelago, while freshwater crayfish are plentiful in lakes and rivers in autumn. A wide variety of mushrooms grow wild all over the country, as well as lingonberries, bilberries and cloudberries.

Cheese
Swedish cheese goes well with herring, such as cheese spiced with cumin (left) or the nutty Västerbotten cheese (right).

Pickled herring, chives, red onion and sour cream.

Gubbröra: anchovy, beetroot, onion, capers, egg yolk.

Pickled herring

Herring marinated in mustard

"Jansson's Temptation" a gratin of anchovies, potatoes, sliced onion and double cream.

Böckling, smoked herring.

Bleak roe with chopped onion and sour cream.

Herring fried and pickled in vinegar and chopped onion.

SMÖRGÅSBORD
This typically Swedish buffet has a variety of dishes but always starts with a selection of herrings prepared in different ways. Cold dishes come next, then hot dishes and finally desserts. Diners help themselves and change plates between courses.

Shellfish Soup
Fresh shellfish such as oysters, mussels, lobsters, shrimps and prawns cooked in white wine, dill, parsley and tomatoes.

Gravad Lax
Salmon marinated for two days in sugar, salt and dill is served with a cold sweet and sour mustard sauce and plenty of dill.

Quiche with Salad
Many cafés serve inexpensive lunches with, for example, a quiche filled with shellfish, ham, cheese or vegetables.

PEAS WITH PORK
Traditionally served on Thursdays, this national dish is yellow pea soup accompanied by lightly salted meat or sausages and mustard. Hot punsch is served on festive occasions. It is followed by pancakes with jam.

Mustard

Hot punsch

Grilled Salmon
Sweden has a rich variety of fish from the sea and the lakes, and they are prepared in more different ways than in most countries. Salmon is served as a starter as well as a main course. It can be boiled, fried, grilled, poached and served cold, marinated, smoked or salted. Here the grilled salmon is served with a selection of lightly cooked vegetables.

Grilled Zander
Freshly caught zander from the Stockholm archipelago or Lake Mälaren is served with shrimps and grated horseradish.

Swedish Meatballs
Always part of a smörgåsbord, *meatballs are also eaten hot with mashed potato, preserved lingonberries and gherkins.*

Brisket of Beef
Boiled salted brisket of beef with root vegetables is one of the most common Swedish "home-cooked" dishes.

Reindeer Calf Fillet
Reindeer meat is very tender, lean and delicious. Here it is grilled with chanterelles, black salsify and cranberries.

Cheesecake and Cloudberries
A traditional dessert made with eggs and almonds, cheesecake is served here with cloudberries from the north or archipelago.

Rosehip Soup
This can be eaten hot or cold, served with whipped cream, vanilla ice cream or parfait and almond biscuits.

Hot Chocolate & Cinnamon Buns
A bun is popular with hot chocolate or coffee.

DRINKS
Sweden imports a huge variety of wine from all over the world, but people usually drink beer or schnapps with herrings or a *smörgåsbord*. Punsch (a sweet arak spirit) is often taken with coffee, or hot with pea soup. Swedish vodka is popular worldwide, but there are also some 60 types of local schnapps flavoured with different herbs and spices. Swedish beer is enjoying a renaissance, from freshly brewed beer to light ale. Blueberry beer is being produced at many new small breweries.

Mineral water **Non-filtered beer** **Aquavit schnapps** **Swedish punsch**

Choosing a Restaurant

THIS LISTING COVERS some 70 restaurants in all price categories selected for their good value, excellent food and/or their interesting setting. Some are located in recommended hotels. The restaurants are listed area by area, starting with the inner city. For map references, see the Street Finder map on pages 198–207. The key to the symbols is on the back flap.

	CREDIT CARDS	OPEN LUNCH TIME	OPEN LATE	FIXED-PRICE MENU	GOOD WINE LIST

GAMLA STAN

COSTAS (Kr)
Lilla Nygatan 21. **Map** 4 B4. 10 12 24.
A tiny restaurant with a mixture of Greek and Mediterranean cuisine. Inexpensive and well-prepared food.
Credit Cards: AE DC MC V · Open Lunch Time ● · Open Late ■

DEN GYLDENE FREDEN (Kr)(Kr)(Kr)
Österlånggatan 51. **Map** 4 C4. 24 97 60.
An artists' restaurant with a long tradition. Excellent Swedish/French cuisine, as well as modestly priced Swedish "home cooking".
Credit Cards: AE DC MC V · Fixed-Price Menu ● · Good Wine List ■

FEM SMÅ HUS (Kr)(Kr)(Kr)
Nygränd 10. **Map** 4 C3. 10 87 75.
Charming and cosy cellar location with many nooks and crannies and larger dining rooms. Elegant modern Swedish cuisine, professional service.
Credit Cards: AE DC MC V · Open Late ■ · Fixed-Price Menu ●

GRILL RUBY (Kr)(Kr)
Österlånggatan 14. **Map** 4 C3. 20 60 15.
Steakhouse with perfectly grilled meat and Texas-style trimmings in attractive medieval cellar vaults.
Credit Cards: AE DC MC V · Open Late ■

KAOS (Kr)(Kr)(Kr)
Stora Nygatan 21 B. **Map** 4 B3. 20 58 86.
Trendy restaurant with sober decor and cramped space between tables. Exciting "cross-over" cuisine and eccentric layout.
Credit Cards: AE DC MC V · Open Lunch Time ● · Open Late ■ · Fixed-Price Menu ●

LEIJONTORNET (Kr)(Kr)(Kr)(Kr)
Lilla Nygatan 5. **Map** 4 B3. 14 23 55.
Stylish but austere decor in a historic medieval cellar. Distinguished cuisine with many Swedish ingredients and excellent desserts. Cheap and good lunches served in the bistro or in the courtyard during the summer.
Credit Cards: AE DC MC V · Fixed-Price Menu ● · Good Wine List ■

MARKATTAN (Kr)(Kr)(Kr)
Stora Nygatan 43. **Map** 4 B4. 440 09 19.
Whitewashed cellar vaults with several charming dining rooms and a separate bar. Modern and well-presented Swedish cuisine. Attractive and quiet location with friendly staff.
Credit Cards: AE DC MC V · Open Late ■

MÅRTEN TROTZIG (Kr)(Kr)(Kr)
Västerlånggatan 79. **Map** 4 C4. 24 02 31.
Several dining rooms and a pleasant courtyard, trendy decor and high gastronomic standards. Swedish and international dishes, knowledgeable staff. "Bakficka" section with lower prices.
Credit Cards: AE DC MC V · Open Lunch Time ● · Open Late ■ · Good Wine List ■

PONTUS IN THE GREENHOUSE (Kr)(Kr)(Kr)(Kr)
Österlånggatan 17. **Map** 4 C3. 23 85 00.
One of Stockholm's virtuoso young chefs creates culinary masterpieces with prices to match. Affluent clientele and cosy location one floor up. Pleasant bistro with lower prices at street level.
Credit Cards: AE DC MC V · Open Lunch Time ● · Open Late ■ · Fixed-Price Menu ● · Good Wine List ■

PRIMO CIAO CIAO (Kr)(Kr)
Skeppsbron 12. **Map** 4 C3. 36 25 00.
Pleasant restaurant in First Hotel Reisen, with maritime-style decor, serving gourmet pizzas and more unusual Mediterranean-inspired dishes.
Credit Cards: AE DC MC V · Open Lunch Time ● · Fixed-Price Menu ●

CITY

BAKFICKAN (Kr)(Kr)
Operahuset. **Map** 4 B1. 676 58 09.
A real little pearl with many regular customers, including artists from the Opera House. Swedish "home cooking" served over the bar counter and other meals from the Operakällaren's legendary kitchen next door.
Credit Cards: AE DC MC V · Open Lunch Time ● · Open Late ■ · Good Wine List ■

Average prices for a three-course meal for one, half a bottle of house wine and unavoidable charges such as service and cover:
(K) under 300 kr.
(K)(K) 300–400 kr.
(K)(K)(K) 40–500 kr.
(K)(K)(K)(K) over 500 kr.

OPEN LUNCH TIME
These restaurants are open for lunch and usually serve inexpensive meals.

OPEN LATE
Restaurants which remain open with their full menu after 10pm.

FIXED-PRICE MENU
A fixed-price menu is available for lunch, dinner or both, usually with three courses.

GOOD WINE LIST
Restaurant has a wide choice of good wines, or a more specialized range.

	CREDIT CARDS	OPEN LUNCH TIME	OPEN LATE	FIXED-PRICE MENU	GOOD WINE LIST
BISTRO JARL (K)(K) Birger Jarlsgatan 7. **Map** 3 D4. (611 76 30. Small luxurious restaurant, a favourite spot for the hip crowd. Mediterranean, Swedish and Asian dishes. The city's only champagne bar. ⚡ Ⓥ Ⓨ	AF DC MC V	●	■		■
BLANDANNAT (K)(K) Norrlandsgatan 33. **Map** 3 D4. (22 47 00. Pleasant modern restaurant with lavish shellfish dishes. Can be cheaper if you create your own menu from the lighter options. ♿ Ⓥ Ⓨ	AE DC MC V	●	■		■
BON LLOC (K)(K)(K)(K) Regeringsgatan 111. **Map** 3 D3. (660 60 60. Food with a Spanish influence. The chef is one of the world's best – a gold-medal winner in the Bocuse d'Or competition. Pleasant, quiet setting. ♿ ⚡ ⚡ Ⓥ Ⓨ	AE DC MC V			●	■
CHIARO (K)(K)(K) Birger Jarlsgatan 24. **Map** 3 D3. (678 00 09. Sober restaurant with large bar and nightclub in the basement. Balanced mixture of "cross-over" and Swedish cuisine, stylish and well prepared. ♿ ♫ Ⓥ Ⓨ	AE DC MC V	●	■		
ETT LITET HAK (K)(K) Grev Turegatan 15. **Map** 3 E4. (660 13 09. Noisy but pleasant local restaurant with trendy Continental cuisine and friendly staff. ⚡ ⚡ Ⓥ Ⓨ	AE DC MC V	●			
FREDSGATAN 12 (K)(K)(K)(K) Fredsgatan 12. **Map** 2 C5. (24 80 52. Star chef Melker Andersson offers a gastronomic experience with his "world cooking", combining the cuisines of many countries. Austere modern decor and trendy clientele. ⚡ Ⓥ Ⓨ	AE DC MC V		■	●	■
GRAND NATIONAL (K)(K) Regeringsgatan 74. **Map** 3 D3. (566 398 00. Located in a legendary dance hall and serving well-prepared Swedish "home cooking" and other classic dishes with background jazz music. ⚡ Ⓥ Ⓨ	AE DC MC V	●	■	●	■
GREITZ (K)(K)(K) Vasagatan 50. **Map** 2 C4. (23 48 20. Pleasant bistro-style restaurant with elegant Continental cuisine and many Swedish classics. Excellent seafood specialities and a large selection of grappa, marc and cognac. ⚡ ⚡ Ⓥ Ⓨ	AE DC MC V	●	■	●	
HALV TRAPPA PLUS GÅRD (K)(K)(K) Lästmakargatan 3. **Map** 3 D4. (611 02 77. Trendy city restaurant with 1970s' decor. Unusual, quirky cuisine with some pleasant surprises. Service outdoors during the summer. ⚡ Ⓥ Ⓨ	AE DC MC V		■		
KB (K)(K)(K) Smålandsgatan 7. **Map** 3 D4. (679 60 32. Classic artists' restaurant with a lived-in atmosphere. Top-class international and Swedish cuisine, good value "home cooking" dishes and excellent lunches. Pleasant bar for cheaper eating. ♿ ⚡ ⚡ Ⓥ Ⓨ	AE DC MC V	●	■	●	■
LAROY (K)(K) Birger Jarlsgatan 20. **Map** 3 D3. (545 037 00. Popular among showbiz and sporting celebrities. The chefs do their best to impress and sometimes succeed. The best on the menu is the dessert page. Ⓥ Ⓨ	AE DC MC V		■	●	■
LYDMAR (K)(K) Sturegatan 10. **Map** 3 D3. (566 113 00. A waterhole for the trendy young and successful. Excellent modern and value-for-money food, served in three different-sized portions. Jazz in the bar, plenty of chatter in the dining room. ♿ ⚡ ♫ Ⓥ Ⓨ	AE DC MC V	●	■		

For key to symbols see back flap

Average prices for a three-course meal for one, half a bottle of house wine and unavoidable charges such as service and cover:
(K) under 300 kr.
(K)(K) 300–400 kr.
(K)(K)(K) 400–500 kr.
(K)(K)(K)(K) over 500 kr.

OPEN LUNCH TIME
These restaurants are open for lunch and usually serve inexpensive meals.

OPEN LATE
Restaurants which remain open with their full menu after 10pm.

FIXED-PRICE MENU
A fixed-price menu is available for lunch, dinner or both, usually with three courses.

GOOD WINE LIST
Restaurant has a wide choice of good wines, or a more specialized range.

		CREDIT CARDS	OPEN LUNCH TIME	OPEN LATE	FIXED-PRICE MENU	GOOD WINE LIST
NORRLAND BAR & GRILL (K)(K) Norrlandsgatan 24. **Map** 3 D4. 611 88 10. Reliable gourmet restaurant with friendly bar, elegant but austere decor and smooth service. Swedish and international cuisine.		AE DC MC V	●	■		■
OPERAKÄLLAREN (K)(K)(K)(K) Operahuset. **Map** 4 B1. 676 58 01. The capital's classic temple of gastronomy. The chefs are young and creative; the dining room with its lavish 19th-century ceiling paintings and the Jugendstil bar are attractions in themselves. Café Opera has lower prices and a famous afternoon cake buffet.		AE DC MC V	●		●	■
PA & CO (K)(K)(K) Riddargatan 8. **Map** 3 E4. 611 08 45. Popular local restaurant and a regular meeting place for celebs and advertising people. Menu on the blackboard offers Thai specialities, as well as French peasant cooking and traditional Swedish food.		AE DC MC V		■		
PRINSEN (K)(K)(K) Mäster Samuelsgatan 4. **Map** 3 D4. 611 13 31. Hundred-year-old restaurant with an extremely lively clientele and food to match. Serves both Swedish and Continental dishes.		AE DC MC V	●			
RESTAURANGEN (K)(K)(K) Oxtorgsgatan 14. **Map** 3 D4. 22 09 52. Choose five dishes at a fixed price and try various wines as well. Exciting food and stylish decor based on light woods.		AE DC MC V	●	■	●	■
ROLFS KÖK (K)(K)(K) Tegnérgatan 41. **Map** 2 C3. 10 16 96. Reliable local restaurant with trend-setting decor and excellent food, both "cross-over" and pure Swedish. Pleasant staff and a loyal clientele.		AE DC MC V	●	■		
SERWITO (K)(K) Regeringsgatan 77. **Map** 3 D3. 796 90 37. One of the better Italians with home-made pasta and varied menus including several Sicilian dishes. Peaceful, with considerate staff.		AE DC MC V	●		●	■
SOPHIES BAR (K)(K)(K) Biblioteksgatan 5. **Map** 3 D4. 611 84 08. Waterhole for the affluent beautiful people in a safari-themed setting. High-class gastronomy with everything from exquisite innovations to more classic cuisine. Professional staff and pleasant bar.		AE DC MC V	●	■		■
STUREHOF (K)(K)(K) Stureplan 2. **Map** 3 D4. 440 57 30. Classic 19th-century seafood restaurant, recently rebuilt. Café and oyster bar, elegant restaurant and outdoor café. Fish and shellfish, delicious snacks and the very best Swedish "home cooking".		AE DC MC V	●	■		■
VASSA EGGEN (K)(K)(K) Kungstensgatan 6. **Map** 2 C2. 21 61 69. Friendly restaurant with sober modern decor, young chefs and innovative international cuisine, beautifully presented. Considerate staff and a pleasant atmosphere.		AE DC MC V		■	●	

BLASIEHOLMEN & SKEPPSHOLMEN

		CREDIT CARDS	OPEN LUNCH TIME	OPEN LATE	FIXED-PRICE MENU	GOOD WINE LIST
BERNS' (K)(K)(K)(K) Berzelii Park. **Map** 3 D4. 566 322 22. Sir Terence Conran has designed this spacious, new restaurant in a building rich in tradition. The restaurant, seating 248, focuses on seafood. The Bar & Grill seats another 110.		AE DC MC V	●	■		■

FRANSKA MATSALEN ⓚⓚⓚⓚ
Grand Hôtel, Södra Blasieholmskajen 8. **Map** 4 C1. 📞 *679 35 84.*
A grandiose dining room with a view of the Royal Palace and an open kitchen
where chefs create culinary masterpieces. A Scandinavian menu is always
available. The service is perfect, as befits a temple of gastronomy. 🔽

	AE		■	●	■
	DC				·
	MC				
	V				

WEDHOLMS FISK ⓚⓚⓚⓚ
Nybrokajen 17. **Map** 4 C1. 📞 *611 78 74.*
A "must" for lovers of seafood. No concessions are made in the selection of ingre-
dients, with no deviation from the classic schools of Swedish or French cuisine.
The decor is sober, the portions are generous and the sauces are irresistible.
Value-for-money lunches and friendly, courteous staff.

	AE	●		●	■
	DC				
	MC				
	V				

DJURGÅRDEN

HASSELBACKEN, RESTAURANG ⓚⓚⓚⓚ
Hazeliusbacken 20. **Map** 6 A3. 📞 *517 343 07.*
Well-prepared traditional restaurant fare is served in a finely restored 1850s
setting. In summer there's a pleasant outdoor café.

	AE	●		●	■
	DC				
	MC				
	V				

WÄRDSHUSET ULLA WINBLAD ⓚⓚⓚ
Rosendalsvägen 8. **Map** 6 A3. 📞 *663 05 71.*
Beautifully located restaurant with olde-worlde atmosphere and well-
prepared classic cuisine, Swedish specialities and some more modern
dishes. The outdoor café is very popular in the summer.

	AE	●			■
	DC				
	MC				
	V				

ÖSTERMALM & GÄRDET

CIAO CIAO GRANDE ⓚ
Storgatan 11. **Map** 3 E4. 📞 *667 64 20.*
Small, busy Italian restaurant with superb pizzas and other Italian dishes.

	AE	●		●	
	DC				
	MC				
	V				

ERIKS BAKFICKA ⓚⓚ
Fredrikshovsgatan 4. **Map** 3 F4. 📞 *660 15 99.*
Pleasant and reliable local restaurant, with menus combining Swedish and French
cuisine. High-class ingredients are prepared with dedication and finesse. Famous
for its desserts. Champagne is served by the glass at modest prices.

	AE	●	■	●	■
	DC				
	MC				
	V				

IL CONTE ⓚⓚ
Grevgatan 9. **Map** 3 E4. 📞 *661 26 28.*
The upper crust's favourite Italian restaurant in a fine location near Strand-
vägen. Charming establishment with excellent food; superb pasta.

	AE		■		
	DC				
	MC				
	V				

LINNEGATAN 18 ⓚⓚⓚ
Linnégatan 18. **Map** 3 E3. 📞 *662 10 18.*
Large-format brasserie with a bar at street level and restaurants in the
basement or one floor up. Neat but rather sober decor with a rather high
noise level. Excellent seafood, professional and courteous young staff.

	AE		■	●	
	DC				
	MC				
	V				

PAUL & NORBERT ⓚⓚⓚⓚ
Strandvägen 9. **Map** 3 E4. 📞 *663 81 83.*
A little gastronomic jewel for gourmets. Elegant, discreet and modern decor,
superb service and excellent seasonal food.

	AE	●		●	■
	DC				
	MC				
	V				

VILLA KÄLLHAGEN ⓚⓚⓚ
Djurgårdsbrunnsvägen 10. **Map** 6 B2. 📞 *665 03 00.*
One of Stockholm's best restaurants with a beautiful waterfront location.
The cuisine is international with the accent on Swedish ingredients.
Pleasant outdoor café.

	AE	●		●	■
	DC				
	MC				
	V				

KUNGSHOLMEN

CAFÉ GÖKEN ⓚ
Pontonjärgatan 28. **Map** 1 C3. 📞 *650 68 37.*
Excellent value for money; everything from Swedish "home cooking" to
"cross-over". Cosy atmosphere, friendly service and splendid view.

	AE	●	■		
	DC				
	MC				
	V				

DUO BAR ⓚⓚ
Norra Agnegatan 39. **Map** 2 A4. 📞 *650 25 00.*
Pleasant small restaurant with exciting cocktails and a variety of snacks
which can be combined as you wish.

	AE	●	■		
	DC				
	MC				
	V				

For key to symbols see back flap

Average prices for a three-course meal for one, half a bottle of house wine and unavoidable charges such as service and cover:
- (k) under 300 kr.
- (k)(k) 300–400 kr.
- (k)(k)(k) 400–500 kr.
- (k)(k)(k)(k) over 500 kr.

OPEN LUNCH TIME
These restaurants are open for lunch and usually serve inexpensive meals.

OPEN LATE
Restaurants which remain open with their full menu after 10pm.

FIXED-PRICE MENU
A fixed-price menu is available for lunch, dinner or both, usually with three courses.

GOOD WINE LIST
Restaurant has a wide choice of good wines, or a more specialized range.

	Price	CREDIT CARDS	OPEN LUNCH TIME	OPEN LATE	FIXED-PRICE MENU	GOOD WINE LIST
KAJPLATS 9 Norr Mälarstrand. **Map** 2 A5. 652 45 45. Maritime-theme decor and fantastic view over the water. Excellent restaurant with high ceilings but little space between tables. Ambitious bourgeois cuisine and knowledgeable staff.	(k)(k)(k)	AE DC MC V	●			■
LA FAMIGLIA Alströmergatan 45 **Map** 1 B2. 650 63 10.. Popular and reliable restaurant, a favourite among children. Classic Italian cuisine, cosy atmosphere and budget prices. Excellent shellfish pasta!	(k)(k)	AE DC MC V			●	
LOKAL Scheelegatan 8. **Map** 2 A5. 650 98 09. Good local restaurant with value-for-money and well-prepared cuisine.	(k)(k)(k)	AE DC MC V				
MÄLARSTRANDSKROGEN Norr Mälarstrand 30. **Map** 2 A5. 653 47 77. An insignificant but highly popular local restaurant with classic French and Swedish cuisine at surprisingly low prices.	(k)	MC V	●			
ROSMARIN Hantverkargatan 14. **Map** 2 A5. 653 87 63. Popular restaurant, best known for its charcoal-grilled meat which is always top quality. Famous for its pork chops.	(k)	AE DC MC V	●			

VASASTAN

	Price	CREDIT CARDS	OPEN LUNCH TIME	OPEN LATE	FIXED-PRICE MENU	GOOD WINE LIST
ALEX VINBAR OCH KÖK Vegagatan 15. **Map** 2 B2. 31 64 40. Elegant and original small restaurant with bar. Superb food, from small snacks to a full-scale meal. All wines can be bought by the glass.	(k)(k)(k)	AE DC MC V		■	●	■
CLAS PÅ HÖRNET Surbrunnsgatan 20. **Map** 2 C2. 16 51 36. Old inn dating from the 18th century. Classic food lovingly prepared in a romantic setting.	(k)	AE DC MC V	●		●	■
HARD ROCK CAFÉ Sveavägen 75. **Map** 2 B2. 16 03 50. Authentic American hamburgers, large steaks and fajitas top the menu. Particularly popular among young people.	(k)(k)	AE DC MC V	●	■		
INDIA GATE CAFÉ Frejgatan 3. **Map** 2 C1. 15 20 30. This restaurant is a real find for anyone who enjoys well-prepared Indian food.	(k)	AE DC MC V	●			
PAUS BAR & KÖK Rörstrandsgatan 18. **Map** 1 C1. 34 44 05. Local restaurant popular among young people with sober decor and elegant, modern and advanced cuisine.	(k)(k)(k)	AE DC MC V		■	●	■
PUGLIESE TARANTINO Roslagsgatan 43. **Map** 2 C1. 15 00 30. Classic Italian cuisine with many tempting dishes in classy surroundings.	(k)	AE DC MC V		■		■
STORSTAD Odengatan 41. **Map** 2 C2. 673 38 00. This is where people go if they want to be seen, and the bar is usually crammed. Minimalist decor, comfortable seating, fanciful and excellent food and courteous staff.	(k)(k)	AE DC MC V		■		■

TRANAN   ⓀⓀ
Karlbergsvägen 14. **Map** 2 B2. 📞 *30 07 65.*
A popular and reliable restaurant in bistro style. International cuisine and top-class Swedish "home cooking". Lively bar on floor below. 🍴 🪑 🅥 🍷
AE · DC · MC · V

WASAHOF   ⓀⓀⓀ
Dalagatan 46. **Map** 2 B3. 📞 *32 34 40.*
Friendly brasserie-style restaurant, popular among theatre and opera folk. The speciality is seafood, but Swedish and international dishes are also on the menu. Adjoins pleasant oyster bar. 🔧 🍴 🪑 🎵 🍷
AE · DC · MC · V

NORRTULL & NORTH OF STOCKHOLM

STALLMÄSTARGÅRDEN   ⓀⓀⓀⓀ
Norrtull. 📞 *610 13 00.*
A 17th-century inn set in an idyllic location on Brunnsviken Bay. The showpiece of Swedish cuisine, with dishes from the charcoal grill and rotisserie. Pleasant outdoor café. 🔧 🍴 🪑 🅥
AE · DC · MC · V

ULRIKSDALS WÄRDSHUS   ⓀⓀⓀⓀ
Ulriksdals Slottspark. 📞 *85 08 15.*
Magnificent location and beautiful legendary inn. Elegant and top-class cuisine. Its collection of wines is the largest in the world, according to *The Guinness Book of Records*. Famous for its outstanding *smörgåsbord*. 🔧 🍴 🪑 🅥 🍷
AE · DC · MC · V

SÖDERMALM

GONDOLEN   ⓀⓀⓀⓀ
Stadsgården 6, top of Katarinahissen. **Map** 9 D2. 📞 *641 70 90.*
Top-class cuisine and location, with the city's most fantastic view. The Gondolen's adjoining Köket restaurant also serves superb food in a rustic setting at significantly lower prices. 🔧 🍴 🪑 🅥 🍷
AE · DC · MC · V

GÄSSLINGEN   ⓀⓀⓀⓀ
Brännkyrkagatan 93. **Map** 8 B2. 📞 *669 54 95.*
Unusual kitsch decor but the culinary level is sky high, with dishes like goose liver, lobster and truffles. 🍴 🅥
AE · DC · MC · V

HALFWAY INN   Ⓚ
Swedenborgsgatan 6. **Map** 8 C2. 📞 *641 94 43.*
Popular pub with unusually good food at unbeatable prices. A 50 kr brunch is served on Sundays. 🪑 🅥 🍷
AE · DC · MC · V

HOSTERIA TRE SANTI   ⓀⓀ
Blekingegatan 32. **Map** 9 D4. 📞 *644 18 16.*
Rustic Italian food and a special atmosphere, with friendly staff and a varied clientele. 🍴 🪑 🅥
AE · DC · MC · V

LO SCUDETTO   ⓀⓀ
Åsögatan 163. **Map** 9 E3. 📞 *640 42 15.*
Top-class traditional and innovative dishes, cheerful service and football pictures on the walls. 🔧 🪑 🅥
AE · MC · V

LONG HORN SMOKE HOUSE   Ⓚ
Sankt Paulsgatan 4 A. **Map** 9 D2. 📞 *702 06 82.*
A tiny establishment which serves perfectly grilled juicy steaks at unbeatable prices. 🅥 🍷
AE · DC · MC · V

MATKULTUR   ⓀⓀ
Erstagatan 21. **Map** 9 F3. 📞 *642 03 53.*
Charming restaurant run by much-travelled enthusiasts who serve food from all over the world. The cuisine is of high quality and exotic. 🪑 🎵 🅥 🍷
AE · DC · MC · V

RINGBOMS   Ⓚ
Hornsgatan 90. **Map** 8 B2. 📞 *429 92 10.*
The evening dish of "home cooking" is nearly always a pleasant surprise. Generous portions at very low prices and a friendly reception. 🔧 🪑 🅥 🍷
AE · DC · MC · V

FURTHER AFIELD

EDSBACKA KROG   ⓀⓀⓀⓀ
Sollentunavägen 220, Solna. 📞 *96 33 00.*
International-class cuisine at an inn dating from 1626, with a setting and service to match. The cuisine is based on the best Swedish ingredients, expertly prepared and beautifully presented. 🔧 🍴 🪑 🅥 🍷
AE · DC · MC · V

Cafés and Pubs

S WEDES LOVE THEIR COFFEE. At work people take a coffee break at around 3pm, and if they are out and about, they are likely to pop into a café. The cake shops (indicated by the sign "Konditori") have a long tradition. They serve typical Swedish pastries, with everything from sweet small buns to tempting gateaux. The best cake shops have their own bakeries and sell a variety of pastries and sandwiches. Cafés were once cheaper and more popular than the elegant cake shops, but the differences have been evened out and there are now many Continental-style cafés serving espresso, cappuccino and caffe latte. Many cafés open for breakfast early in the morning, and they usually serve lunch as well. The old Swedish "beer cafés" have been replaced by the city's many pubs, which also serve simple dishes at reasonable prices.

CAFÉS AND CAKE SHOPS

C AFÉ CULTURE is flourishing in Stockholm, and the style ranges from American or Italian to traditional Swedish and classic cake shops. The café is a good choice if you feel peckish between meals, need to rest your legs or simply want a meeting place. Apart from coffee, sandwiches and cakes, nearly all serve simple lunches – quiches and salad, for example – soft drinks and ice cream. Typical cafés serve Swedish-style strong coffee, along with sandwiches, buns and cakes. Don't miss the delicious *prinsesstårta* cream cake, by far the most popular one. Cafés usually close at around 6pm.

Many cafés have tables outside in the summer. If you feel like sitting under a fruit tree where you can enjoy the birdsong, **Rosendals Träd-gårdscafé** on Djurgården is the place. The salad buffet is a feast for the eye and the palate, consisting of organically grown vegetables and home-baked bread. It is open only during the summer and in December. **Lasse i Parken** is another rustic idyll in the city with home-baked bread and delicious cheesecakes.

Sturekatten is a classic cake shop decorated in the style of an early 20th-century upper-class home with many small rooms and unrivalled pastries. **Vete-Katten** is one of Stockholm's most authentic cake shops. Its pastries are outstanding and chocaholics

won't be able to resist the home-made pralines. After a hectic day's shopping, ladies head for the restful **Diplomat Tea House**, which serves English-style afternoon tea. Another oasis in the shopping district is **Gateau**, one floor up in Sturegallerian. The pastries are delicious and the gentle piano music relaxing.

Rather more unusual is **Hemma hos Seyhmus**, which serves Middle Eastern vegetarian delicacies with bio-dynamic bread. Another one is **Hemma hos Julia**, where excellent fresh cheeses are home-made. It also serves excellent hot chocolate and provides a choice of eight different cheesecakes, all of them mouth-watering.

Stortorgets Kaffestuga is a genuine traditional Swedish café serving porridge for breakfast, good soup for lunch, and buns or sandwiches with salami sausages. Another pleasant place for breakfast is **Cinnamon**, which has its own bakery and serves fresh sandwiches and cakes.

Wayne's Coffee is Södermalm's most popular meeting place with giant sandwiches and cakes, comfortable armchairs and an elegant clientele. **Coffee Cup** serves bagels with various fillings and many different types of coffee. At **Tabac** you can mingle with the locals as you enjoy a café au lait and home-baked brownies. Absolutely the finest espresso is served at **Tinta-rella di Luna**, an authentic Italian café which also has the

city's best *panini*. Coffee connoisseurs should not miss **Robert's Coffee**, where they roast their own beans. They also stock a range of exclusive beans which you can buy to take home.

PUBS

T HE OLD SWEDISH beer cafés have either closed down, transformed into a local restaurant (Tranan at Odenplan is a typical example – *see p163*) or are now pubs with an international flavour. Irish, Scottish or English pubs are all popular, but there are also influences from Belgium, the Czech Republic, Germany, Australia and the USA.

Stockholmers have a great interest in beer, so the pubs usually have a wide selection of brews and the staff are knowledgeable. Try some of the beers from three new small, acclaimed, quality breweries: Tärnö, Stockholm's own brewery; Slottskällan in Uppsala; and Pilgrimstad from northern Sweden.

One of the busiest and most traditional pubs is the **Tudor Arms**, opened in the 1960s, where English is the normal language and many of the regular customers are British. Scots and Americans head for the **Bagpiper's Inn**, where bagpipes are provided on the upper floor and Scottish beers are available. One floor down is the **Bald Eagle** where drinkers can enjoy rock music, and there is usually a queue for the billiards table. The adjoining pub, **Boomerang**, features music from Down Under, everyone is "mate", and the staff are Australian. The steakhouse serves kangaroo or ostrich steaks.

Anyone feeling homesick for Ireland only needs to go through the door of **Limerick** to enjoy some Guinness or Kilkenny. Irish music is performed there at weekends. **The Loft** has many Irish regulars and also serves excellent food. **The Dubliner** is yet another Irish pub, with a large selection of malt whiskeys. Live music contributes to the atmosphere. On Södermalm, **Soldaten**

Svejk specializes in Czech draught beer and offers rustic country cooking.

Beer connoisseurs or whisky drinkers should head for **Akkurat**, which has about 400 different types of whisky and beer from all over the world, but particularly from Belgium. Mussels are always on the menu, but there is also a good choice of other hot dishes and delicious snacks. Beer and whisky tastings take place frequently, the staff are knowledgeable and service is quick. **Oliver Twist** is reckoned to be one of the city's best pubs for draught beer, imported from all over the world. The staff here are also dedicated and knowledgeable. Business people head for **Man in the Moon** after work, and the atmosphere is rather more refined than at most other pubs. A

pleasant rural feel pervades the **Anchor Pub**, which specializes in unusual beers and has live music 3–4 nights a week.

Lundgrens is one of Sweden's best lagers and can be enjoyed on Kungsholmen, where it is brewed by the Tärnö brewery. It is served on draught at both **Mackinlay's** and **Kings Head**, two pleasant local pubs. **Tennstopet** was once a meeting place for journalists and some have remained loyal customers. It is pleasant but noisy, and there is a darts board. Swedish "home cooking" is available. The clientele is typically in the upper middle-age bracket.

Like their predecessors, the beer cafés, the pubs serve not just drinks but also snacks and value-for-money hot food from lunchtime till late in the evening. Many Stockholmers now regard going out to the

pub as a pleasant and often less expensive alternative to their local restaurant.

Most pubs are open daily. Many open for lunch and usually close at 11pm, while a few remain open to midnight or 1am *(see also pp170–71)*.

FAST FOOD

IF YOU ARE LOOKING for a quick snack, there are plenty of street kiosks selling hot dogs, hamburgers or kebabs. Several of them are open 24 hours. The Kungshallen complex at Hötorget has a lot of restaurants and fast-food outlets – particularly useful for groups who are undecided on the type of food they want to eat. There are also plenty of pizzerias of varying standards, as well as Chinese restaurants where you can eat well and inexpensively.

DIRECTORY

CAFÉS AND CAKE SHOPS

Cinnamon
Verkstadsgatan 9.
Map 1 C5.
[669 22 24.

Coffee Cup
Birger Jarlsgatan 9.
Map 3 D4.
[678 75 22.

Diplomat Tea House
Strandvägen 7 C.
Map 3 E4
[459 68 02.

Gateau
Sturegallerian. **Map** 3 D4.
[611 65 93.

Hemma hos Julia
S:t Eriksgatan 15.
Map 1 B3
[651 45 15.

Hemma hos Seyhmus
Hornsgatan 80.
Map 8 B2
[669 35 35.

Lasse i Parken
Högalidsgatan 56.
Map 1 B5
[658 33 95.

Robert's Coffee
Kungsgatan 44.
Map 2 C4.
[791 88 80.

Rosendals Trädgårdscafé
Rosendalsterrassen 2.
Map 6 C3.
[662 28 14.

Stortorgets Kaffestuga
Stortorget 22. **Map** 4 B3.
[20 59 81.

Sturekatten
Riddargatan 4.
Map 3 D4.
[611 16 12.

Tabac
Stora Nygatan 46.
Map 4 B4.
[10 15 34.

Tintarella di Luna
Drottninggatan 102.
Map 2 C3.
[10 79 55.

Wayne's Coffee
Götgatsbacken 31.
Map 9 D2.
[644 45 90.
Kungsgatan 14.
Map 3 D4.
[791 00 86.

Vete-Katten
Klara Norra Kyrkogata 26.
Map 2 C4.
[20 84 05.

PUBS

Akkurat
Hornsgatan 18.
Map 8 C2.
[644 00 15.

Anchor Pub
Sveavägen 90.
Map 2 C2.
[15 20 00.

Bagpiper's Inn/Bald Eagle
Rörstrandsgatan 21.
Map 1 C1.
[31 18 55.

Boomerang
Rörstrandsgatan 23.
Map 1 C1.
[33 04 11.

The Dubliner
Smålandsgatan 8.
Map 3 D4
[679 77 07.

Kings Head
Fleminggatan 49
Map 2 A4.
[652 15 50.

Limerick
Tegnérgatan 10.
Map 2 C3.
[673 43 98.

The Loft
Regeringsgatan 66.
Map 3 D4.
[411 19 91.

Mackinlay's
Fleminggatan 85.
Map 1 C2.
[650 83 20.

Man in the Moon
Tegnérgatan 2 D.
Map 2 C3
[458 95 00.

Oliver Twist
Repslagargatan 6.
Map 9 D2.
[640 05 66.

Soldaten Svejk
Östgötagatan 35.
Map 9 D3.
[641 33 66.

Tennstopet
Dalagatan 50.
Map 2 A2.
[32 25 18.

Tudor Arms
Grevgatan 31.
Map 3 F4.
[660 27 12.

ENTERTAINMENT IN STOCKHOLM

WITHIN THE PAST couple of decades Stockholm has become an important city for entertainment. The capital, which was once said to have a "cold beauty", is now a vibrant, trend-setting metropolis full of theatres, bars and music venues. International stars increasingly put Stockholm on their touring schedule, not least because of the magnificent indoor arena, Globen. Another

Jazz musician

factor is Swedish pop music's great position on the world stage which has made it an important export item. A wide range of entertainment is on offer and the short distance between venues is another benefit. The Royal Opera House, for instance, is only a few minutes' walk from the intimate clubs of Gamla Stan. Stockholm also has a rich cultural life with concerts, drama and exhibitions.

Kungliga Operan (Royal Opera House), Gustav II Adolfs Torg *(see p64)*

ENTERTAINMENT LISTINGS

A RELIABLE SOURCE of information about special events is the official guide *What's On Stockholm* which is available free of charge at most hotels, conference centres and tourist information offices. It is published 10 times a year in both English and Swedish. Daily newspapers also have detailed information on forthcoming events in a special section or in weekend supplements (but only in Swedish).

The Internet has several good sites with up-to-date information on special events. **Stockholm Information Service**, SIS *(see p182)* has an official "tourist site" (www.stockholmtown.com) which is constantly updated with detailed information and includes some useful links. **www. alltom stockholm.se** gives a wealth of information about entertainment and events in Stockholm, including everything from museums and restaurants to concerts.

A third extremely useful and userfriendly site on entertainment in the capital is **www.rival.se**. Information on all three websites is partly in English.

Stampen, in Stora Nygatan, one of Stockholm's great jazz clubs *(see p171)*

BOOKING TICKETS

TICKETS FOR EVENTS can usually be bought at the ticket office of the relevant theatre or sports arena. But to be sure of reserving a seat it is advisable to book in advance either with the help of your hotel or one of the Stockholm Information Service tourist offices, located at Sweden House adjoining Kungsträdgården and at the Hotellcentralen office in the Central Station. You can also use one of the city's ticket agencies, for example **Biljett Direkt**, which can make bookings by telephone for theatres, concerts, sporting events and excursions. A booking fee of 10–15 kr is charged. Tickets for various events can also be bought over the counter at the centrally located **Boxoffice**. Tickets booked direct can also be picked up here.

OUTDOOR CONCERTS AND FESTIVALS

MAJOR OUTDOOR events get under way in mid-May with the annual **Kungsträdgården** programme. This includes a wide variety of music with regular lunchtime and evening concerts. In the second week of June the **Slottsgalorna** event takes place at Ulriksdals Slott with international stars and the country's top musicians. **Skansen** stages a wide range of music, especially in July, with jazz on Monday evenings. The **International Jazz & Blues Festival** is held on Skeppsholmen in

A sea of people at the Royal Philharmonic Orchestra's outdoor concert

DIRECTORY

EVENTS LISTINGS

Stockholm Information Service
Sweden House, Hamngatan.
Map 3 D4.
█ 789 24 00.
w www.stockholmtown.com

Other good Internet sites:
w www.alltomstockholm.se
w www.rival.se

TICKET BOOKINGS

Biljett Direkt
█ 077-170 70 70.

Boxoffice
Norrmalmstorg. **Map** 3 D4.
█ 10 88 00.

STOCKHOLM FOR CHILDREN

Aquaria p95
Fjäderholmarna p144
Gröna Lund p95
Junibacken p88
Kulturhuset p67
Medeltidsmuseet p59
Skansen pp96–7
Naturhistoriska Riksmuseet/ Cosmonova p124
Leksaksmuseet p131
Vasamuseet pp92–3

mid-August, and attracts the big names in jazz and blues.

For classical music lovers, the **Royal Philharmonic Orchestra**'s outdoor concert at Sjöhistoriska (the National Maritime Museum) on the second Sunday in August is one of the summer's highlights. The concert is an annual tradition and attracts audiences of 25,000–30,000.

Other events include the **Restaurant Festival** at Kungsträdgården on the first weekend in June, the **American Festival** on the third weekend in June, and the **Boules Festival** on the first weekend in July.

NIGHT-TIME TRANSPORT

THE TUNNELBANA stops around 1am Sunday to Thursday nights, but on Friday and Saturday nights it runs until 4am. It is replaced by night buses. Several night buses depart from Sergels Torg, and most bus stops have maps showing the night routes. Taxis are usually not difficult to find, even on a Saturday evening *(see p193).*

STOCKHOLM FOR CHILDREN

COMPARED WITH many major cities, Stockholm is an extremely child-friendly place and ideal for family visits.

It is easy to take prams and pushchairs on to the new buses, and there is plenty of space for them inside.

Most of the museums have children's corners with special activities. Museums and other important sights often have a cafeteria or restaurant with special menus or smaller portions for children. Toilets with a baby-changing table are frequently available.

Many of the favourite places for children are on Djurgården. **Junibacken** has an exciting journey through the fantastic world of the children's author Astrid Lindgren. The nearby **Vasamuseet** is also child-friendly as well as the **Aquaria** water museum only a short walk away. For decades the **Gröna Lund** funfair has been a mixture of traditional and exciting new attractions, making it an ideal excursion for families with

Gröna Lund's roller-coaster

both teenagers and younger children. The open-air museum **Skansen**, with all its animals and exciting activities, can keep a family happily occupied for a whole day.

Special children's weeks are organized on **Fjäderholmarna**, a group of islands which can be reached from the city centre in only 25 minutes.

Leksaksmuseet (the Toy Museum) on Söder is a safe bet for children. In the city centre **Kulturhuset** has a variety of children's activities with a cultural content.

Naturhistoriska Riksmuseet (the Swedish Museum of Natural History) is an interesting excursion in its own right. It houses the Cosmonova planetarium and IMAX cinema which is a big attraction for children and young people.

Drama and Classical Music

Stockholm's year as Cultural Capital of Europe in 1998 was a well-deserved honour, as all the city's various areas of culture reflect a high degree of dedication and talent. This applies particularly to the world of music, which has seen many top-class international artists emerge from the capital's stages. As a result opera, ballet and classical music is well supported by Stockholmers who have a wide home-grown repertoire to enjoy, which is complemented by a number of guest artists from all over the world.

BALLET AND DANCE

Classical ballet of the highest quality is mainly staged at the over 100-year-old **Kungliga Operan** (see pp64–5). Every season three of the best-known ballets, for example *The Nutcracker*, *Swan Lake*, and *Romeo and Juliet*, are performed to packed houses. Thanks to the choreographer Birgit Cullberg, now deceased, Stockholm has also become a noted centre for modern dance. Many established dance companies make guest appearances at **Dansens Hus** (see p69) which has taken over the previous home of Stadsteatern. **Moderna Dansteatern** in the old torpedo factory on Skeppsholmen is another important stage for modern dance.

OPERA

Traditional productions in their original language are staged mainly at **Kungliga Operan**. Lunchtime operas or concerts are sometimes performed in the Gustav III opera café. During the summer, major operas are presented at **Drottningholms Slottsteater** (see pp140–3). Dating from the 18th century, the theatre's stage settings and scene-shifting machinery are preserved in their original condition and are still in good working order. All the operas performed here are also from the 18th century, and over the years the theatre has revived several unknown works by Mozart, using instruments typical of that era. The theatre is open for guided tours.

Sweden's oldest Rococo theatre, **Confidencen**, is located near Ulriksdal (see p125). Between June and September weekly opera and ballet performances are held here. Another genre of classical opera is staged at **Folkoperan**, which performs the classics in Swedish and without elaborate scenery. **Regina-Stockholm Operamathus** is a rebuilt cinema where audiences can dine in comfort while enjoying the opera.

THEATRES AND MUSICALS

Stockholm has a flourishing theatrical life, but performances are usually in Swedish. **Kungliga Dramatiska Teatern**, often known simply as "Dramaten" (see pp72–3), is Sweden's national theatre and has five stages. International and Swedish classics are regularly performed here, from Shakespeare to Strindberg, as well as modern foreign and Swedish productions. Ingmar Bergman was the theatre's director from 1963–6, and he has returned as an acclaimed guest director many times since then.

Södra Teatern (see p128) often presents modern productions despite having roots that go back to the 19th century. **Stockholms Stadsteater**, based in Kulturhuset (see p67), has a widely varied programme. A summer speciality is the popular series of **Parkteatern** productions in several of the city's parks with drama, dance and children's theatre. **Judiska Teatern** has a repertoire of new Jewish drama, as well as dance, poetry and film shows. **Teater Galeasen** is Stockholm's avant-garde stage for new Swedish and foreign

drama. **Marionetteatern** has puppet shows for both children and adults, along with a puppet museum on the same premises. **Pantomimteatern** is a theatre company which performs not only in Stockholm but tours rural areas, too.

Light-hearted plays are often staged at **China-Teatern**, and its programmes include some highly popular musicals and some much-loved plays for children. High quality musicals are also performed at **Oscars-Teatern**, **Göta Lejon** and **Cirkus**.

CLASSICAL MUSIC

World-standard classical music is regularly performed at **Berwaldhallen** (see p106). The hall is dedicated to the great Swedish composer Franz Berwald (1796–1868) and is home to the Swedish Radio Symphony Orchestra which has thrived under musical directors like Sergiu Celibidache and Esa-Pekka Salonen. The Swedish Radio Chorus, which is regarded as one of the world's great *a cappella* ensembles, is based here, too. Concerts are also given in the hall by other symphony orchestras and smaller ensembles.

Konserthuset (see p68) is the home of the Royal Philharmonic Orchestra, an internationally acclaimed 100-piece orchestra whose season runs from August to May. Its programme includes a couple of chamber music series and a jazz series, as well as performances for families on Saturdays. An annual composition festival is held every November.

Nybrokajen 11 (see p83) was formerly the home of the Musical Academy. Apart from July and August, its large hall is now used almost daily for concerts. In addition to classical music, you can hear performances of jazz, choral music and folk music. **Music at the Palace** is an annual summer series at the Royal Palace (see pp50–53) with two concerts every week, usually classical music but sometimes other styles. The concerts are normally staged in the Hall of

State or the Royal Chapel. The majestic staircase of **National-museum** *(see pp82–3)* is the setting for summer concerts. **Riddarhusmusik** at Riddar-huset *(see p58)* is a series by the Stockholm Sinfonietta .

FOLK AND CHURCH MUSIC

R URAL FOLK MUSIC still flour-ishes in the capital, and this tradition is particularly

fostered at **Skansen** *(see pp96–7)*, where fiddlers and folk dance teams play a major role in the various festivals held there *(see pp26–7)*. Folk music is also on the pro-gramme at **Nybrokajen 11**.

Concerts are regularly given in the city's churches, for example visitors can relax and enjoy beautiful church music in the tranquil surroundings of **Jacobs Kyrka** in Kungsträd-gården *(see p64)* every

Saturday at 3pm. Afternoon concerts usually take place in **Storkyrkan** *(see p49)* on Saturday and Sunday during spring and autumn.

BOOKING TICKETS

T ICKETS FOR Stockholm's theatres and concert halls can be booked through **BiljettDirekt**; directly at the relevant box office; or ordered by telephone *(see p166)*.

DIRECTORY

BALLET & DANCE

Dansens Hus
Barnhusgatan 12–14.
Map 2 C3.
📞 796 49 10.
FAX 10 87 90.
🌐 www.dansenshus.se
@ biljett@dansenshus.se
Tickets on sale: noon–6pm Mon–Sat, noon–4pm Sun (during performances).

Kungliga Operan
Gustav Adolfs Torg.
Map 4 B1.
📞 24 82 40.
Tickets on sale: noon–6pm Mon–Fri.

Moderna Dansteatern
Slupskjulsvägen 32,
Skeppsholmen.
Map 5 E2.
📞 611 32 33.
🌐 www.mdt.a.se
Tickets on sale: directly from Dansteatern/home page, or by phone.

OPERA

Confidencen
Ulriksdals Slottsteater.
📞 85 70 16.

Drottningholms Slottsteater
Drottningholm Palace,
Lovön.
📞 660 82 25.

Folkoperan
Hornsgatan 71.
Map 8 B2
📞 616 07 50.
FAX 84 82 84.
Tickets on sale: noon–6pm Mon–Fri, noon–4pm Sun.

Kungliga Operan
Gustav Adolfs Torg.
Map 4 B1.
📞 24 82 40.
Tickets on sale: noon–6pm Mon–Fri.

Regina-Stockholm Operamathus
Drottninggatan 71 A.
Map 2 C3.
📞 411 63 20.
Tickets on sale: noon–6pm Mon–Fri.

THEATRE

China-Teatern
Berzelii Park 9.
Map 3 D4.
📞 566 323 50.
Tickets on sale: 11am–6pm Mon–Fri, noon–6pm Sat.

Cirkus
Djurgårdsslätten.
Map 6 A4.
📞 660 10 20.
Tickets on sale: 10am–6pm Mon, 10am–7pm Tue–Fri, 3:30–6pm Sat, 1:30–4pm Sun. Telephone bookings (not for same day). 10am–6pm weekdays.

Kungliga Dramatiska Teatern
Nybroplan.
Map 3 E4.
📞 667 06 80
FAX 667 84 00
Tickets on sale: 10am–6pm Mon, 10am–7pm Tue–Fri, 3:30–6pm Sat, 1:30–4pm Sun.

Drottningholms Slottsteater
Drottningholm Palace,
Lovön.
📞 660 82 25.

Göta Lejon
Götgatan 55.
Map 9 D3.
📞 642 40 20.
Tickets on sale: 10am–6pm Mon–Tue, 10am–7:30pm Wed–Sat.

Judiska Teatern
Djurgårdsbrunnsvägen 59.
Map 7 E2.
📞 660 02 71.
🌐 www.judiskateatern.org

Marionetteatern
Brunnsgatan 6.
Map 3 D3.
📞 411 71 12.

Oscars-Teatern
Kungsgatan. 63.
Map 2 B4.
📞 20 50 00.
FAX 20 77 76
Tickets on sale: 11am–6pm Mon– Fri, noon–7:30pm Sat.

Pantomimteatern
Gästrikegatan 14.
Map 2 A2.
📞 31 54 64.

Parkteatern
📞 506 202 92.

Stockholms Stadsteater
Sergels Torg. **Map** 2 C4.
📞 506 202 00.
Tickets on sale: 11am–6pm Mon, 11am–7pm Tue–Fri, 11am–6pm Sat, noon–4pm Sun.

Södra Teatern
Mosebacke Torg 1–3.
Map 9 D2.
📞 644 99 00.
Tickets on sale: noon–6pm Mon–Fri, 2–6pm Sat, 2–6pm Sun (during performances).

Teater Galeasen
Slupskjulsvägen 32,
Skeppsholmen.
Map 5 E2.
📞 611 09 20.

CLASSICAL MUSIC

Berwaldhallen
Strandvägen 69.
Map 6 A2.
📞 784 50 00.

Konserthuset
Hötorget.
Map 2 C4.
📞 10 21 10.
🌐 www.konserthuset.se

Music at the Palace
The Royal Palace,
Slottsbacken.
Map 4 C2.
📞 10 22 47.

Nationalmuseum
Södra Blasieholmskajen.
Map 5 D2.
📞 519 543 00.

Nybrokajen 11
Nybrokajen 11
Map 4 C1.
📞 407 16 00.

Riddarhusmusik
Riddarhuset,
Riddarhustorget 10.
Map 4 A3.
📞 723 39 90.

CENTRAL TICKET AGENCY

BiljettDirekt
📞 077-170 70 70.
🌐 www.biljett.se

Nightlife and Entertainment

IN COMMON WITH MOST capitals, Stockholm has a rich variety of nightlife and entertainment, with something for everyone. Pop music is one of the country's biggest exports so there is no shortage of groups following in the footsteps of ABBA. Top-class musical entertainment is provided on a large scale in Globen or on a smaller more intimate basis in the pubs, clubs and bars. The Swedish jazz scene thrives in several venues where live music is played nightly.

ROCK AND POP

STOCKHOLM'S **Globen** is the city's biggest stage for rock and pop music. It attracts all the biggest international artists as well as leading Swedish groups. **Cirkus** and **Södra Teatern** (see p168) are other favourite venues for rock and pop, and they stage both musical and theatrical productions in beautiful settings. **Münchenbryggeriet**, a former brewery, also provides a great venue. Hard rock enthusiasts are well-catered for at **Anchor Pub** three or four times a week.

Nalen is a traditional old-time music hall, built in the 1880s. Its heyday was between the 1920s and 1960s, and now it has been re-opened offering a variety of live music on several stages.

JAZZ MUSIC

A WIDE CHOICE OF jazz can be found in Stockholm. **Fasching Jazzklubb** has an international reputation for good music with performances virtually every day of the week. Another classic jazz spot is **Stampen** in Gamla Stan which attracts a rather older clientele. The bar at the **Lydmar Hotel** has one of the city's best stages, where top-class artists often give impromptu performances to a young and fashionable crowd. **Nalen** holds frequent jazz events, and usually provides live music to dance to on Sundays. **Glenn Miller Café** has a cosy atmosphere, with jazz nightly from Monday to Saturday. During the summer the vintage steamboat **SS Blidösund** (see p137) operates special jazz cruises around the archipelago four times a week.

MUSIC PUBS

LIFE IN STOCKHOLM'S pubs and bars has changed in recent years as a number of establishments have introduced live music. Irish bands often play at **The Dubliner** (see p164), and live music is also performed at the **Engelen** and **Akkurat** pubs. Engelen has a variety of music while the accent is on rock at Akkurat.

Apart from these musical watering holes, there are plenty of traditional British and Irish pubs in the capital, generally with a wide choice of beer and whisky and snack meals (see pp164–5).

BARS

THE BEST BARS ARE usually found in the hotels and restaurants, but those in the latter are often noisier and smokier. The most fashionable tend to have a long queue, supervised by a doorman, waiting to enter. For a quieter atmosphere with comfortable armchairs, hotel bars are the best bet. The minimum age for buying alcohol is 18, and young customers must be prepared to show proof of age.

The **Cadier Bar** in the Grand Hôtel (see pp79 & 151) undoubtedly has the most elegant clientele because this is where the rich and famous stay. From the verandah there is a fine view of the Royal Palace and the archipelago boats and in the background gentle music is played on the white grand piano.

Operabaren is a sight in itself with well-preserved Jugendstil decor, marble tables and leather sofas. The regulars often include authors, artists and intellectuals.

Gondolen at the top of Katarinahissen (see p127) offers arguably the most beautiful view of Stockholm and is a perfect place for a drink at sunset. It has comfortable leather armchairs, skilled bartenders and a relaxing atmosphere. **Sky Bar**, high up in the Royal Viking Hotel, has a panoramic view of the city, seen at its best after dark when the lights come on. The **Sheraton Lobby Lounge** is a classic international bar where business people from all over the world relax to the accompaniment of piano music while skilled bartenders fix their favourite cocktails.

Lydmar Hotel has a bar in its lobby which has become a popular meeting place for artists, designers and musicians. Live bands play soft jazz, and the bartenders always know which drinks are in fashion. **Sturehof Bar** is a sophisticated and modern nightspot, particularly popular with people from the advertising and media worlds and other local night owls.

NIGHTCLUBS

MOST OF STOCKHOLM's best nightclubs are located around Stureplan (see pp70–71). The traditional discotheque evenings are Friday and Saturday, and on other days of the week they are often hired by various clubs providing particular styles of music. The nightlife scene is changing all the time as new clubs come and go. **Café Opera**, Stockholm's most historic international-class nightclub, is located to the rear of Kungliga Operan (see pp64–5). It has a mixed clientele of both the young and trendy and a more soberly dressed older generation. **Sturecompagniet** is a large disco on several floors which also has a rock bar at street level. **Fasching Jazzklubb** opens its doors to salsa lovers on Fridays and excellent DJs provide soul from the 1960s and 1970s on Saturdays. **Spy Bar** is the place to rub shoulders with Swedish celebrities and international artists on tour. However, it is often crowded and a membership card may be necessary. **Tiger** is another "in" place with a fashion-conscious clientele. The younger generation enjoy dancing to a variety of music at **Chiaro**.

CABARETS

G OOD FOOD AND top-class entertainment are on the menu at **Hamburger Börs**,

which features cabaret shows performed by leading Swedish artists. **Wallmans Salonger** offers musical entertainment provided by the waiters and waitresses along with the food.

FILM

F ILMS ARE NOT dubbed into Swedish, so non-Swedish speaking visitors can more often than not go to a cinema

and enjoy a film that is in their own language. Films in languages other than English are usually screened at **Zita**, and **Sture** is also a good venue for cineasts. There are both classic cinemas like **Röda Kvarn**, showing quality international drama, and multi-screen complexes like **Filmstaden Sergel** which screens most of the current Hollywood repertoire.

DIRECTORY

ROCK AND POP

Anchor Pub
Sveavägen 90. **Map** 2 C2.
[15 20 00.
[] 3pm–3am Mon–Fri,
1pm–3am Sat,
1pm–2.30am Sun.

Cirkus
Djurgårdsslätten.
Map 6 A4.
[587 987 00.

Globen
Globentorget 2.
[725 10 00.

Münchenbryggeriet
Söder Mälarstrand 29.
Map 8 B1.
[658 00 20.

Södra Teatern
Mosebacke Torg 1–3.
Map 9 D2.
[644 99 00.

Tre Backar
Tegnergatan 12–14.
Map 2 C3. [673 44 00.
[] 11am–midnight Mon–
Wed, 11am–1am Thu–Fri,
6pm–1am Sat.

JAZZ

Fasching Jazzklubb
Kungsgatan 63.
Map 2 B4.
[21 62 67.
[] 7pm–midnight Mon–
Thu, 8pm–4am Fri–Sat,
8pm–midnight Sun.

Glenn Miller Café
Brunnsgatan 21 A.
Map 3 D3. [10 03 22.
[] 5pm–midnight
Mon–Thu, 5pm–1am
Fri–Sat; [] from 8pm.

Lydmar Hotel
Sturegatan 10.
Map 3 D3.
[566 113 00.
[] 11.30am–1am
Mon–Thu, 11.30am–3am
Fri, 1pm–3am Sat,
1pm–1am Sun.

Nalen
Regeringsgatan 74
Map 3 D3.
[453 34 01

Stampen
Stora Nygatan 5.
Map 4 B3.
[20 57 93.
[] 8pm–2am Mon–Sat,
1pm–5pm Sun.

SS Blidösund
Skeppsbron 10.
Map 4 C2.
[411 71 13.
[] May–mid Sep: boat
departing at 7pm
Mon–Thu.

MUSIC PUBS

Akkurat
Hornsgatan 18.
Map 8 C2.
[644 00 15.
[] 11am–1am Mon–Fri,
noon–1am Sat,
6pm–2am Sun.

The Dubliner
Smålandsgatan 8 .
Map 3 D4.
[679 77 07.
[] 4pm–3am Tue–Sat.
[] from 10pm; 4pm–1pm
Sun–Mon, [] from
9.30pm.

Engelen
Kornhamnstorg 59 B.
Map 4 B4.
[20 10 92.
[] 4pm–3am Mon–Sun.

BARS

Cadier Bar
Grand Hôtel, Södra
Blasieholmshamnen 8.
Map 4 C1. [679 35 00.

Gondolen
Stadsgården 6.
Map 4 C5.
[611 70 00.

Lydmar Bar
Sturegatan 10.
Map 3 D3.
[566 113 88.

Operabaren
Kungsträdgården.
Map 4 B1.
[676 5808.

**Sheraton Lobby
Lounge**
Tegelbacken 6.
Map 4 A1.
[412 34 75.

Sky Bar
Vasagatan 1. **Map** 2 B4.
[506 540 37.

Sturehof Bar
Stureplan 2.
Map 3 D4.
[440 57 30.

NIGHT CLUBS

Café Opera
Operahuset, Kungsträd-
gården. **Map** 4 B2.
[676 58 07
[] 11.30am–3am
Mon–Sat, 1pm–3am Sun.

Chiaro
Birger Jarlsgatan 24.
Map 3 D3.
[678 00 09.
[] 5pm–midnight Mon–
Wed, 5pm–1am Thu,
4pm–5am Fri, 7pm–
5am Sat.

Fasching Jazzklubb
Kungsgatan 63.
Map 2 B4. [21 62 67
[] Latino club: 10.30pm–
4am Fri; Soul club: mid-
night–3am Sat.

Tiger
Kungsgatan 18.
Map 3 D4. [24 47 00.
[] 10pm–5am Mon Tue,
7pm–5am Wed–Sat.

Spy Bar
Birger Jarlsgatan 20.
Map 3 D3.
[611 65 00.
[] 10pm–5am Wed–Sat.

Sturecompagniet
Sturegatan 4. **Map** 3 D3.
[611 78 00.
[] 11.30am–1am or 3am
Mon–Wed, 11.30am–5am
Thu–Sat.

CABARETS

Hamburger Börs
Jakobsgatan 6. **Map** 3 D5.
[787 85 00.

Wallmans Salonger
Teatergatan 3. **Map** 3 E5.
[611 66 22.

FILM

Filmstaden Sergel
Hötorget. **Map** 2 C4.
[562 600 00.

Röda Kvarn
Biblioteksgatan 5.
Map 3 D4. [562 600 00.

Sture
Birger Jarlsgatan 28–30.
Map 3 D3. [678 85 48.

Zita
Birger Jarlsgatan 37.
Map 3 D3. [23 20 20.

OUTDOOR ACTIVITIES

Hot-air balloon over Stockholm

As a city built around water and where the countryside reaches into the centre, Stockholm is ideally positioned for all kinds of open-air pursuits. The great outdoors plays an important role in the Swedish lifestyle, and the capital offers a plethora of activities throughout the year – for the energetic and not so energetic – from walking, cycling and ice-skating to fishing, skiing and hot-air ballooning. In spring, summer and autumn around 80 golf courses are open to visitors, as well as well-planned jogging and cycle tracks. Outdoor swimming pools are popular on hot summer days, and in winter long-distance skating between the islands and cross-country and downhill skiing are the things to do.

In many cases, it is simple to make your own contacts, but the Stockholm Information Service (SIS) will be able to advise you *(see p182)*.

Hagaparken, an inviting area for exercise and recreation *(see pp122–3)*

JOGGING, WALKS AND CYCLING

It can be both practical and rewarding to take some exercise while exploring the capital. Everything in the city centre is within easy walking distance, including major sights, beautiful parks and

Fishing at Blasieholmskajen in the centre of the city

modern shopping malls. A walk in Stockholm always takes you close to the water or some unusual sight. The organized walks in the city are usually conducted in Swedish but there are also tours of Gamla Stan with English-speaking guides. Contact Stockholm Information Service (SIS) for advice on a route.

Even if you want to head out of the city centre, there is no need to travel far. The No. 47 bus goes out to Djurgården, where you can have a walk or jog along the shores, through the avenues under the oak trees, or over green fields. Walking paths along the city's waterfronts *(see pp40–41)* provide both good routes and stunning views. There are many floodlit jogging tracks, and plenty of fun-run events to choose from *(see pp26–9)*.

Those who prefer to move at a gentler pace can head for **Skansen** open-air museum *(see pp96–7)* or the **Gröna Lund** amusement park *(see p95)*, both suitable for the whole family, providing a day out in the open air.

Djurgården has plenty of cycle paths and bicycles can be hired from **Cykel Mopeduthyrningen** or **Skepp & Hoj** *(see p197)*, near Djurgårdsbron *(see p98)*. Roller-blades can also be hired near the bridge.

Cyclists planning to take a longer tour should visit SIS and ask to be put in touch with the Cykelfrämjandet cycling organization.

HORSE RIDING

Several riding schools near the city centre, such as **Stockholms Ridhus**, offer lessons. For those who prefer to discover Stockholm's surrounding areas, tours on Icelandic ponies are operated from quite a few stables.

Friluftsryttarna hires out horses to experienced riders to explore the Tyresö nature reserve, southeast of the city, after an initial briefing.

WATER SPORTS

There are excellent opportunities for water sports. Canoes, rowing boats, pedalos and larger boats for longer tours, can be hired from **Tvillingarnas Båtuthyrning** and **Skepp & Hoj** *(see p197)*, both near Djurgårdsbron. A good area for canoeing is the canal near Karlberg *(see pp118–19)*, where **Kanotbryggan** hires out canoes.

SWIMMING

DURING THE SUMMER there are plenty of outdoor swimming pools to choose from. They include **Eriksdalsbadet** in Södermalm, **Kampementsbadet** at Gärdet and **Vanadisbadet** in Vasastan. There are several good places for a swim along the Kungsholmen shores of Riddarfjärden. And on Långholmen there are both sandy beaches or rocks to swim from (see p132).

For a completely different bathing experience, try the Japanese **Yasuragi** at Hasseludden. For indoor pools, try Centralbadet (see p69) or Sturebadet (see p71).

GOLF

GOLFERS WILL FIND about 80 golf courses within easy reach of the city centre. The closest, such as **Djursholms Golfklubb**, are in delightful settings.

The courses are popular and advance bookings are recommended. Golf information is available on Stockholm's official website (www.stockholmtown.com).

OTHER ACTIVITIES

BRIGHTLY COLOURED hot-air balloons hovering over the city are a common sight in the evening. Several companies operate charter trips in balloons. You can book via SIS or directly with a company such as **City Ballong**.

Game fishing for salmon and trout is possible right in

Vanadisbadet in Vasastan

the city centre near the Royal Palace. Suitable tackle can be hired at **Fiskarnas Redskapshandel**. The **Anglers' Association** can provide information on fishing in and around Stockholm.

Outdoor tennis courts are available at several places, including **Kungliga Tennishallen**, where the Stockholm Open ATP indoor tournament is held every November.

You can go scuba-diving around Stockholm too. Contact SIS for details of diving schools and equipment hire.

Ice-skaters are in their element once the open waters of the archipelago have frozen over. Meanwhile, the artificial rink at Kungsträdgården is open throughout the winter, and hires out skates.

The outdoor activities organization **Friluftsfrämjandet** provides information on skating and skiing in the area. Visitors with disablities can find out more about the availability of outdoor pursuits by contacting **De Handikappades Riksförbund** (see p183)

(see p183)

One of Stockholm's many golf courses

DIRECTORY

HORSE RIDING

Friluftsryttarna
Rundmars Gård, Tyresö.
📞 770 08 35.

Stockholms Ridhus
Storängsvägen 29. **Map** 3 F1.
📞 664 61 79.

WATER SPORTS AND FISHING

Anglers' Association
📞 19 78 20 (10am–1pm).

Fiskarnas Redskapshandel
S:t Paulsgatan 2–4. **Map** 8 C2.
📞 641 82 14.

Kanotbryggan
Karlbergs Strand 4. 📞 82 82 80.

SWIMMING

Eriksdalsbadet
Hammarby Slussv. 8.
Map 9 D5. 📞 508 402 75.

Kampementsbadet
Sandhamnsgatan (Gärdet).
📞 661 62 16.
🕐 25 May–25 Aug.

Vanadisbadet
Vanadislunden. **Map** 2 B1.
📞 34 33 00.
🕐 25 May–31 Aug.

Yasuragi
Hasseludden Konferens & Yasuragi.
🚂 35-min journey from Slussen.
📞 747 61 00. 🕐 7am–11pm.

GOLF

Djursholms Golfklubb
Hagbardsvägen, Djursholm.
📞 755 14 77.

OTHER ACTIVITIES

City Ballong
Gästrikegatan 8. **Map** 2 A3.
📞 33 64 64.

Kungliga Tennishallen
Lidingövägen.
📞 459 15 00.

Friluftsfrämjandet
📞 556 307 40.
🌐 www.frilufts.se

SHOPPING IN STOCKHOLM

STOCKHOLM IS WORTH visiting for the shopping alone. All the best shops in the central area are within easy walking distance and they stock virtually everything anyone could want. There are plenty of small boutiques for fashion and interiors, as well as antique shops, luxury international designer outlets and well-stocked department stores.
Shopping is good all over the city. Exclusive shops can be found in fashionable Östermalm. Gamla Stan is a good place for handicrafts and unusual knick-knacks. Södermalm and Vasastan have antique and second-hand shops. Cameras, mobile telephones, furs, children's clothing, toys and Swedish glass are cheaper in Sweden than in most other countries. No expedition is complete without a visit to one of the city's splendid market halls which sell Swedish delicacies like reindeer and elk meat, caviar and cloudberries.

Dala horse
(see p176)

OPENING TIMES

MOST SHOPS USUALLY open at 10am and close at 6pm, although many in the city centre remain open until 7pm. Most shops are open until 2pm on Saturdays, and the major department stores stay open until 5pm. Large stores, shopping malls and a number of shops in central Stockholm are open on Sundays. Market halls are closed on Sundays and public holidays. Larger supermarkets are open daily until 8pm.

PAYMENT

ALL THE MAIN CREDIT cards and travellers' cheques are accepted at most Stockholm shops. If you are paying by card you may be asked for proof of identity. Goods can be exchanged if you produce the receipt. Purchases can usually be made on a sale-or-return basis, providing this is noted on the receipt.

VALUE ADDED TAX

VALUE ADDED TAX ("moms" in Swedish) is charged on all items except daily newspapers. The VAT rate is 25%, except on food, for which the rate is only 12%. VAT is always included in the total price.

TAX-FREE SHOPPING

RESIDENTS OF countries outside the European Union are entitled to a refund of the VAT they have paid on their purchases. Tax-free shopping with Global Refund gives visitors a cash refund of 15–18 per cent on their departure from the EU. Look for the "Tax-free shopping" sign. Global Refund is at all departure points, including Arlanda Airport.

Biblioteksgatan, an attractive shopping street in Stockholm

SALES

TWICE A YEAR Stockholm's shops and department stores have sales with reduced prices on clothing, shoes and other fashion goods. Sales are indicated by the *rea* sign. The year's first sales start after Christmas and continue throughout January. The second sales period lasts from late June to the end of July.

SHOPPING CENTRES AND DEPARTMENT STORES

STOCKHOLM'S best-known superstore is **IKEA**, which has become a popular tourist attraction in its own right. It sells not just furniture but also everything else for the home, and all at attractive prices. The textiles section is particularly good, as well as the kitchenware and porcelain departments. IKEA's store is located outside the city but is

NK, Stockholm's most exclusive department store

Nordiska Kristall, a major outlet for Swedish glass in Stockholm

easy to reach by a free shuttle bus from Regeringsgatan 13 to Kungens Kurva, hourly on weekdays from 10am to 5pm.

Another well-known store is the fashion house **H&M** (Hennes & Mauritz), which has branches in many European cities and several outlets in Stockholm. H&M stocks the latest fashions at low prices. It has its own designers and makes clothing for women, men, teenagers and children. The shops also sell accessories, jewellery, underwear, perfume and cosmetics.

Nordiska Kompaniet (NK) on Hamngatan is Stockholm's leading department store, where many well-known names in fashion and cosmetics have their own shops. NK also stocks Swedish-designed products, jewellery, handicrafts and souvenirs as well as cameras, films, books and CDs.

PUB on Hötorget is another established department store with a wide selection of goods.

One of Arsenalsgatan's fine antique shops

The **Duka** boutique chain has a good choice of table coverings and decorations, both classic and modern.

Most shopping items can be bought inexpensively at **Åhlens** department store in City, Vasastaden, Kungsholmen and Östermalm, as well as some suburbs.

There are several indoor shopping malls. **Gallerian** on Hamngatan is the largest and the prices are lower than in the elegant **Sturegallerian** near Stureplan with its many trendy boutiques. Also there are shopping centres in most suburbs where nearly all the retail chains are represented.

MARKETS

A TRADITIONAL Christmas market is held at Skansen *(see p96)* every Sunday in December. Stortorget in Gamla Stan *(see p54)* also has a delightful market at Christmas.

Vegetables, fruit and flowers are sold from Monday to Friday at Hötorget *(see p68)*, Östermalmstorg *(see p71)* and Medborgarplatsen *(see p131)*. Street stalls along Drottninggatan and around Sergels Torg sell watches, clocks, toys and other knick-knacks.

Stockholm's flea market, **Skärholmens Loppmarknad,** offers a wide variety of clothes, practical objects and bric-a-brac for sale.

WINES AND SPIRITS

THE ONLY SHOPS selling alcohol in Sweden are run by Systembolaget, the State monopoly chain. They are open Monday to Friday 10am–6pm (some open on

DIRECTORY

SHOPPING CENTRES & DEPARTMENT STORES

Duka Aveny
Kungsgatan 41.
Map 2 C4.
(20 60 41.

Fältöversten
Karlaplan 13.
Map 3 F3.
(528 098 11.

Gallerian
Hamngatan/Regeringsgatan.
Map 3 D4.
(585 918 51.

H&M
Hamngatan 22. **Map** 3 D4.
(796 54 34.
Sergels Torg 12. **Map** 2 C4.
(796 54 70.

IKEA
Kungens Kurva, Skärholmen.
(744 83 00.
Barkarby, Järfälla.
(795 40 00.

NK
Hamngatan 18–20. **Map** 3 D4
(762 80 00.

PUB
Hötorget. **Map** 3 C4.
(23 99 15.

Sturegallerian
Grev Turegatan 9.
Map 3 D4.
(611 46 06.

Åhléns
Klarabergsgatan 50.
Map 2 C4.
(676 60 00.
Fridhemsplan. **Map** 1 B2.
(617 97 00.
Nybrogatan 37. **Map** 3 E3.
(553 401 00.
Odenplan. **Map** 2 B2.
(728 53 00.

MARKETS

Skärholmens Loppmarknad
P-huset. Skärholmen.
(710 00 60.
 11am–6pm Mon–Fri,
9am–3pm Sat, 10am–3pm Sun.

Saturdays 10am–2pm, but not on a public holiday weekend). The minimum age for buying alcohol at Systembolaget shops is 20 *(see also p183)*.

What to Buy in Stockholm

Elk candlestick

THE DALA WOODEN HORSE must be the most typical Swedish souvenir. But it is facing strong competition from the elk, which has become a symbol for a country with vast tracts of unspoilt countryside. The Swedes love the great outdoors, so there are plenty of shops selling top-class sporting equipment. Swedish glass and crystal are renowned around the world. Orrefors and Kosta are just two of several glassworks producing both classic and modern glassware. Educational toys in natural materials are a Swedish speciality and so are clogs, which can be found in many shoe shops.

Hand-painted clogs

HANDICRAFTS & DESIGN

Modern Swedish design is a familiar concept in many households worldwide, even for simple everyday items (*see pp38–9*). Handicrafts have a long tradition in Sweden and contemporary designers often use wrought-iron work, weaving, pottery and woodcarving.

Dala Horse and Cockerel
Originally the brightly painted Dala horses and cockerels were toys carved from left-over fragments of wood. Later the horse became a national symbol and is sold in many variants.

Swedish Glass
Hand-blown sets of glass-ware are made in Sweden's glassworks, as well as artistic crystal creations and beautiful objects for everyday use.

Nobel **glass carafe from Orrefors by Gunnar Cyrén**

Traditional schnapps glasses

Tray with design by Josef Frank, Svenskt Tenn

Cheese slicer and knife by Michael Björnstierna

Designer Objects
The larger department stores often commission well-known designers for porcelain, glass, textiles and household items which make highly desirable gifts.

Mama, **a humorous clothes hanger**

Crux **rug by Pia Wallén**

Children's Toys
Colourful wooden children's toys from Brio are worldwide favourites. Educational picture books, games and puzzles are all excellent gifts for children.

OUTDOOR GEAR

Many Swedes enjoy outdoor pursuits like fishing, hunting, sailing, golf, camping and all types of winter sports, so there are many well-equipped sports shops around. Unique items include Lapp handicrafts beautifully made from reindeer horn or skin.

Hand Knits
Caps and gloves with attractive designs, known as lovikka, *are made from a special wool which gives good protection in cold or wet conditions.*

Reindeer Skin Rucksack
Rucksacks are popular for both adults and children. This exclusive model is made in Lapland.

Drinking vessel
in carved wood

Spinning Reel and Lures
ABU-Garcia makes top-quality fishing tackle perfect for Sweden's long coastline, countless lakes and rivers with their rich and varied fishing.

Lapp Handicrafts
A hunting knife with a sheath of reindeer horn, or a kåsa, *a drinking vessel carved in birch, are not only attractive but useful when out walking in the wild.*

SWEDISH DELICACIES

Popular preserves are made from wild berries such as bitter lingonberries (for meatballs) or sweet cloudberries (served with whipped cream). Herring, crispbread and ginger biscuits can be bought in all groceries, and sweets are sold loose. Schnapps miniatures come in gift packs.

Lingonberry preserve   Cloudberry jam

Pickled Herring
Pickled herring should be enjoyed with new potatoes cooked with dill, chopped chives and crème fraîche. Versions flavoured with mustard, dill or other herbs or spices are also available.

Swedish schnapps gift-pack miniatures

"Raspberry boat" candy   Salt liquorice   Crispbread   Box of ginger biscuits

Where to Shop in Stockholm

CLOTHING FROM ALL the well-known international fashion houses can be found in Stockholm, and many have their own shops. If you want something rather different it is worth seeking out the creations of younger Swedish fashion designers. Swedish interior design is famous for its clean lines, functionalism and the use of pale wood, and Stockholm is a paradise for anyone interested in design. Handicrafts are of a high quality. Leisurewear and sports goods offer excellent value for money.

FASHION

STOCKHOLM'S TOP places for fashion are in the "golden triangle" bounded by Sture-plan, Nybroplan and Norr-malmstorg. Clothing at more moderate prices can be bought around Sergels Torg.

If you are looking for Swedish designers, **NK** has a selection of clothing created by younger designers as well as mainstream local products. Classic men's clothing of high quality is designed by Oscar Jacobsson, while Stenström shirts are sold in department stores and the more elegant menswear boutiques. **Björn Borg** has his own shops sell-ing men's and women's clothing and underwear, per-fume and accessories. **Johan Lindeberg** produces unusual fashions for the daring man, while fashion-conscious young people shop at **elleGAL-illEGAL**. The designer **Filippa K** produces smart clothing for trendy women. **Anna Holt-blad** has a good selection of stylish women's garments, while **Thalia** in Östermalm has a good range of exclusive party outfits.

DESIGN AND INTERIOR DECORATION

THE CITY CENTRE, Östermalm and Hornsgatan in Söder-malm have a number of interior decoration shops selling the products of young designers and artists. To see the latest on offer, visit **DesignTorget**, where young designers display their work. **R.O.O.M** on Kungsholmen, **Asplund** in Östermalm and **Norrgavel** in City are just a few of the most up-to-date shops and they all have a good selection of products.

Svenskt Tenn is the city's oldest shop for interior decoration, with both new and classic designs. **Nordiska Galleriet** has exclusive mo-dern furniture and decoration items while **Georg Jensen** specializes in silver. **Kao-Lin**, **Nutida Svenskt Silver**, **Blås&Knåda** and **Galleri Metallum** stage exhibitions and sell Swedish-designed products. Modern printed textiles can be found at **Tio-Gruppen** in Södermalm. **Svenskt Glas** and **Nordiska Kristall** both have a wide choice of Swedish glassware, which can also be found at the various department stores.

ANTIQUES

A LARGE NUMBER of antique shops can be found along Odengatan, Upplandsgatan and Roslagsgatan in Vasastan. Gamla Stan also has many shops offering collectables. Shops selling art, silver and porcelain of a more exclusive variety are on Arsenalsgatan on Blasieholmen, and also around Östermalmstorg. Södermalm has small shops selling bric-a-brac.

MUSIC AND MULTIMEDIA

MANY SWEDISH pop bands now have an internatio-nal reputation. Exciting new talents continue to find their way into the charts, and the latest products can often be bought in the record shops before they become available outside Sweden. Apart from pop and rock, Sweden has a long folk-music tradition, as well as many skilled jazz musicians and opera singers. **Mega Skivakademien** has a wide selection of CDs, as do the large department stores.

SPORT AND LEISURE

THE SWEDES devote a lot of time to outdoor sports and activities. **Naturkompaniet**, **Friluftsbolaget** and **Peak Performance** have an exclusive selection of sportswear and equipment. **Stadium** and **Alewalds** have a varied choice of sports clothing and equipment at attractive prices. Equipment and exclusive clothing for hunting or fishing can be bought at **Walter Borg**.

SOUVENIRS AND HANDICRAFTS

GLASSES FOR SCHNAPPS, silver jewellery, hand-painted clogs, Lapp (*Same*) crafts, hand-knitted woollen gloves and caps, hand-made candles, Christmas decorations and wrought-iron products can all be bought in the main department stores as well as at Gamla Stan shops like **Carl Wennberg Sameslöjd** and **Kilgren Knives and Clothing**. **Svensk Hemslöjd** and the various museum gift shops are also good places to shop. Visitors to Skansen (*see pp96–7)* can buy handicrafts made in its shops. **Sweden Shop** sells Swedish hand-icrafts and quality souvenirs.

BOOKS

PHOTOGRAPHY books, cookery books, books on Swedish design and children's books make good souvenirs to take home. Apart from the **NK Bookshop** and at other department stores, **Heden-grens Bokhandel** has a large foreign-languages department. The **Sweden Bookshop** at Sweden House has a good selection of books on Stock-holm and Sweden in English.

TOYS AND BABY EQUIPMENT

IT IS WORTH BUYING high-quality baby prams and pushchairs produced by Emmaljunga and baby equipment by Babybjörn. **Babyland** and **Bonti** have a wide selection of these and other well-made products for children. Brio's wooden toys and other attractive toys are also favourite presents. **Bulleribock** and **Stor & Liten** offer a wide choice. Practical children's clothing can be found at **Polarn och Pyret** or at the larger department stores.

SWEDISH DELICACIES

THE CAPITAL HAS three superb market halls: **Östermalmshallen**, **Hötorgshallen** and **Söderhallarna**. Delicacies on sale include salmon, bleak roe, smoked eel and smoked reindeer meat, which are all delicious culinary souvenirs. The food sections of the major department stores sell tinned herrings, lingonberry or cloudberry jam, crispbread, gingerbread and sweets, which make good presents.

DIRECTORY

FASHIONS

Anna Holtblad
Grev Turegatan 13.
Map 3 E4.
[545 022 20.

Björn Borg
Birger Jarlsgatan 25.
Map 3 D3.
[411 54 20.

elleGAL-ilLEGAL
Odengatan 89.
Map 2 B3.
[30 71 00.

Filippa K
Grev Turegatan 18.
Map 3 E4.
[545 888 88.

Johan Lindeberg
Grev Turegatan 9.
Map 3 D4.
[678 61 65.

NK
Hamngatan 18–20.
Map 3 D4.
[762 80 00.

Thalia
Karlavägen 62.
Map 3 E3.
[660 54 30.

DESIGN AND DECORATION

Asplund
Sibyllegatan 31.
Map 3 E3.
[662 52 84.

Blås&Knåda
Hornsgatan 26.
Map 4 B5.
[642 77 67.

DesignTorget
Kulturhuset, Sergels
Torg 3. Map 2 C4.
[508 315 20.
Götgatan 31.
Map 9 D2.
[462 35 20.

Galleri Metallum
Hornsgatan 30.
Map 4 B5.
[640 13 23.

Georg Jensen
Birger Jarlsgatan 13.
Map 3 D4.
[611 85 22.

Kao-Lin
Hornsgatan 50.
Map 8 C2.
[644 46 00.

Konsthantverkarna
Mäster Samuelsgatan 2
Map 3 D4.
[611 03 70.

Nordiska Galleriet
Nybrogatan 11.
Map 3 E4.
[442 83 60.

Nordiska Kristall
Kungsgatan 9.
Map 3 D4.
[10 43 72.

Norrgavel
Birger Jarlsgatan 27.
Map 3 D3.
[545 220 50.

Nutida Svenskt Silver
Arsenalsgatan 3.
Map 3 D4.
[611 67 18.

R.O.O.M
Alströmergatan 20.
Map 1 C2.
[692 50 00.

Svenskt Glas
Karlavägen 61.
Map 3 E3.
[679 79 09.

Svenskt Tenn
Strandvägen 5.
Map 3 E4.
[670 16 00.

Tio-Gruppen
Götgatan 25.
Map 9 D2.
[643 25 04.

MUSIC AND MULTIMEDIA

Mega Skivakademien
Sergels Torg.
Map 2 C4.
[566 157 00.

SPORT AND LEISURE

Alewalds
Kungsgatan 32.
Map 6 D3. [21 90 00.

Friluftsbolaget
Kungsgatan 26.
Map 3 D4.
[24 19 96.

Naturkompaniet
Kungsgatan 4. Map 3 D4.
[723 15 81.

Peak Performance
Biblioteksgatan 18.
Map 3 D4.
[611 34 00.

Stadium
Sergelgatan 8.
Map 2 C4.
[14 09 90.

Walter Borg
Klara Norra Kyrkogata 26.
Map 2 C4.
[14 38 65.

SOUVENIRS AND HANDICRAFTS

Carl Wennberg Sameslöjd
Svartmangatan 11,
Map 4 B3.
[20 17 21.

Kilgren Knives and Clothing
Västerlånggatan 45.
Map 4 B3.
[20 46 80.

Svensk Hemslöjd
Sveavägen 44.
Map 2 C3
[23 21 15.

Sweden Shop
Sverigehuset. Hamngatan
27. Map 3 D4.
[789 24 06.

BOOKS

Hedengrens Bokhandel
Stureplan 4. Map 3 D4.
[611 51 28.

NK Bookshop
Hamngatan 18–20.
Map 3 D4.
[762 80 39.

Sweden Bookshop
Sverigehuset, Hamngatan
27. Map 3 D4.
[789 21 31.

TOYS AND BABY EQUIPMENT

Babyland
Karlbergsvägen 40.
Map 2 A2. [31 58 00.

Bonti
Norrtullsgatan 33.
Map 2 B2. [30 69 16.

Bulleribock
Sveavägen 104.
Map 2 C2.
[673 61 21.

Polarn och Pyret
Gallerian, Hamngatan 35.
Map 3 D4. [411 22 47.

Stor & Liten
Gallerian, Hamngatan 35.
Map 3 D4.
[545 154 40.

SWEDISH DELICACIES

Östermalmshallen
Östermalmstorg.
Map 3 E4.

Hötorgshallen
Hötorget. Map 2 C4.

Söderhallarna
Medborgarplatsen.
Map 9 D3.

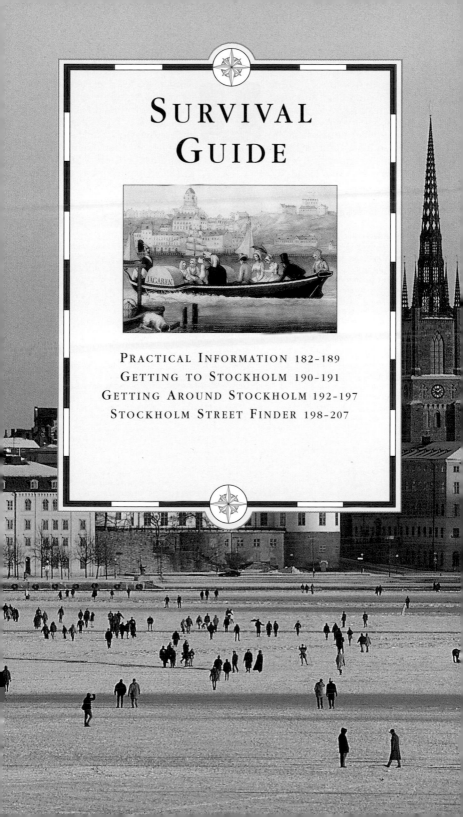

SURVIVAL
GUIDE

PRACTICAL INFORMATION 182–189
GETTING TO STOCKHOLM 190–191
GETTING AROUND STOCKHOLM 192–197
STOCKHOLM STREET FINDER 198–207

PRACTICAL INFORMATION

WITH STOCKHOLM growing rapidly as an important destination for tourism and special events in recent years, service standards in the tourist industry and in shops have improved greatly. It is easy to be a foreign visitor in the city, not least because most people speak English. The city's official tourism organization, Stockholm Information Service

Tourist office symbol

(SIS), provides an excellent range of services and its printed and Internet information material, as well as that of most attractions, is nearly always available in English and often in other languages, too. In international terms, Stockholm is a small capital, but it still has its share of pickpockets, and it's wise to take care at night in the deserted business and shopping area in the centre.

TOURIST INFORMATION

STOCKHOLM'S OFFICIAL tourist information organization is **Stockholm Information Service** (SIS). It offers a year-round service at its main office in Sweden House on Hamngatan *(see pp63, 64)*, while some additional offices are open only during the peak holiday season, usually at the more important attractions or in particular city areas. The green "i" sign indicates an authorized tourist information office. Hotel staff are often well informed. Most hotels, as well as many department stores and museums, stock the brochure *What's On Stockholm*, which is distributed every month free of charge.

The Stockholm police are always pleased to help visitors, as are most Stockholmers who are familiar with their city. Swedes usually speak English reasonably fluently.

Visitors can obtain the latest information about Stockholm on the Internet before travelling to Sweden. The city's official tourism website, www.stockholmtown.com, can probably answer the most

▾ STOCKHOLM INFORMATION SERVICE

The logo of Stockholm Information Service (SIS)

common questions. The majority of museums also have their own excellent websites, and www.stockholmsmuseer. com is a useful site with a large number of links that give an excellent overview of the city's museums. Visitors can frequently book hotel accommodation on the Internet, check the city's calendar of special events, and book tickets. This guide quotes web addresses for all the most important sights.

PASSPORTS & CUSTOMS

CITIZENS OF virtually all countries can enter Sweden without a visa. From 2001, passports will not be needed by visitors from European countries which have signed the Schengen agreement.

Differing rules often apply between travellers from the European Union (EU) and

those from other countries. Travellers from within the EU are able to bring for their private consumption 1 litre of spirits or 3 litres of fortified wine, 26 litres of wine, 32 litres of strong beer and 400 cigarettes. Travellers from outside the EU may only bring (again, for private consumption) 1 litre of spirits or 2 litres of fortified wine, 2 litres of wine, 15 litres of strong beer and 200 cigarettes.

The rules governing the importing of food also differ. All visitors can take in canned foods, but EU citizens can also take in a maximum of 15 kg (33 lb) of fresh food per person, while visitors from other areas must have a certificate from a recognized exporter. Visitors from non-EU countries can take in goods up to a value of 1,700 kr in addition to normal travel-related items.

Dogs and cats from other EU countries can be taken into Sweden, although a veterinary certificate from the animal's home country is needed. The animal must also have an identification marking, as well as an import permit issued by the Swedish Agricultural Authority (available from Swedish embassies).

Tax-free sales in Sweden are permitted only for travellers with a final destination outside the EU.

OPENING HOURS

MOST MUSEUMS and other sights are open between 10am or 11am and 5pm or 6pm all year, and they often have longer opening hours in the summer. They are usually

The tourist information office at Sweden House on Hamngatan

◁ **The ice-covered waters of Riddarfjärden, transformed into walking grounds**

Toilet for handicapped, parents of small children, women and men

closed on Monday. Information on current activities is available in the brochure *What's On Stockholm*, available at tourist information offices, hotels and department stores.

DISABLED VISITORS

UNDER SWEDISH LAW, public areas have to be accessible by physically or visually disabled people, as well as those suffering from allergies. Stockholm is a long away ahead of many other big cities in this respect. Disabled visitors from abroad can obtain information in English before their stay from **De Handikappades Riksförbund**.

The Tunnelbana underground network is adapted for disabled passengers, and most buses "kneel" at bus stops to give a reasonable height for passengers to get on or off. Disabled car drivers with a disability permit from their home country can park in special areas. Some useful brochures with detailed information about facilities for disabled visitors at theatres, cinemas, museums and libraries can be found at tourist information offices.

ADMISSION CHARGES

ENTRANCE FEES to Stockholm's museums are generally between 50 and 70 kr. Discount prices are usually available for students, children and senior citizens. The Stockholm Card (*Stockholmskortet*) gives free admission to more than 70 museums and other attractions along with free travel on local buses, Tunnelbana trains and local trains. It also offers

The Stockholm Card, giving free admission to museums

free parking at official city parking areas, as well as seasonal special offers.

Tickets for theatres, concerts and sports events can be bought at the venue or on the Internet. Tickets can also be bought in the Excursion Shop at **Sweden House**. Ticket agencies such as **Box Office** and **Biljett Direkt** also sell tickets *(see p167)*.

ETIQUETTE

BANS ON SMOKING are increasingly common throughout Sweden. Smoking is generally not permitted in public places, including all local transport and queues at bus stops and railway stations. Restaurants are obliged to provide no-smoking areas.

The Swedes queue patiently, but guard their place jealously. They are usually friendly and glad to help foreign tourists. The use of first names is the norm and a friendly "Hej!" is a familiar greeting.

Casual clothing is acceptable almost everywhere, including restaurants, particularly in the summer. Tips are always included in restaurant prices, but it is usual to round up the bill by up to 10 per cent for good service.

The logo of Systembolaget, the State-owned liquor store

ALCOHOL

SWEDISH POLICY towards alcohol is restrictive. Wines and spirits can be bought only in the relatively few shops of the State monopoly Systembolaget. They are open Monday–Friday from 10am to 6pm, and also at a limited number of shops from 10am to 2pm on Saturday. Queues tend to be long, particularly on Friday. The minimum age for buying liquor in these shops is 20, and young people may be asked to produce proof of their age. In restaurants the minimum age for

DIRECTORY

TOURIST INFORMATION

Sweden House/ Sverigehuset
Hamngatan 27 (Kungsträdgården).
Box 7542, 103 93 Stockholm.
Map 4 E1. ☉ *Jun–Aug:* 8am–7pm *Mon–Fri,* 9am–5pm *Sat–Sun; Sep–May:* 9am–6pm *Mon–Fri; Apr–May & Sep: also* 9am–3pm *Sat–Sun.*
📞 *789 24 90, from abroad* +46 8 789 2495. ℻ *789 24 91.*
🌐 www.stockholmtown.com
@ info@stoinfo.se

Hotellcentralen
(hotel bookings)
Centralstation, 111 20 Stockholm.
Map 4 E1. ☉ *Oct–Apr:* 9am–6pm; *May–Sep:* 7am–9pm.
📞 *789 24 25.* ℻ *791 86 66.*

De Handikappades Riksförbund
(information for disabled visitors)
📞 *28 30 30.* @ dhrs@algonet.se

SIGHTSEEING

City Sightseeing
(guided tours by bus)
Gustav Adolfs Torg, **Map** 4 F1.
📞 *411 70 23.*

Stockholm Sightseeing
(guided tours by boat)
Strömkajen, Grand Hôtel.
Map 2 D5. 📞 *587 140 20.*

Taxiguidning
(taxi guides) 📞 *789 24 96.*

EMBASSIES AND CONSULATES

United Kingdom
Skarpögatan 6–8. 📞 *671 90 00.*

United States
Dag Hammarskjölds väg 31.
📞 *783 53 00.*

buying liquor is 18. Most restaurants and pubs stop selling alcohol at 1am, but some city centre bars stay open till 5am.

With the maximum permitted blood alcohol level of only 0.2 per mil, drinking is effectively totally banned for car drivers.

The Swedish custom of "skåling" confounds many visitors. To "skål", look the person straight in the eye, raise your glass, drink, then repeat the eye contact before putting your glass down.

Personal Security and Health

Police symbol

STOCKHOLM IS OUTSTANDINGLY safe compared with virtually any other major city. To a great extent the city has been spared the scourges of violence and terrorism, and natural disasters like earthquakes and severe storms do not occur. But it is worth noting that in recent decades the city centre has been given over mainly to offices and public buildings, so the area tends to be deserted at night, with all the risks that entails. Sweden has a well-developed network of emergency services which visitors can naturally call on. Rescue services and hospital emergency clinics are highly efficient.

Policeman   Security guard

Police car

PROTECTING PROPERTY

ALTHOUGH STOCKHOLM is basically a safe city, tourists can naturally run into trouble at times. Especially in the summer months, the many popular events attract bag-snatchers and pickpockets. Visitors should be particularly careful to keep an eye on their property in crowded public areas, especially handbags and cameras.

It is advisable to leave your passport and travel documents at the hotel when going out. Valuables and personal documents should always be locked in your room safe or in the hotel strongbox. There is no need to carry large amounts of cash when exploring the city. All the main credit and debit cards are accepted in virtually all shops and restaurants, and cash-card machines can be used for any amounts.

It is equally important not to leave any valuables in your car;

ideally, choose a hotel with its own parking facilities.

Visitors to Stockholm with their own car should ensure they have an international Green Card for insurance.

PERSONAL SAFETY

POLICE IN STOCKHOLM are generally extremely helpful and speak good English. Police patrolling on foot or in cars are a routine sight in the city centre, and mounted police are often used at special events. There are police stations in every part of the city, and also at the

Mounted police officers

Central Station/T-Centralen. In addition to the police, uniformed security guards are a common feature at central Tunnelbana stations and in department stores, as well as in office reception areas.

Stockholm is a good city for tourists because of the compact size of the central area and the fact that it is easy to explore on foot. In addition, the Tunnelbana (underground railway) is efficient and comfortable as well as being safe at most times, but avoid empty carriages. TV security systems are installed at some Tunnelbana stations, the Central Station, main squares, department stores and many shops.

Visitors need to be careful about using unauthorized taxis, particularly when arriving at Arlanda Airport or at night in the city centre.

For some years it has been illegal to buy sexual services in Sweden so it is the buyer, not the prostitute, who is prosecuted. As a result of this law and increased police activity, street prostitutes are now a very rare sight indeed in the inner city.

LOST PROPERTY

LOST OR STOLEN property should be reported to the nearest police station. The **Police Lost Property Office** (Polisens Hittegodsexpedition) is open Monday–Friday from 9am to noon. Telephone enquiries can be made during the same hours. **Swedish State Railways** (Statens Järnvägar) has its own lost property office at the Central

Station for items lost on long-distance or local trains. For property lost on a bus or a Tunnelbana train, check with the **SL Lost Property Office** (Hittegodsavdelning), open Monday–Friday between 10am and 5pm.

EMERGENCIES

THE EMERGENCY telephone number for police, fire or ambulance is 112. It can be dialled free of charge from all public telephones, but should be used only in emergencies. For minor illnesses or concerns, ring the **Healthcare Information Service** (Sjukvårdsupplysningen).

HEALTHCARE

NO SPECIAL vaccinations are needed by anyone planning a visit to Sweden. Several city hospitals have accident and emergency clinics, including **Karolinska Sjukhuset**, **Astrid Lindgrens Barnsjukhus** (children), **Danderyds Sjukhus**, **S:t Eriks Sjukhus** (eye and dental emergencies), **S:t Görans Sjukhus** (privately owned) and **Södersjukhuset**.

Patients should not report to individual emergency clinics without contacting the **Healthcare Information Service** beforehand.

The information service can provide advice in English. Its staff have up-to-date knowledge about the current situation in the city's hospitals and can assign patients to a suitable hospital or duty doctor. It is always advisable to make use of this central information service, otherwise there can be long waiting times for those with minor ailments who go direct to a hospital emergency clinic.

For severe toothache, patients should report to **S:t Eriks Sjukhus** between 7:45am and 8:30pm, or to the **Emergency Dental Clinic** after 8:30pm.

Foreign visitors are advised to take out medical insurance before departure to cover medical care or hospital inpatient treatment.

Citizens of other EU countries are entitled to free

Pharmacy sign

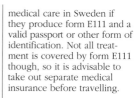

Ambulance

medical care in Sweden if they produce form E111 and a valid passport or other form of identification. Not all treatment is covered by form E111 though, so it is advisable to take out separate medical insurance before travelling.

MEDICINES

PHARMACIES CAN dispense medicines for most minor ailments without a prescription, and the staff can usually give good advice on suitable medication. Pharmacies are normally open Monday–Friday from 8:30am to 4pm or 6pm. Some also open on Saturday. The **C W Scheele** pharmacy near the Central Station is open 24 hours.

MOSQUITOES AND TICKS

MOSQUITOES CAN be a nuisance between June and late September, especially at dusk. This is particularly the case in parks, along waterways and, above all, in the archipelago. Ticks can also give a nasty bite. Pharmacies can supply mosquito repellent. Ticks should be removed from the skin with tweezers as quickly as possible. If the redness around the bite area persists a doctor should be consulted.

DIRECTORY	S:t Eriks Sjukhus	24-hour Pharmacy	LOST PROPERTY
EMERGENCIES	Map 1 C2. **(** 672 31 00.	**C W Scheele** Klarabergsgatan 64. Map 2 C4. **(** 454 81 00 (24-h).	**Police Lost Property Office** Bergsgatan 39. Map 1 C3. **(** 401 07 88.
Ambulance, Police, Fire Brigade **(** 112.	**Södersjukhuset** Map 8 B4. **(** 616 10 00.		
HEALTHCARE	**Astrid Lindgrens Barnsjukhus** Map 2 A1. **(** 517 771 02.	**24-HOUR HEALTHCARE INFORMATION**	**Swedish State Railways Lost Property Office** Central Station, Vasagatan. Map 2 C4. **(** 762 25 50.
Danderyds Sjukhus **(** 655 50 00 (24 h).		**Healthcare Information Service** **(** 463 91 00 (24-h).	
Karolinska Sjukhuset Map 2 A1. **(** 517 700 00 (24 h).	**Emergency Dental Clinic** S:t Eriks sjukhus Map 1 C2. **◯** 7:45–8:30pm: **(** 545 512 20. After hours: 24-h dentist **(** 463 91 00.	**Poisons Information Service** **(** 33 12 31 (24-h).	**SL Lost Property Office** Klara Östra Kyrkogata 4. Map 2 C5. **(** 412 69 60.
S:t Görans Sjukhus Map 1 A2. **(** 587 010 00.		**Pharmaceutical Information** **(** 020 66 77 66 (24-h).	

Banking and Local Currency

WHILE SWEDEN REMAINS OUTSIDE the European Monetary Union (EMU), goods are priced only in Swedish kronor and not in euros. Visitors can change currency in banks, which provide an efficient service, but better rates can often be obtained at bureaux de change, which have longer opening hours and are strategically sited in the city centre. Automatic cash machines can be found outside most banks and in larger shopping centres. Credit and debit cards are accepted virtually everywhere, and the larger stores will accept traveller's cheques and sometimes also the most important foreign currencies.

The logo of Forex, a bureau de change with many branches

Bankomat, the joint cash-machine system of the business banks

BANKS

THERE ARE PLENTY of banks in the city centre, all providing an excellent service. Their opening times vary, but the normal hours are 9:30am–3pm. Some banks stay open until 6pm at least once a week. All banks are closed at weekends and on public holidays, as well as the day before a public holiday.

Automatic cash machines operate efficiently. There are two types: *Bankomat* machines are the joint system of the business banks, while *Uttag* machines belong to

Föreningssparbanken. Foreign visitors can use all the city's cash machines provided that they have a bank card with a PIN code that is linked to, for example, Visa or MasterCard. Machines usually have instructions in several languages. The charge for withdrawing cash varies according to the type of card.

CURRENCY EXCHANGE

VARIOUS BUREAUX de change chains are represented in Stockholm. Generally they provide a better exchange rate than the banks.

Changing money in your hotel is the most expensive option. It is always worth checking exchange rates and commission charges because the differences can be significant. An advantage of the specialist bureaux de change is that they are easily accessible. In the city centre there is always an office close at hand.

Currency can be changed at Arlanda Airport from 5:30am, and from 7am at the Central Station, and both these outlets are open for more than 12

The head office of Handelsbanken at Kungsträdgårdsgatan, City

hours daily. At the Central Station there are foreign-exchange offices both in the main entrance hall and on the underground train level.

There is a Forex branch at the tourist information office in Sweden House (see p183), so visitors can change money while checking on current events in the city.

CREDIT CARDS

ALL THE WELL-KNOWN credit cards like **Visa**, **Master-Card**, **American Express** and **Diners Club** are accepted not just by the larger hotels and restaurants but by virtually all shops and services. One notable exception is the State-owned chain of liquor stores, Systembolaget, where only Swedish debit cards or cash are accepted. If you pay by credit card, you may sometimes be asked to produce proof of identity.

Cash machines can be used to make withdrawals using an internationally accepted credit card with a PIN code.

TRAVELLER'S CHEQUES

IF YOU ARE PLANNING any large purchases, traveller's cheques are a useful method of payment. They are not accepted in all shops but can be changed at banks. When buying cheques in your home country, it is worth checking the procedure if you lose any of your cheques. It is sensible to keep a receipt showing the serial numbers of the cheques in a separate place.

CURRENCY

SWEDEN'S CURRENCY is the krona (plural kronor). The krona (abbreviated as SEK or kr) is divided into 100 öre. The smallest coin is 50 öre, available in two versions, and the largest note is 1,000 kronor, which is not used much. If possible, it is advisable not to carry notes of more than 500 kr.

While Sweden remains outside the European Monetary Union (EMU), it is unlikely that the euro will be accepted for the time being.

20 kronor

Notes
Swedish currency notes are issued in denominations of 20, 50, 100, 500 and 1,000 kronor. They depict historic Swedish artists, authors, scientists and monarchs.

50 kronor

100 kronor

500 kronor

1,000 kronor

Coins
Coins are issued in values of 50 öre, and 1, 5 and 10 kronor. The 1 kr coin depicts Sweden's monarch on the obverse side while the 5 kr has his monogram on the reverse side. The 50 öre piece incorporates the State "three crowns" symbol.

50 öre   1 krona   5 kronor   10 kronor

Telecommunications, Post and Media

Mobile phone

SWEDEN HAS A FIRST-CLASS public telephone system. A top-ranking telecommunications industry and high living standards have placed the Swedes among the world's biggest users of mobile telephones, and there is a high level of Internet usage. The "Inform@fon" system can be used not just to make a phone call but also as a text telephone, to send a fax or e-mail, or to surf the Internet. Telephone cards – and usually credit or debit cards – can be used to make a call from a public kiosk. There is no risk of being cut off from the world when you visit Stockholm.

MAKING A PHONE CALL

PUBLIC TELEPHONE kiosks are usually operated by card only and owned by the State-owned Telia company. The cards can be bought at newspaper kiosks and in shops and are available for 30, 60, or 100 units. For a local call, one unit buys one minute while other calls cost two units per minute. Normal credit cards or international telephone cards like Access can also be used. It is possible to make reverse-charge (collect) calls from all public phones, as well as calls

to the emergency number 112 (free of charge).

Instructions on how to use public telephones are shown in English, but phone directories are not often available. Numbers can be obtained by ringing Telia directory enquiries on 118 118.

The prefix for international calls from Sweden is 00, after which one dials the country code, the area code (omitting the initial 0), followed by the local number.

Coin-operated phones are very rare but have instructions in English. Coins accepted are 1 kr, 5 kr and 10 kr.

Partly state-owned Telia card-operated phone kiosk

MOBILE PHONES

THE NUMBER OF telephone kiosks in Sweden has shown a marked decline in recent years because virtually every Swede now has a mobile phone. In most cases foreign visitors can use their GSM phone in Sweden. Within the Stockholm area you dial the area code 08 before the local number – the country code is not needed. The GSM network also has good coverage outside the cities.

FAX, TELEGRAMS AND E-MAIL

AN ADVANCED NEW telecommunications system, "Inform@fon", has been introduced in Stockholm. It is located indoors at more than 100 points including airports, railway stations, shopping centres and other public areas. The system can be used as a normal telephone, text telephone and fax, or to send e-mails, surf the Net and leave a message on a GSM-connected mobile phone. The system is particularly useful for the hard of hearing: one simply writes a message via the keyboard. Payment can be made by a normal phone card or credit/debit card.

The larger hotels offer guests fax, telegram and e-mail services.

E-mail messages can be sent or picked up at the **Kulturhusets Internetcafé** in Sergels Torg (*see p67*).

USING A CARD TELEPHONE

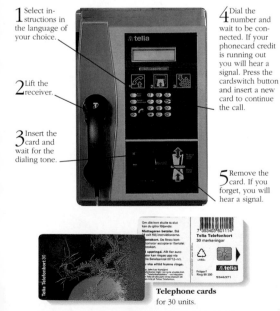

1 Select instructions in the language of your choice.

2 Lift the receiver.

3 Insert the card and wait for the dialing tone.

4 Dial the number and wait to be connected. If your phonecard credit is running out you will hear a signal. Press the cardswitch button and insert a new card to continue the call.

5 Remove the card. If you forget, you will hear a signal.

Telephone cards for 30 units.

Swedish postage stamps in values of 5 kr, 7 kr and 8 kr

POST

LOCAL POST OFFICES can be found in all parts of the city and the suburbs. They are generally open from 10am to 6pm on weekdays and 10am to 1pm on Saturdays. The post office at the Central Station is open on weekdays from 7am to 10pm and from 10am to 7pm on Saturdays and Sundays. Stamps can be bought at post offices, Pressbyrån kiosks and tourist information offices. It costs 5 kr to send a postcard or letter under 20 g (0.04 lb) within Sweden; to other European countries 7 kr; and to the rest of the world 8 kr. Postboxes are painted in different colours. The yellow boxes should be used for mail going abroad, and the blue boxes for letters within the Stockholm area (post codes starting with "1"). There are also red boxes for local post, but these need a special stamp which can be bought at Pressbyrån

Post office logo

Yellow postbox for national and international, blue for local mail

kiosks. White boxes are used only for giro payments. Collection times are shown on the postbox.

Letters can be received by using the Poste Restante service. The address has to show the recipient's name, and the name and post code of the post office where the mail will be collected. These letters are retained for up to one month after receipt.

Most international courier services are represented in Stockholm and special services are also operated by the Swedish post office.

TV AND RADIO

VIRTUALLY ALL HOTELS provide television in their rooms with both national and foreign channels. The most commonly used are the Swedish SVT1, SVT2, TV3, TV4 and Channel 5, as well as the international CNN, Sky News, MTV and Eurosport. SVT1 and 2 are State-run public-service channels. SVT2 and TV4 broadcast local programmes in the morning and evening which include weather forecasts.

There are a number of local radio stations, broadcasting mainly international and Swedish music. P6, Stockholm International, has English- and German-language programmes on 89.6 MHz.

NEWSPAPERS AND MAGAZINES

MOST OF THE important foreign newspapers and magazines can be bought in Stockholm. For the widest choice visit Press Point, Press Center and Press Specialisten. The many Pressbyrån kiosks and tourist information offices around the city stock only a limited selection of foreign publications.

Pressbyrån kiosks, for the purchase of stamps

DIRECTORY

TELECOMMUNICATIONS

International Operator
C 11 81 19.

Sending Telegrams
C 020-0021 (Telia).

Directory Enquiries
C 118 118 (Telia).

International Directory Enquiries
C 118 119 (Telia).

Wake-up Call
C 90 180.

E-MAIL SERVICES

Kulturhusets Internetcafé
Sergels Torg. **Map** 2 C4.
C 508 314 89.

COURIER SERVICES

DHL
C 020-345345

Federal Express
C 797 99 60.

TNT
C 020-960 960.

FOREIGN NEWSPAPERS

Press Point
Kungsgatan 14. **Map** 3 D4.
C 21 91 03.

Press Center
Gallerian, Hamngatan 37.
Map 3 D4. C 723 01 91.

Press Specialisten
Sveavägen 52. **Map** 2 C3.
C 21 91 13.

GETTING TO STOCKHOLM

STOCKHOLM'S POSITION at the centre of the Baltic region has made it an important transport interchange. The capital now has daily direct flights to and from most major European and North American cities. Arlanda Airport is one of the most efficient in the world. It is served by about 60 international and domestic airlines. Sweden's infrastructure is constantly being improved, with new motorways being built and the railway system being upgraded for high-speed trains. Car ferries operate to Stockholm from Finland and other points in the Baltic in about 11–15 hours. From Sweden's west and south coasts the capital can be reached by high-speed trains and motorways in no more than six hours. Sweden has a direct link to the Continent via the new Öresund road and rail bridge to Denmark in the south.

Aircraft of Scandinavian Airlines (SAS)

ARRIVING BY AIR

MOST MAJOR EUROPEAN cities have direct flights to the Swedish capital. Many of the world's leading airlines and Swedish domestic flights serve Arlanda Airport, located about 40 km (25 miles) north of the city centre.

Stockholm is served by two other airports. Bromma, close to the city centre, is used by a few of the smaller domestic airlines. Passengers flying with **Malmö Aviation** from London via Malmö also arrive here. Skavsta, about 100 km (62 miles) south of Stockholm near Nyköping, is used by **Ryanair** for budget-price flights to and from London Stansted Airport. A bus takes travellers into Stockholm.

Services between Stockholm and North America are operated by **SAS** (Scandinavian Airlines) and **Finnair** and by the US airlines Delta and American. The charter airline Premiair has frequent flights across the North Atlantic.

The Arlanda Express, linking Arlanda Airport with the city

GETTING FROM AND TO ARLANDA AIRPORT

THERE ARE SEVERAL ways of getting to the city centre from Arlanda Airport. The "Flygbussarna" bus service which operates every five minutes at peak times takes 45 minutes to the City Terminal at Central Station and costs about 60 kr. An onward journey by taxi can be booked

SAS logo

on the bus. The taxi journey into town from the airport is quicker but more expensive. Most taxi firms have a fixed charge of about 350 kr to the city centre. Visitors should avoid the so-called "black taxis" and should check the fare before departure. The shortest journey time is by the Arlanda Express train, which costs about 120 kr for the 20-minute trip to Central Station. There are two stations at the airport: one for terminals 2, 3, 4 and the other for terminal 5. Arlanda's Sky City station is served by long-distance trains.

AIR FARES

FARE OPTIONS are many and varied, particularly if you are flexible about departure and arrival dates, or can book well in advance. SAS, for example, has low-cost fares which must be booked at least seven days before departure and require a Saturday night stay at the destination. Bookings using this type of ticket cannot usually be changed.

Increased competition between the airlines has meant that it is sometimes possible to fly to Stockholm from London for a return fare of less than £100.

Scheduled airlines generally maintain their basic fare structure throughout the year, but special offers are frequently available. Newspaper advertisements and travel companies' websites often have details of last-minute deals.

Terminal 5 (International) at Stockholm's Arlanda Airport

Ferry from Finland on the way to its terminal at Stadsgården

TRAVEL BY TRAIN OR COACH

RAIL OR COACH TRAVEL from the Continent to Stockholm is relatively quick, inexpensive and comfortable. Journey times have been speeded up with the opening of the Öresund bridge between Denmark and Sweden which carries both rail and road traffic. Travel agencies can give more information on the options available.

Within Sweden the State-owned railway company **Statens Järnvägar** operates many of the long-distance trains. Some routes are run by private companies, notably **Tågkompaniet** (Stockholm–northern Sweden). In recent years air travel between Stockholm and Malmö or Gothenburg has faced strong competition from the X 2000 high-speed train. The journey time by train from Malmö to Stockholm is about 5 hours and from Gothenburg it takes about 3 hours.

The same routes are served by express coaches such as **Swebus**. Journey times are naturally longer (about 7

SJ

Swedish Railways logo

hours from Gothenburg and about 9 hours from Malmö), but fares are generally much lower and advance booking is not required.

TRAVEL BY FERRY

LARGE PASSENGER/CAR ferries sail to Stockholm from Finland. Both **Viking Line** and **Silja Line** operate daily services and have their own terminals at Stadsgården near the city centre and Värtahamnen respectively. The journey from Helsinki takes about 15 hours and from Turku 11 hours. Both shipping lines offer excellent passenger facilities, including good food, entertainment and shopping. From Tallinn in Estonia **EstLine** operates daily to the Värtahamnen terminal.

TRAVEL BY CAR

VISITORS DRIVING from Denmark can use the spectacular new Öresund toll bridge between Copenhagen and Malmö. On the Swedish side the bridge connects with the E4, a 550-km (340-mile) motorway to Stockholm. Another option is the 20-minute car ferry from Helsingør in Denmark to Helsingborg in Sweden.

Car ferries to Gothenburg operate from Denmark (Frederikshavn) and Germany (Kiel), with an onward journey on the E3 to Stockholm, about 450 km (280 miles). The fastest route from Germany to Sweden is the

Arrival hall at Stockholm Central Station

DIRECTORY

AIRLINES

SAS
📞 020 72 75 55.
📞 0845 607 27 727 (UK).

British Airways
📞 0200 770098.
📞 0345 222111 (UK).

Malmö Aviation
📞 020 55 00 10.
📞 0207 473 1043 (UK).

Finnair
📞 020-78 11 00.
📞 0207-408 1222 (UK).

Ryanair
📞 22 15 00.
📞 0541-569 569 (UK).

RAILWAYS

Statens Järnvägar (SJ)
📞 020-75 75 75.

Tågkompaniet (Svenska)
📞 020-444 111.

FERRY LINES

Silja Line
📞 22 21 40.

Viking Line
📞 452 40 00.

EstLine
📞 667 00 01.

EXPRESS COACHES

Swebus
📞 0200-21 82 18.

catamaran ferry from Rostock to Trelleborg in southern Sweden, then the E6 to Malmö and E4 to Stockholm. Speed limits on Swedish motorways are 110 km/h (68 mph), and 90 km/h (56 mph) on other main roads. The limit in built-up areas is 50–70 km/h (31–43 mph). When driving in the countryside, take care at dawn and dusk especially, since elk and deer can then suddenly appear on the road.

Warning, elk on the road

Getting around Stockholm

STOCKHOLM IS A PERFECT city for pedestrians. Distances between sights are usually short, and around every corner there is always something interesting to discover. The capital extends across a large number of islands, offering eye-catching vistas and waterfront scenes. There are many cycle lanes, although not everywhere in the busy city centre, and for inexperienced visitors it might

Pedestrian and cycle route

be safer to stick to green areas like Djurgården. Public transport on buses, underground trains, trams and local trains is efficient and covers the entire city and surrounding region. Apart from the area of Gamla Stan, and during the rush hours, driving a car in Stockholm is relatively easy and indoor parking facilities are adequate. But the best way of exploring the city centre is on foot.

Stockholm on Foot

IN LARGE PARTS of central Stockholm, walking is the best way to see the sights, but one needs to be aware of the regulations. Pedestrians are not allowed to cross a road against a red light, but motorists must stop and give way to pedestrians at zebra crossings without traffic lights (always look carefully). If you are waiting at a crossing with lights press the button, otherwise you are likely to wait a long time before the light changes to green.

The clear street signs make it easy to find one's way around, and Stockholmers are always glad to help visitors. There are walking and cycling routes everywhere in the city, as well as plenty of pedestrian precincts and parks.

Gamla Stan is a popular area for exploring on foot, and there is always something to see around Kungsträdgården as well. A stroll along the quayside opposite the Grand Hôtel and Nationalmuseum, followed by a walk around Skeppsholmen, makes

Pedestrians crossing signals: red for wait and green for go

Taking a waterfront stroll along Djurgårdsbrunnsviken

an interesting route. Another delightful area is Djurgården, with a host of attractions set in parkland only a short distance from the centre.

Those who like to walk along the waterfront can follow the quaysides, for example from Stadshuset along Norr Mälarstrand and the Riddarfjärden bay. You will not lack company – jogging is a popular pastime in Stockholm. Fjällgatan *(see p129)* is also recommended, not least for its magnificent view of the city.

Guided walks are organized regularly, often with a special theme – history, architecture or parks, for example. Sometimes they are available in different languages, especially during the summer months. Most walks take in the Old Town, but there are a number of other routes – tourist information offices will have details *(see Directory, p183)*.

Driving in Stockholm

ANYONE FAMILIAR WITH driving in large cities will have no problems in Stockholm. It is relatively easy to find one's way around by car, except during the rush hours (7.30–9.30am, 12 noon to 1pm, and 3.30–6pm). Cars are not really necessary in the city centre because of the short distances between sights and excellent public transport. However, a car is an advantage if you want to explore further afield.

The speed limit is usually 50 km/h (31 mph), but near schools, for example, it is 30 km/h (19 mph). Speeds up to 70 km/h (43 mph) are permitted only on the main roads in and out of the city. Fines for speeding are high, and even if the limit is only slightly exceeded, you can lose your driving licence. Drivers and passengers must always wear seat belts. Drink-drive laws are zero-tolerance: the maximum permitted blood alcohol level is 0.2 per mil. Motorists must give way to pedestrians at crossings without traffic lights. The yellow light means "Stop".

Pedestrian crossing sign

Reading Street Signs

Street name

Roslagsgatan

kv. Ingemar **46-34**

Block

Street number range in block

CAR RENTAL

MOST OF THE international car-rental firms have offices in Stockholm, as well as several local operators. The larger hotels and the tourist information office at Sweden House *(see p183)* can arrange a car which can be delivered at your convenience. The only documentation needed is a national driving licence which must be shown when you sign the rental contract.

PARKING

THERE ARE PLENTY of parking spaces on the streets and in multistorey car parks, but it can sometimes be difficult to find a vacant spot, particularly in summer. If you plan to park on the street you need to familiarize yourself with the various road signs. In the city centre it often costs 10 kr or more per hour to park. Parking in many streets is free, particularly at weekends, or between 5pm and 9am except on street-cleaning nights as indicated on road signs. Major attrac-

Parking warden

No parking sign permits short stop to set down or pick up (5–10 min).

No stopping zone, indicated by yellow line by pavement.

Parking zone

Parking charge 9am–5pm; free at other times

No parking on weekday night indicated, midnight 6am

tions like museums often have their own car parks, which are subject to a charge throughout the week.

The city's parking wardens are diligent. Any breach of regulations can involve a fine of 400 kr or more, and it costs 700 kr if one parks within 10 m (33 ft) of a crossing. Do not leave valuables in the car, even in multistorey car parks.

PARKING METER

Rates & Times | Coin slot

Green button: non residential parking | Yellow button: residential parking

Day and date | Time of expiry

Parking ticket for non-residents

GETTING AROUND BY TAXI

WITH THE SHORT distances between places in the city centre, the need for a taxi is not so important, but it is convenient and for brief journeys relatively cheap.

There are usually plenty of taxis available, particularly at stations and sights, with the exception of the rush hours. One can also hail an empty taxi, indicated by the illuminated sign on the car roof. The best method is to order a taxi by telephone or book one in

Taxi sign lights up when available

Taxi sign

advance. The initial charge is usually 30 kr, with an additional 60–100 kr for a journey within the central area. It is always worth enquiring what the fare is likely to be.

One should be careful about using the unauthorized so-called "black taxis", especially at night.

A Stockholm taxi

DIRECTORY

TAXI

Taxi Stockholm
(15 00 00.

Taxi Kurir
(30 00 00.

Taxi 020
(020-93 93 93.

CAR RENTAL

Avis
(020-78 82 00.

Europcar
(020-78 11 80.

Hertz
(020-211 211.

Statoil
(020-252525.

Getting around by Tunnelbana and Bus

Stockholm Tunnelbana logo

V̲irtually all stockholm's sights and attractions can be reached easily by Tunnelbana (underground train) or bus. The map below shows the Tunnelbana network, and a map of inner-city bus routes is on the inside back cover. Along with other operators, SL is responsible for public transport by Tunnelbana, bus and local shuttle train. The various types of transport complement each other and cover Greater Stockholm.

Full-price Tunnelbana coupon (top) and SL's one-day ticket

TUNNELBANA

I̲n the late 1940s work started on the building of Stockholm's first underground railway. Since then the network has been extended and now has 100 stations on three main routes – the green, red and blue lines. These link up at T-Centralen adjoining Central Station.

Of the 100 stations, 19 are located in the inner city, and nearly all the sights described in this guide can be reached by Tunnelbana or the main bus routes. The Tunnelbana system has four zones, with the inner zone covering a large part of the city centre. This means that one can travel direct to many of the sights for less than 20 kr. Most ticket barriers are manned.

A modern SL Tunnelbana train

Apart from single tickets, there are travelcards for one day, three days or a month. Cards are valid for all zones. You can also use the Stockholm Card *(see p183)*. It can pay to buy a book of discount coupons valid for 10 journeys in the inner-city zone for about 100 kr. Tickets can be bought at Pressbyrån kiosks, the SL central ticket office, or at stations. Tickets for a single journey can be bought at Tunnelbana stations or on buses.

Sunday to Thursday nights the Tunnelbana operates until 1am while on Friday and Saturday nights it runs until 4am. At other times there are night bus services.

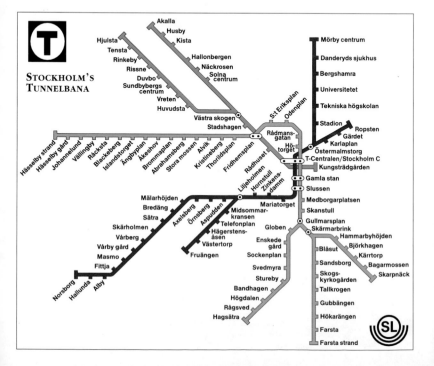

GETTING AROUND BY BUS

THE NETWORK OF "red" city buses is built up around a number of "blue" feeder routes which complement the Tunnelbana network. Many streets in the city centre have special bus lanes which speed up the traffic. The buses are all modern and comfortable, with easy access for prams, and frequently use environmentally friendly fuels like ethanol and gas.

Travelling by bus is a pleasant and economical way of seeing the city. A two-coupon single ticket gives two hours' travel, with an unlimited number of changes. The best routes for sightseeing are 3, 4, 46, 47, 62 and 69. These cover most of the central area

Restored vintage tram, a popular way of getting to Djurgården

and stop near many sights. Routes 47 and 69 from, for instance, Normalmstorg are particularly useful for reaching sights not served by Tunnelbana. Route 47 takes visitors to Djurgården with its attractions including Skansen, Gröna Lund, Vasamuseet and Nordiska Museet, continuing to Waldemarsudde. Route 69 goes to southern Gärdet with its four important museums and Kaknästornet, continuing via Thielska Galleriet to Blockhusudden at the easternmost tip of Djurgården.

Red city bus and blue "feeder" bus

VINTAGE TRAMS

A CHARMING WAY of travelling to Djurgården, particularly in the summer, is to take one of the lovingly restored vintage trams. Trams ceased to operate in Stockholm in 1967, when Sweden switched over to right-hand driving, but since 1991 a voluntary organization of tram enthusiasts has operated services on the former route 7 between Normalmstorg and Djurgården, where 14 trams are stabled.

Every year more than 300,000 passengers enjoy a trip using this popular method of travel. Refreshments are served on some services.

ART ON THE TUNNELBANA

S TOCKHOLM'S Tunnelbana network is an attraction in itself. From the start, time and money were invested in decorating the stations artistically. Today about 130 artists are represented by sculptures, mosaics and paintings. SL has an artistic advisory board which is responsible for choosing new works of art and has an annual budget of 3 million kronor. Some stations are particularly worth seeing, including the following:

Kungsträdgården
Sculptures, waterfall, arch paintings, etc (Ulrik Samuelson, 1977–87.)

Fridhemsplan *Homage to Carl von Linné* glazed wall and terracotta sculpture (Dimas Macedo, 1997).

Zenith, a painted steel sculpture by Leif Tjerned at Gullmarsplan station

Östermalmstorg Reliefs on the theme *Women's rights, and the peace and environmental movements* (Siri Derkert, 1965).

Stadion Wooden sculptures linked to the 1912 Olympic Games, Stockholm Stadium, and the Royal Musical Academy (Enno Hallek, Åke Pallarp, 1973).

Universitetet *The United Nations Declaration of*

Human Rights, wall decoration in ceramics (Françoise Schein, 1998), video installation (Fredrik Wretman, 1998).

Rissne *Time axis from the pyramids to the present day* (Madeleine Dranger, Rolf H Reimers, 1985).

A guide in English to art on the Tunnelbana is available at the SL central ticket office or tourist information offices.

Getting Around by Ferry and Boat

Waxholms-bolaget's logo

STOCKHOLM'S LOCATION between Lake Mälaren and the Baltic archipelago means that its waterways play an important role in city life. Boats and ferries are a familiar feature of the Stockholm scene and provide a delightful way of getting to know the city and its surroundings. A large number of scheduled boat services, ferries and sightseeing tours offer visitors almost endless opportunities to enjoy Stockholm from the water. Motor and rowing boats, pedalos and canoes can also be hired for a personal voyage of discovery.

Sightseeing boat crossing Stockholms Ström

GETTING AROUND BY FERRY

FOR MANY DECADES it has been a tradition to visit the attractions of Djurgården by ferry from the city centre. This pleasant service links with bus and Tunnelbana routes, and can be used free of charge by holders of SL's 1-day or 3-day card (the Stockholm Card is not valid).

There is a year-round ferry service from Slussen via Skeppsholmen to Allmänna Gränd near Gröna Lund from 7.30am until after midnight. From May to August there is a route from Nybroplan to Vasamuseet, Skeppsholmen and Gröna Lund from 9am–6pm. Both these ferries operate at frequent intervals. During the summer **Strömma Kanalbolaget**'s neat little

ferries ply between the jetties around Brunnsviken alongside the Haga Park *(see p121)*.

SIGHTSEEING BY BOAT

A PLEASANT WAY of enjoying Stockholm from the water is to take an excursion run by Stockholm Sightseeing (**Strömma Kanalbolaget**). A "Round Kungsholmen" tour departs hourly from the quayside near the City Hall from

Djurgården ferry in front of Nordiska Museet

10.30am to 4.30pm. Tickets costing about 100 kr can be bought on the quay. Guides speak both English and Swedish and sometimes a third language.

The "Under Stockholm's Bridges" and "Round Djurgården" tours depart hourly from Strömkajen near the Grand Hôtel, and passengers are also picked up from Nybroplan. Tickets can be bought at both these points. The former tour operates between 10am and 8pm and costs about 150 kr, the latter between 10.30am and 6pm for about 100 kr. A commentary is provided on headsets in a variety of languages. All tours are available during summer only apart from "Round Djurgården" which runs to December. Information and tickets can be obtained from tourist information offices.

FERRY AND SIGHTSEEING ROUTES

Waxholmsbolaget's Djurgården ferries operate on the inner city's waterways on two routes: Slussen–Skeppsholmen–Allmänna Gränd plus (May–August) Nybroplan–Vasamuseet–Skeppsholmen–Allmänna Gränd as shown on the map (right). The most popular Stockholm Sightseeing tours are shown on the larger map. The longest tour goes to Drottningholms Slott.

KEY

— Djurgårdsfärjan *(see inset map)*

— Under Stockholm's Bridges (May–Sep)

— Historical Canal Tour (Jun–Aug)

— Royal Canal Tour (Apr–Dec)

— Drottningholm Tour (Jun–Aug)

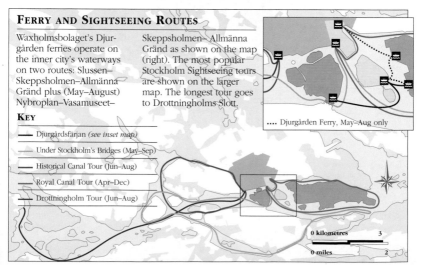

.... Djurgården Ferry, May–Aug only

0 kilometres   3

0 miles   2

HIRING BOATS AND CANOES

E NJOYING THE CITY from the water on one's own is an exciting experience. Rowing boats, canoes, kayaks, pedalos and small boats with an outboard motor can be hired near the Djurgården bridge at **Tvillingarnas Båthyrning** and **Skepp & Hoj**. The gentle waters of the Djurgården Canal are ideal for rowing or canoeing. A motor-boat trip round Djurgården takes about an hour. Larger boats for exploring the archipelago can be rented by the hour or day.

EXCURSIONS BY BOAT

T HE MANY SCHEDULED public transport boat services operated by **Waxholms-bolaget** generally sail year-round, but most frequently between June and mid-August. An excellent way of exploring the archipelago independently is to take one of the regular services from Strömkajen which call at countless picturesque jetties along the way. The ferry company and tourist information offices can suggest suitable itineraries.

Organized excursions both in the archipelago and on Lake Mälaren are run by **Strömma Kanalbolaget** and other operators. You can, for instance, take a gastronomic evening cruise to Vaxholm, departing at 7pm and returning at 9.45pm, and other attractive options are available.

Gourmet steamer cruise in the archipelago with top-class Swedish cuisine

A number of sights which can be reached by fast passenger boats or traditional steamers are listed on pages 134–145.

are listed on pages 134–145.

DIRECTORY

ARCHIPELAGO AND SIGHTSEEING BOATS

Gripsholms-Mariefreds Ångf. AB
Stadshusbron. **Map** 2 C5.
⬛ 669 88 50.

Strömma Kanalbolaget
Nybrokajen. **Map** 3 E4.
⬛ 587 140 00.

Waxholmsbolaget
Strömkajen. **Map** 3 D5.
⬛ 679 58 30.

BOAT AND BICYCLE RENTAL AND MAPS

Cykel & Mopeduthyrningen
Strandvägen, quay berth No. 24.
Map 3 F4. ⬛ 660 79 59.

Cykelstallet
S:t Eriksgatan 34. **Map** 1 C2.
⬛ 650 08 04.

Djurgårdsbrons Sjöcafé
Galärvarvsvägen 2. **Map** 3 F5.
⬛ 660 57 57.

Kartbutiken
Kungsgatan 74. **Map** 2 B4.
⬛ 20 23 03.

Kartcentrum
Vasagatan 16. **Map** 2 C5
⬛ 411 16 97.

Tvillingarnas Båtuthyrning
Djurgårdsbron. **Map** 3 F4.
⬛ 663 37 39.

Getting Around by Bicycle

Nynäsleden
Suggested bicycle tour

T HE CAPITAL'S NETWORK of bicycle tracks is increasing all the time, but you need to be an experienced city cyclist if you want to explore the central area from the saddle. Otherwise Stockholm and its surrounding area are tailor-made for cycling. Anyone wanting to go out into the countryside and enjoy the fresh air and beautiful surroundings does not need to travel far from the city centre.

V ISITORS WHO WANT to find out more about the cycling possibilities in Stockholm in advance can check **www.rent bike.com** on the Internet. Otherwise the SIS tourist information office at Sweden House (see p183) can put cyclists in touch with a local cycling organization which will be pleased to give some useful suggestions.

Two bicycle-hire firms, **Djungårdsbrons Sjöcafé** and **Cykel & Mopeduthyrningen**, are located on Strandvägen near the Djurgården bridge. From there it is only a short ride to Djurgården with its gently graded cycle tracks and roads which are mostly free of cars.

Gärdet, Lilljanskogen and Haga are other good areas for biking, and there are also marked routes which stretch further out from the city centre. It is also possible to cycle in parts of Ekoparken (see p121) which are virtually traffic-free.

Rollerblades can be hired at the same outlets as bikes, while **Cykelstallet** is the best place to go for mountain bike rental.

Maps can be bought from, among others, **Kartcentrum** and **Kartbutiken**.

Cycling on the peaceful Djurgården

STOCKHOLM STREET FINDER

THE MAP BELOW shows the areas of Stockholm covered by the street map. Gamla Stan (Old Town) is shown on a larger scale than the rest of the city. The map references listed in the guide for many sights, restaurants, hotels, shops and entertainment spots refer to the maps in this section. The first figure of the refer-

Japanese visitors

ence indicates the map page, while the letter and following figure shows its location on the map grid. All the more important sights are marked so that they are easier to find. The key below explains other symbols on the map, including post offices, tunnelbana stations and churches. An overview map of Stockholm is on pp12–3.

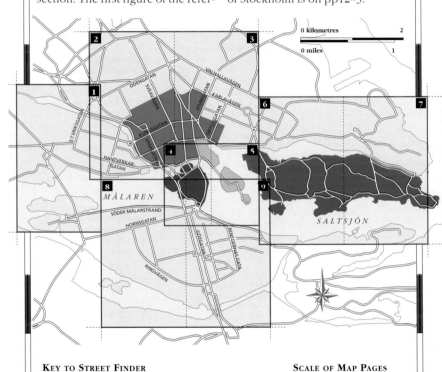

KEY TO STREET FINDER

▦	Major sight	ℹ	Tourist information office
▦	Place of interest	✚	Hospital
▦	Other building	🚓	Police station
🚆	Train station	✝	Church
Ⓣ	Tunnelbana station	✡	Synagogue
🚌	Main bus stop	⊠	Post office
🚍	Coach station	✲	Viewpoint
⛴	Ferry boarding point	—	Railway line
🚋	Tram stop	–	One-way street
P	Car park	▬	Pedestrian street

SCALE OF MAP PAGES 1–3 OCH 6–9

0 metres   250

0 yards   250

SCALE OF MAP PAGES 4–5

0 metres   250

0 yards   250

Street name index on
pp208–10

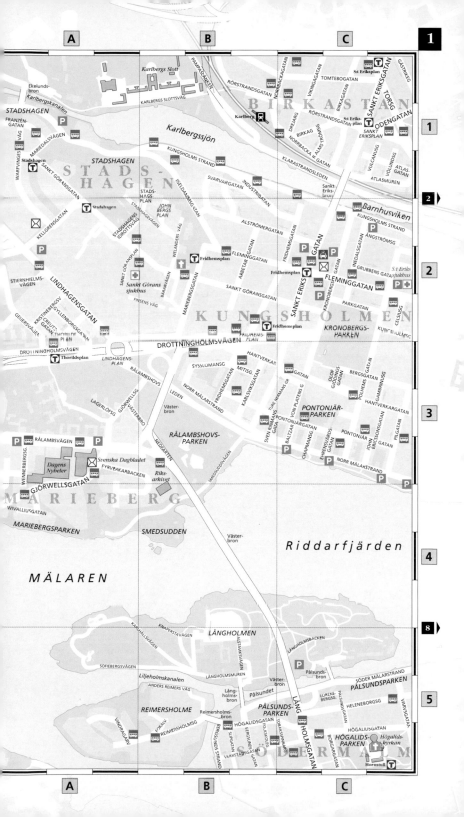

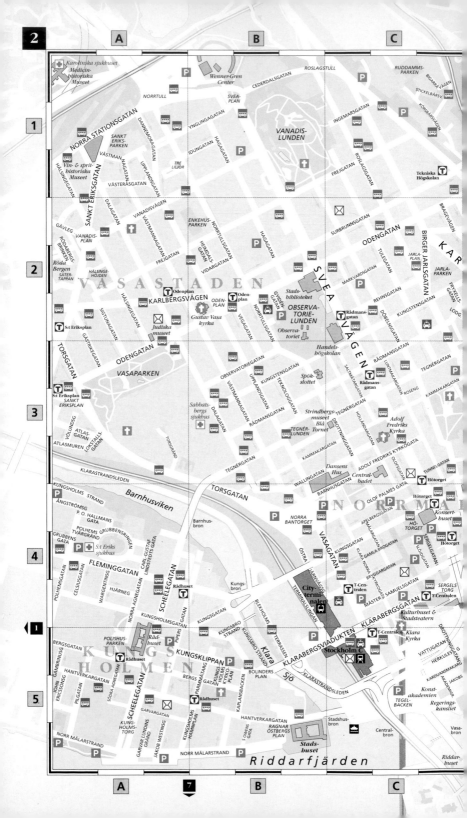

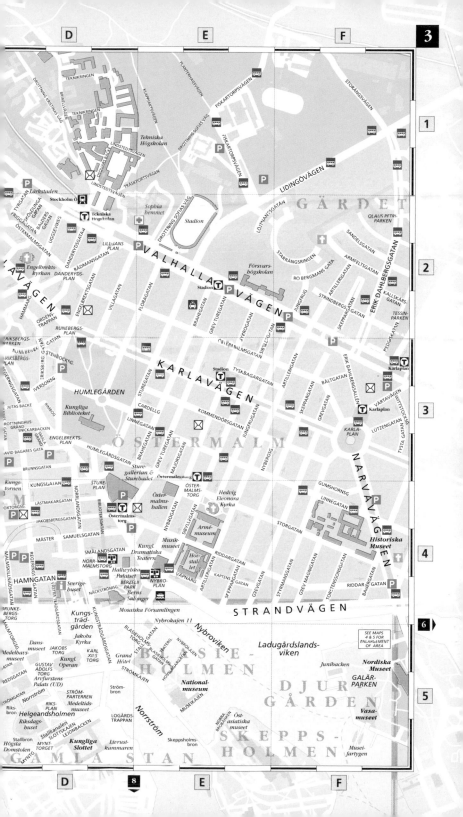

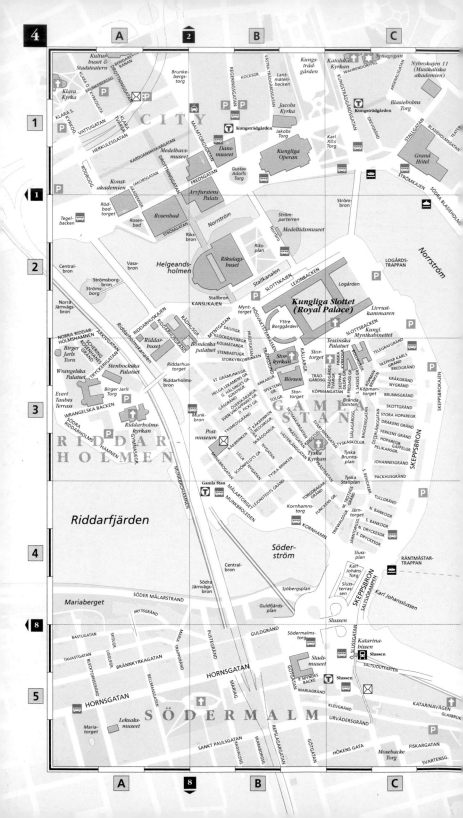